The Passivity of Law

Luigi Corrias

The Passivity of Law

Competence and Constitution
in the European Court of Justice

 Springer

Luigi Corrias
Faculty of Law
Legal Theory and Legal History
VU University Amsterdam
De Boelelaan 1105
1081 HV Amsterdam
The Netherlands
l.d.a.corrias@vu.nl

ISBN 978-94-007-1033-7   e-ISBN 978-94-007-1034-4
DOI 10.1007/978-94-007-1034-4
Springer Dordrecht Heidelberg London New York

Printed on acid-free paper

Springer is part of Springer Science+Business Media (www.springer.com)

Acknowledgements

This book is the adapted version of my doctoral thesis written between 2003 and 2009 and defended at Tilburg University in February 2010. The department of Legal Philosophy formed not only an excellent environment to carry out this research, it also provided me with the chance to work with a lot of inspiring people. I would like to use this opportunity to thank a number of them. First of all, I owe a lot to my supervisor Bert van Roermund. He has taught me so much more than can be expressed here, or in the pages to follow. Let me just say that I am proud that I have had the chance to work with him. I am also very grateful to the people who were so kind to be part of the doctoral committee, all of which I admire as great scholars. In alphabetical order, these are Gilles Labelle (University of Ottawa), Hans Lindahl (Tilburg University), Sacha Prechal (Utrecht University), Jenny Slatman (Maastricht University) and Wouter Veraart (VU University Amsterdam). Presently, I am part of a young and enthusiastic group of scholars at VU University Amsterdam. In particular, I would like to thank Bart van Klink who invited me to work there. Furthermore, I am very grateful to my friends and family for all their support over the years. In this respect, a special word of thanks goes to my brothers and, of course, to my parents for all the sacrifices they have made for me. Finally, I would like to thank Irina for showing me every day what is really important in life. Without her absolutely nothing would be possible.

Amsterdam   Luigi Corrias
December 2010

Contents

Introduction

Europe's constitutional journey has not been a smooth one. On the contrary, it is not an exaggeration to say that Europe's search for a constitution has turned out to be an opening of Pandora's box: In the controversy surrounding the European Constitution, all kinds of quarrels and debates are cast on issues ranging from the enlargement of the European Union to its legal-political nature, from the legitimacy of the Union to its very identity, from the role the Union should play in the world to the way its actions influence daily life in its smallest regions.[1] Anyway, the Constitution has proved tougher than expected. Its proclaimed 'death by (double) referendum' did not make it disappear. Indeed, the Treaty of Lisbon, so lawyers seem to agree, is to an important degree, similar to the 'dead' constitutional treaty stripped from its most 'constitution-like' characteristics. Is this problematic? There is surely no easy answer to this question. What seems less difficult to ascertain, however, is that the project of a constitution for Europe embodied a desire to improve the legitimacy of the Union and the way in which the citizens value the reality of an ever further integrated Europe.[2] The Treaty of Nice had not tackled some important problems, and the constitution was being enacted, amongst other motives, precisely to come up with solutions to these issues. A 'better division and definition of competence in the European Union' was one of the four core problems to which the new Constitution had to find a solution, as the Laeken Declaration stated:

---

[1] As this book will use both the terms 'European Union' and 'European Community', their distinction should be explained from the beginning. Between 1993 and 2009, the European Union encompassed three pillars. The first pillar consisted of the three (now two) European Communities: The European Atomic Energy Community (EAEC or EURATOM), the European Community (EC) and the now-expired European Coal and Steel Community (ECSC). The second pillar was formed by the Common Foreign and Security Policy (CFSP) and the third pillar was made up of the Police and Judicial Cooperation in Criminal Matters (PJCC). With the coming into force of the Treaty of Lisbon (1 December 2009) the pillar structure has been abolished.

[2] The Laeken Declaration speaks of three challenges for the European Union: the democratic challenge, bringing Europe closer to its citizens and giving Europe a new role in a globalised world. See: Presidency Conclusions of the Laeken European Council (14 and 15 December 2001): Annex I: Laeken Declaration on the future of the European Union, in Bulletin of the European Union. 2001, No 12, pp. 19–23, available at: http://ec.europa.eu/justice_home/unit/charte/en/declarations-laeken.html [visited on 29 October 2009].

Thus, the important thing is to clarify, simplify and adjust the division of competence between the Union and the Member States in the light of the new challenges facing the Union. (…)
A first series of questions that needs to be put concerns how the division of competence can be made more transparent. (…)
The next series of questions should aim, within this new framework and while respecting the 'acquis communautaire', to determine whether there needs to be any reorganisation of competence. (…)
Lastly, there is the question of how to ensure that a redefined division of competence does not lead to a creeping expansion of the competence of the Union, or to encroachment upon the exclusive areas of competence of the Member States and, where there is provision for this, regions. How are we to ensure at the same time that the European dynamic does not come to a halt? In the future as well, the Union must continue to be able to react to fresh challenges and developments, and must be able to explore new policy areas. Should Articles 95 and 308 of the Treaty be reviewed for this purpose in the light of the 'acquis jurisprudentiel'?[3]

It is this problem of 'creeping competences' that forms the starting point of this book.[4] After the rejection of the European Constitution, the answer to this question was laid down in the Treaty of Lisbon. Given the importance of this Treaty and its resemblance to the old constitution, it may not come as a complete surprise that it received no warm welcome in all Member States.[5] In Germany, several people brought constitutional complaints against the act ratifying the Treaty of Lisbon to the Federal Constitutional Court (FCC). Surely, it was not the first time that the FCC was asked to give its opinion on a decisive step in the integration process, and because of its critical attitude, the judgment was awaited with anxiety. This judgment came by the end of June 2009, and in the considerations of the FCC, we find some hints about the depth of the legal-political problems lying at the heart, not simply of the Treaty of Lisbon, but of the very endeavour that is Europe's constitutional quest.

So what does the FCC think? Has the 'creeping expansion of the competence of the Union' indeed come to a halt? What limits to European competences does the German court put forward? Time and again, the FCC has stressed that the EU legal order is a derived order (i.e., derived from that of the Member States). Accordingly, its competences are also of a derived nature, and this is reflected by the main principle regulating the legal powers of the Union, the principle of conferral. This principle, also known as the principle of conferred powers, holds that the Union only possesses those competences that are given to it. Now, according to the FCC, this entails that there is at least one hard limit to the competences of the Union, that of constituent power: 'The constituent power of the Germans, which gave itself the Basic Law, wanted to set an insurmountable boundary to any future political development.

---

[3] Ibid. Note that the numbering of the articles has changed. Article 95 EC is now Article 114 of the Treaty on the Functioning of the European Union (TFEU). Article 308 EC is now Article 352 TFEU.

[4] Cf. M.A. Pollack, 'Creeping Competence: The Expanding Agenda of the European Community', *Journal of Public Policy*, vol. 14 (1994), pp. 95–145.

[5] The Irish people only accepted the Treaty of Lisbon in a second referendum held on 2 October 2009.

(...) The so-called eternity guarantee takes the disposal of the identity of the free constitutional order even out of the hands of the constitution-amending legislature. The Basic Law thus not only assumes sovereign statehood but guarantees it.'[6] Any transfer of powers, as has taken place by joining the project of European integration, is, therefore, necessarily limited in nature: 'The Basic Law does not grant the German state bodies powers to transfer sovereign powers in such a way that their exercise can independently establish other competences for the European Union. It prohibits the transfer of competence to decide on its own competence (Kompetenz-Kompetenz).'[7] Nevertheless, an interpretation of EU powers, in order to safeguard their 'effet utile', is admitted by the German court. In other words, the FCC says that it has no problems with the doctrine of implied powers[8], as long as the principle of conferral is respected.[9] It is under these conditions that Germany can go on with the project of European integration, because the Member States remain the masters of the Treaties.[10] The doctrine of implied powers appears to be a borderline case, thus it is the last admissible form of broad interpretation of the European competences that the ECJ may use. In any case, the constituent power of the Member States is to be protected. Hence, granting the EU 'Kompetenz-Kompetenz' would go too far.[11]

At this point, my questions begin to surface. What are these 'creeping competences'? What makes them creep? What to make of these implied powers? In what way are they the last admissible instrument for the ECJ, the bridge it may cross just before reaching 'a bridge too far'? What, if anything, may serve as an argument by which to assign this doctrine such an important role? In this respect, the nature of this doctrine 'on the threshold' may be exemplified by the fact that the FCC seems to have changed its opinion on implied powers. In its judgment on the Treaty of Maastricht, the FCC had rejected the doctrine as an interpretation tool that went too far.[12] But this makes the questions only more pertinent. What to make of these implied powers as a borderline concept? What makes them distinguishable from 'Kompetenz-Kompetenz', a power which the FCC explicitly says that the EU does not possess, and should not possess? What exactly is the German court trying to protect when it points to the untouchable constituent power of the German people? The most interesting feature of the FCC's judgment on the Treaty of Lisbon is, perhaps, that it does not only address strictly legal questions, but that it also connects these questions with fundamental issues in legal and political philosophy. In this way, the FCC shows that there is more to 'creeping competences' than meets the (legal) eye. Indeed, (not even so deep) under the surface, 'creeping competences' pose

---

[6] BVerfG, 2 BvE 2/08 vom 30.6.2009, Absatz-Nr. (1–421), par. 216. The preliminary English translation is available at: http://www.bverfg.de/entscheidungen/es20090630_2bve000208en.html [visited on 29 October 2009].

[7] Ibid., par. 233.

[8] Ibid., par. 237.

[9] Ibid., par. 238, 240 and 265 amongst others.

[10] Ibid., par. 298 amongst others.

[11] In par. 322 the FCC holds that the Treaty of Lisbon does not give the EU 'Kompetenz-Kompetenz'.

[12] See Chap. 1, Sect. 1.5.

questions that invite us to dwell at the very centre of legal and political philosophy. In my opinion, it is no exaggeration to say that 'creeping competences' give food for thought. What, then, lies at the beginning of this study? Starting from the hypothesis that the FCC is right in connecting the problem of 'creeping competences' with issues like implied powers, constituent power and 'Kompetenz-Kompetenz', this book is an attempt to elucidate these problems in their mutual relationships in order to shed new light on them.

A Note on Methodology

This is a work in Philosophy of Law. Therefore, I will start by identifying the problems as they appear *in* law, and first articulate them in the language *of* law. Only at a second stage will I connect these problems to more general issues in legal and political philosophy. Finally, at a last stage, I will come back to the legal level in order to show what the philosophical detour has given us. The general methodology of the book is conceptual analysis. In order to understand the phenomenon of 'creeping competences', I will start by describing how competences, or legal powers, are regulated in the European legal order. In this context, special attention will be devoted to the pivotal role played by the European Court of Justice (ECJ). As the example of implied powers shows, the ECJ's case law has become essential to any understanding of competences in the European Union.[13] Here, it should immediately be noted that there exist different meanings of the concept of an implied power. One can distinguish at least two formulations, both of which are important for our purposes: 'According to the narrow formulation, the existence of a given power implies also the existence of any other power which is reasonably necessary for the existence of the former; according to the wide formulation, the existence of a given *objective* or *function* implies the existence of any power reasonably necessary to attain it.'[14] Some other chapters of the case law of the ECJ will also be analysed in order to show that, when it comes to competences, there is more room for manoeuvre than a strict reading of the Treaties suggests.

Discussing these cases, and some other problems with the current regulation of competences, will automatically bring us to the concepts of 'Kompetenz-Kompetenz' and constituent power. Since these notions address the same legal-political problem, I will continue with the concept of constituent power since it is more common in constitutional theory. Indeed, constitutional theory usually starts from the distinction between constituent or constituting power (the power to give the constitution) on the one hand, and constitutional or constituted power (the power given by the constitution) on the other. Competence or legal power can then be equated with constituted

---

[13] Cf. G. Conway, 'Conflicts of Competence Norms in EU Law and the Legal Reasoning of the ECJ', *German Law Journal*, vol. 11 (2010), pp. 966–1005.

[14] T.C. Hartley, quoted in: P. Craig & G. de Bùrca, *EU Law. Text, Cases, and Materials* (4th edition), Oxford (etc.): Oxford University Press 2008, p. 90 [Italics in the original].

power. Given the recent processes of 'constitutionalisation' in Europe (on the level of the EU, but also in several East-European countries) and in international organisations, the concept of constituent power has received quite some attention recently.[15] In that sense, this thesis takes up a problem that is central to contemporary legal theory. At the same time, it is also necessary to show how the conceptual problems encountered in the sphere of EU competences have developed in the history of constitutional thinking. Hence, a part of this study will be devoted to analysing important moments of this history in order to understand how constituent power and the relation with constituted power have been conceptualised. Furthermore, I will argue that the concept of constituent power represents the specific legal-political version of a more general philosophical problem: How are we to understand the creation or constitution of something meaningful?

Casting the problem of constituent power in these terms allows me to address it at a deeper level. What is at stake are the very foundations of constitutional theory. In order to reconceptualise these foundations, I take my cue from a movement in philosophy called phenomenology, and especially from the work of Maurice Merleau-Ponty (1908–1961). Phenomenology is the movement in Western philosophy that starts from, and aims to, articulate the viewpoint of the first person. This entails, in the words of Charles Taylor, taking the stance of radical reflexivity: 'What matters to us is the adoption of the first person standpoint. (…) The world as I know it, is there for me, is experienced by me, or thought about by me, or has meaning for me. Knowledge, awareness is always that of an agent. (…) In our normal dealings with things, we disregard this dimension of experience and focus on the things experienced. But we can turn and make this our object of attention, become aware of our awareness, try to experience our experiencing, focus on the way the world is *for* us. This is what I call taking a stance of radical reflexivity, or adopting the first-person standpoint.'[16] This stance of the first person, singular or plural, is of central importance for law and legal theory because it acknowledges the necessity of knowledge of identity, of oneself for legal discourse.[17] In other words, the importance of phenomenology for law and legal theory is that it articulates this primordial intersection between me and the world that is only found in experience,

---

[15] Cf. M. Loughlin and N. Walker (eds.), *The Paradox of Constitutionalism: Constituent Power and Constitutional Form*, Oxford (etc.): Oxford University Press 2007, and N. Tsagourias (ed.), *Transnational Constitutionalism. International and European Perspectives*, Cambridge (etc.): Cambridge University Press 2007.

[16] C. Taylor, *Sources of the Self. The Making of the Modern Identity*, Cambridge (etc.): Cambridge University Press 1989, p. 130 [Italics in the original].

[17] Cf. B. van Roermund, 'Introduction: Law - the Order and the Alien,' *Ethical Perspectives: Journal of the European ethics network*, vol. 13 (2006), pp. 331–357, at pp. 332–333: 'Legal discourse provides ample evidence of this "self-based" conceptual geography. Without silently recalling the experience of one's own existence, it is incomprehensible why certain rights should be regarded as "fundamental." Without the internal view on a legal order as "one's own", there is no reason why some assertions should count as "normative", and some form of authority as "supreme". Without appreciating the reflexive overtones of the "proper", one would be unable to understand the concepts of "property" or of "trespassing". Phenomenology basically explicates this starting point, as it pervades all our thinking, speaking and acting.'

and that is central to law. For the concept of legal power this means that a phenomenological approach is able to understand legal power from the first person stance; to grasp a fundamental sense of self or identity that is presupposed in any account of legal power.

The oeuvre of Merleau-Ponty comprises texts on subjects such as perception, language, history, painting, expression, politics, ontology, nature, pedagogy and behaviour. Merleau-Ponty did not explicitly address legal problems. Yet, his work has formed the inspiration for Claude Lefort, one of the most important contemporary French political philosophers.[18] Not unlike Lefort, I will use the work of Merleau-Ponty to analyse the concepts central to this study: constituent power and constituted power. For this purpose, I will put emphasis on certain aspects of Merleau-Ponty's work, leaving others aside. Furthermore, I will confront his works with that of others in order to unveil their full potential for the themes of this inquiry. It is important to stress that this is not an inquiry into the value of Merleau-Ponty's thoughts for legal philosophy in general, nor a book on the political philosophy of Merleau-Ponty himself.[19] Rather, I would like to see my engaging with Merleau-Ponty's work as in accordance with his own way of philosophising, taking up an 'unthought' of his thought.[20] In this way, the theme of constituent power can be traced back to its philosophical foundations. From there, a new light may be cast on the problem of how to make sense of the 'competence creep'. As a philosophical study, this book makes no pretentions of coming up with solutions to the problem of creeping competences. Its aim is more modest. Philosophy of Law may help elucidate problems in law and can point a way, or offer an alternative framework, wherein these legal problems can be articulated and solutions might be found. This study hopes to develop such a framework for the problem of creeping competences in the EU.

---

[18] For the intellectual relationship between Merleau-Ponty and Lefort, see: G. Labelle, 'Maurice Merleau-Ponty et la genèse de la philosophie politique de Claude Lefort', *Politique et Sociétés*, vol. 22 (2003), pp. 9–44, available at: http://id.erudit.org/iderudit/008849ar [visited 29 October 2009] and D. Loose, *Democratie zonder blauwdruk. De politieke filosofie van Claude Lefort*, Best: Damon 1997, Chap. I.

[19] There are also some other publications that use Merleau-Ponty's work to analyse problems in the field of legal philosophy: W. S. Hamrick, *An Existential Phenomenology of Law: Maurice Merleau-Ponty*, Dordrecht (etc.): Nijhoff 1987, B. van Roermund, 'We, Europeans. On the Very Idea of a Common Market in European Community', in B. van Roermund, F. Fleerackers, & E. van Leeuwen (eds.), *Law, Life and the Images of Man*, Berlijn: Duncker & Humblot 1996, pp. 455–467, and H. Lindahl, 'Acquiring a Community: The Acquis and the Institution of European Legal Order', *European Law Journal*, vol. 9 (2003), pp. 433–450.

[20] M. Merleau-Ponty, *The Visible and the Invisible*, trans. A. Lingis, Evanston, Ill.: Northwestern University Press 1968, p. 199/M. Merleau-Ponty, *Le visible et l'invisible*, Paris: Gallimard 2003 [1964], pp. 249–250: '[C]an one put to a philosophy questions that it has not put to itself? (…) My point of view: a philosophy, like a work of art, is an object that can arouse more thoughts than those that are "contained" in it (can one enumerate them? Can one count up a language?), retains a meaning outside of its historical context, even *has* meaning only outside of that context' [Italics in the original]. For the notion of 'unthought', see: M. Merleau-Ponty, *Signs*, trans. R.C. McCleary, Evanston, Ill.: Northwestern University Press 1964, p. 160/M. Merleau-Ponty, *Signes*, Paris: Gallimard 2001 [1960], p. 260.

Outline of the Book

Concluding this introduction, let us take a look at what awaits us in the pages to come. The first chapter will describe the central problem of this book: What are we to make of the competence creep of the European Union? This chapter will thus be a legal account of the competence creep, and the role the ECJ plays in it. For that purpose, the present division of competences, and the main principles regulating it, will be sketched. Central to an understanding of creeping competences is the ECJ's doctrine of implied powers as an emblematic case of this phenomenon. What lies at the core of this doctrine is the relationship between constituent and constituted power. This becomes clear when we reread parts of the Maastricht-judgment of the German Federal Constitutional Court. Chapter 2 will address the relationship between constituent power and constituted or constitutional power from the viewpoint of the history of constitutional theory. Making the distinction between a tradition of constituent power, on the one hand, and a tradition of constitutionalism, on the other, I will argue that this relationship is traditionally conceptualised in a dualistic way. The work of several authors will be discussed in this context. Yet, since this dualism cannot make sense of the phenomenon of creeping competences, the present theories need to be rejected as far as this aspect is concerned.

Proceeding to the next stage of this inquiry, I will rethink the concepts of constituent and constituted power, and sketch an alternative theory of their relationship in Chaps. 3 and 4. Borrowing a term from Merleau-Ponty, I will call my alternative 'chiastic'. Accordingly, I will show what a chiastic understanding of legal power amounts to. Chapter 3 will first explore an alternative way of understanding constitution by taking it as a form of expression. In the fourth chapter, I will argue that this goes with a specific understanding of rule-following. In this respect, Merleau-Ponty's work offers important insights to help make sense of what Wittgenstein called the 'animal' character of rule-following. In the fifth and last chapter, I will return to the legal problem of 'creeping competences' and show that this alternative theory (a theory of chiastic power) can make sense of the Court's role in the competence creep, in general, and the doctrine of implied powers, in particular. Indeed, implied powers as a borderline case reveals that in constitutional settings, legal power moves between power *in* and power *over* law. Hence, there can be no strict distinction between constituent power (or politics) on the one hand, and constitutional power (or law) on the other. Several other case studies concerning competences will also be discussed to sustain this claim. Finally, the conclusion will summarise the main argument of this book.

Chapter 1
Competences and Authority in the European Legal Order

European integration is no longer an idea that is taken for granted, much less taken as gospel. Especially in the last couple of years, with the European Union trying to adopt its own constitution, one can witness growing reservations about the process of European integration. Often, this reticence goes hand in hand with a criticism of the growing power of Brussels, and the lack of democratic legitimacy. Central to these debates is the concept of legal competence, the power to impose binding norms. The criticism against European integration is often expressed in terms of a 'competence creep', as if Brussels is the head of a giant octopus that, in the name of integration, usurps more and more national powers. This study is to be an inquiry into these 'creeping competences'. How can we legally make sense of them? In what way are they creeping at the cost of national powers? At what cost will national powers come if integration is the issue? What are the philosophical problems hiding in the background of this phenomenon? In this chapter, I will give an overview of how the issue of competence lies at the heart of politico-legal developments in the European Union. In this respect, I will pay attention to the monitoring role that the European Court of Justice (ECJ) plays as the highest judge of the Union. I will also discuss the so-called doctrine of implied powers, as an emblematic case of 'creeping competencies'. Furthermore, I will analyse the problem of competences, and will show how a strictly legal solution does not suffice. However, I will start by sketching the present division of competences between the European Union and its Member States.

1.1 The Division of Competences Between Union and Member States

Any inquiry into the problem of competence in the European Union should start with an analysis of what the Treaty says on the issue of competence. What remains of the story of a power-usurping Union when we take into account the legal documents? Where do we, legally speaking, stand today?[1] In this respect, two important principles need to be distinguished. The first appears in Article 13, paragraph 2 Treaty on European Union, or TEU (ex Article 7 EC) that governs the horizontal division of competences, i.e., the division between the different institutions of the EU. It holds that '[e]ach institution shall act within the limits of the powers conferred upon it by this Treaty.'[2] Accordingly, each institution has only those powers attributed to it and in the Union one may speak of an 'institutional balance'.[3] Its importance notwithstanding, Article 13 TEU does not say which powers the institutions of the Union hold. A first answer to this question may be found when we take a look at the so-called principle of conferred powers, also known as the principle of attribution or conferral. This is the main principle governing the competences of the European Union. We find it in Article 5 TEU, paragraph 2 (ex Article 5 EC, paragraph 1) that states: 'Under the principle of conferral, the Union shall act only within the limits of the competences conferred upon it by the Member States in the Treaties to attain the objectives set out therein. Competences not conferred upon the Union in the Treaties remain with the Member States.'[4]

The principle says that the Union only has the power to act within the fields and by the means explicitly mentioned. Therefore, the Union has no general competence to act within the framework of the Treaty. The direct consequence of the principle of conferred powers for the European Union is that all its actions must depend on a prior legal basis in the Treaty. The rationale underlying this requirement is the idea that the Union itself has no power to create competences, but that its powers derive from the Member States. In other words, all competences of the European institutions are retraceable to the Member States. This view is also supported by the case law of the ECJ: With the signing of the Treaties, the Member States have 'limited their sovereign rights, albeit within limited fields.'[5] Because of this, a transfer of competences for an indefinite period has taken place.

---

[1] For the sake of clarity, I will also refer to the Treaty establishing a Constitution for Europe, C 310/1. This constitution had structured and laid down the existing case law of the ECJ on the division of competences in a better way. For an excellent analysis of the way in which the European Constitution had dealt with the issue of competence, see: Z.C. Mayer, 'Competences – Reloaded? The Vertical Division of Powers in the EU and the new European Constitution', *International Journal of Constitutional Law*, vol. 3 (2005), pp. 493–515.

[2] It should immediately be noted that an important kind of competence creep takes place here. The 'competences of EU institutions' are often confused with matters that fall 'within the scope of EU law'. It is important to note that we are dealing here with two different things. A matter 'within the scope of EU law' does not necessarily entail a competence of an EU institution. However, by claiming that a certain matter falls 'within the scope of EU law', the ECJ contributes to a loss of power for the Member States. On this issue see: S. Prechal, S. de Vries and H. van Eijken, 'The Principle of Attributed Powers and the "Scope of EU Law"', in L. Besselink, F. Pennings and S. Prechal (eds.), *The Eclipse of Legality in Europe*, Kluwer Law International, forthcoming 2011.

[3] Cf. J-P. Jacqué, 'The Principle of Institutional Balance', *Common Market Law Review*, vol. 41 (2004), pp. 383–391.

[4] Cf. Article 5 EC, paragraph 1 stated: 'The Community shall act within the limits of the powers conferred upon it by this Treaty and of the objectives assigned to it therein.' See also Article I-11, paragraph 2, of the Treaty establishing a Constitution for Europe.

[5] Case 26/62, *Van Gend & Loos* [1963] ECR 1.

The importance of the requirement of a prior legal basis comes into sight when we consider its two different, but interrelated, functions.[6] First of all, it works as a guarantee. The legal basis of a decision contains the scope of the competence, the authorized institution, the required decisionmaking procedure and the instruments that must be used. With these specific requirements, the competences of an institution can be distinguished from those of other institutions, or the powers of Member States. In this way, citizens, Member States and other institutions can be protected against unauthorized actions of an institution. This protection is reflected in Article 296 TFEU (ex Article 253 EC) that demands to state the reasons on which the acts of an institution are based. As this is an essential procedural requirement in the sense of Article 263 TFEU (ex Article 230 EC), the Court can declare void actions that do not comply with it. The second function of the requirement of a prior legal basis is instrumental. Since the institutions of the European Union do not have a general competence, they can only act using the specific competences that were explicitly given to them. In other words, the competences of an institution are the 'legal limbs' with which it can act.[7] Yet, sometimes there seems to be more than one legal basis for a certain action. In this respect, it is important to stress that the institutions do not possess a wide-ranging discretionary power to choose the applicable legal basis. In its case law, the ECJ has determined that the choice of the legal basis must depend on objective factors which are the purpose and the content of the decision.[8]

The following division of legislative competences between the institutions of the European Union and the Member States can be sketched. In the current system, one may draw a distinction between exclusive competences of the Member States, exclusive competences of the Union, competences that are shared or concurrent and complementary competences of the Union.[9] Beginning with the **exclusive competences of the Member States**, we can make a further distinction between two groups. First, there are domains that the Treaties do not cover. In these areas, Member States remain exclusively competent.[10] The second group of exclusive com-

---

[6] R. Barents & L.J. Brinkhorst, *Grondlijnen van Europees Recht*, Deventer: Kluwer 2006, pp. 146–149.

[7] One could also say that the specific competences granted to the Community are 'the legal expedient created to enable them to proceed with the task stipulated in their constitutive acts.' Cf. A. Goucho Soares, 'The Principle of Conferred Powers and the Division of Powers between the European Community and the Member States', *Liverpool Law Review*, vol. 23 (2001), pp. 57–78, at p. 57.

[8] As Van Ooik comments: 'The European Court of Justice (ECJ) has always played an important role in monitoring the division of competence, both between the Member States and the EU institutions (vertical competence disputes), and between the EU institutions themselves (horizontal battles over might and power). Most of these types of disputes reach the ECJ in the form of a legal basis case (...)'. See: R. van Ooik, 'The European Court of Justice and the Division of Competence in the European Union', in: D. Obradovic and N. Lavranos (eds.), *Interface between EU Law and National Law*, Groningen: Europa Law Publishing 2007, pp. 11–40, at p. 13.

[9] Van Ooik, o.c., also distinguishes the residual competence of the Union, i.e. Article 308 EC (now Article 352 TFEU). I will come back to this provision in the next Section of this Chapter.

[10] The implied powers of the European Community are not yet taken into account. I will turn my attention to them in the next Section of this Chapter.

petence of the Member States consists of those domains where their competence is explicitly mentioned, or where the Union is prohibited from acting. Examples can be found in Articles 114, 154 and 169 TFEU (ex Articles 95, 138 and 153 EC). There are very few areas in which the Member States are exclusively authorized to enact legislation. It is also important to notice that we are not dealing with large, clearly demarcated domains, but only with specific aspects of certain fields. Legislation concerning acquiring and forfeiting nationality makes a good example. The competence in this area is exclusively reserved for the Member States.[11]

Just like the Member States, the European Union is exclusively competent in only a small number of fields. This follows from the principle of conferred powers: an **exclusive power of the Union** can never be the rule. An exclusive competence of the EU is defined in Article 2 TFEU, paragraph 1: 'When the Treaties confer on the Union exclusive competence in a specific area, only the Union may legislate and adopt legally binding acts, the Member States being able to do so themselves only if so empowered by the Union or for the implementation of Union acts.' In this context, 'the concept of an "area" is essentially built up by a collection of Treaty provisions enabling the EC [/EU, LC] institutions to adopt secondary legislation on the various aspects of a certain substantive matter.'[12] This exclusivity applies even if the Union has not yet taken any legislative action in the field. Therefore, were a Member State to enact legislation in an area belonging to the exclusive competences of the Union, a citizen of a Member State could lodge a complaint with the national judge referring directly to the exclusivity of the Union competence. The judge will have to declare the national rule not applicable. However, it remains possible that Member States are allowed to act in these domains. The Union may explicitly authorize the Member States, or the competence may be delegated to them. In total, there are five areas where the Union is exclusively competent. The Treaty on the Functioning of the European Union enumerates the areas in which the Union has exclusive competence in Article 3, paragraph 1: '(a) customs union; (b) the establishing of the competition rules necessary for the functioning of the internal market; (c) monetary policy for the Member States whose currency is the euro; (d) the conservation of marine biological resources under the common fisheries policy; (e) common commercial policy.'[13] Lawyers agree that these areas are not new, but that the Union was already exclusively competent in these domains.[14] To some extent the Treaty on the Functioning of the European Union only confirmed what was already known from the case law of the European Court of Justice. In its case law the ECJ had recognized two of these areas of exclusive competence. The first of these

---

[11] The Declaration on nationality of a Member State, attached to the Maastricht Treaty, states that: '(...) wherever in the Treaty establishing the European Community reference is made to nationals of the Member States, the question whether an individual possesses the nationality of a Member State shall be settled solely by reference to the national law of the Member State concerned.'

[12] R. van Ooik, o.c., p. 15.

[13] See also: Article I-13 of the Treaty establishing a Constitution for Europe.

[14] Cf. Van Ooik, o.c., p. 14. The external exclusive competences of the Community will be treated separately.

was the common commercial policy as defined in Article 207 TFEU (ex Article 133 EC).[15] The protection of maritime resources and the conservation of marine biological resources under the common fisheries policy was the second one.[16]

The largest category of competences consists of those shared by the Union and the Member States; **the concurrent or shared competences**.[17] Sharing competence is almost the default practice for the internal division of competences between the Union and the Member States.[18] The formulation of Article 4, paragraph 1 TFEU also makes this clear: 'The Union shall share competence with the Member States where the Treaties confer on it a competence which does not relate to the areas referred to in Articles 3 and 6.' The definition of a shared competence may be found in Article 2, pargarph 2 TFEU: 'When the Treaties confer on the Union a competence shared with the Member States in a specific area, the Union and the Member States may legislate and adopt legally binding acts in that area. The Member States shall exercise their competence to the extent that the Union has not exercised its competence. The Member States shall again exercise their competence to the extent that the Union has decided to cease exercising its competence.'[19] In other words, in a specific area both the Member States and the Union may enact legislation. Immediately, the question arises about the relationship between the two levels in case of conflict. Keeping this question in mind, we can draw a further distinction within this category taking into account whether or not a Union competence is exhaustible.

So-called *exhaustible or joint competences*[20] exist in areas where both the Member States and the Union are competent, but where the Union, by enacting legislation, can exhaust this competence, thereby claiming it exclusively for itself. In the case that EU institutions have not yet acted, Member States remain competent to adopt legally binding rules. Of course, they may only do so while complying with their obligations following from the Treaty. This situation, nevertheless, changes when the EU decides to exercise its shared competence and legislate. As a consequence, a competence hitherto shared by Union and Member States may, from now on, only be exercised by the Union. The Member States may only follow by legisla-

---

[15] Opinion 1/75 [1975] ECR 1355, Case 41/76, *Suzanne Donckerwolcke v Procureur de la République* [1976] ECR 1921 and Opinion 1/94 [1994] ECR I-05267.

[16] Case 804/79, *Commission v United Kingdom* [1981] ECR 1045 and Joined cases 3, 4 and 6/76, *Kramer* [1976] ECR 1279.

[17] The Court already used the term 'shared competence' in Opinion 2/91 [1993] ECR I-1061 and in Opinion 1/94 [1994] ECR I-5267.

[18] Cf. S. Weatherill, 'Competence' in B. de Witte (ed.), *Ten Reflections on the Constitutional Treaty for Europe*, European University Institute, Robert Schuman Centre for Advanced Studies and Academy of European Law, San Domenico di Fiesole 2003, pp. 45–66, at p. 47. This is exactly why, according to Weatherill, a hard list of EU competences is not a good solution to improve the transparency of the present division of competences.

[19] See also: Article I-14 of the Treaty establishing a Constitution for Europe.

[20] The Court uses the phrase 'joint competence' in its case law, for example in Opinion 2/91. The French version speaks of '(...) *une compétence des États membres parallèle à celle de la Communauté*.' Note that the distinction between exhaustible and non-exhaustible shared competences is not made in the Treaties.

tion implementing the rules of the Union. In other words, a transformation occurs: The EU pre-empts action of the Member States, making a shared competence into a *de facto* exclusive competence of the Union after exhaustion.[21] This also explains why the Union may not exercise these shared competences unconditionally; it must always take into account the principles of subsidiarity and proportionality.[22] Lastly, the situation may occur that the EU stopped adopting legislation in a specific field. On these (rare) occasions, there is a possibility that the Member States may once again exercise their competence.[23]

The category of exhaustible Union competences includes the following fields: internal market, social policy; economic, social and territorial cohesion; agriculture and fisheries, with the eclusion of marine biological resources; environment; consumer protection; transport; trans-European networks; energy; area of freedom, security and justice; common safety concerns in public health matters.[24] Then there is a small group of shared competences that are *non-exhaustible*. In areas with this type of competence, the Union cannot exhaust it and, as a consequence, both the Union and the Member States remain authorised to adopt legislation. The areas with this kind of competence are research, technological development and space and, furthermore, development cooperation and humanitarian aid.[25]

The final category of Union powers is that of **the competences to carry out supporting, coordinating or complementary action**. As Article 4, pargraph 5 TFEU makes clear: 'In certain areas and under the conditions laid down in the Treaties, the Union shall have competence to carry out actions to support, coordinate or supplement the actions of the Member States, without thereby superseding their competence in these areas. Legally binding acts of the Union adopted on the basis of the provisions of the Treaties relating to these areas shall not entail harmonisation

---

[21] See also: R. Wessel, 'Integration by Stealth: On the Exclusivity of Community Competence. A Comment on the Ronald van Ooik Contribution,' in: D. Obradovic and N. Lavranos (eds.), *Interface between EU Law and National Law*, Groningen: Europa Law Publishing 2007, pp. 41–49, at p. 46. For the doctrine of pre-emption in EC law, see: R. Schütze, 'Supremacy without Pre-emption? The very slowly emergent Doctrine of Community Pre-emption', *Common Market Law Review*, 43 (2006), pp. 1023–1048. This article also points to older literature. Strangely enough, both Van Ooik and Wessel do not refer to this doctrine in their contributions. Yet, Wessel's neofunctional approach seems very close to 'the spirit' of pre-emption.

[22] Article 5, paragraphs 3 and 4 TEU (ex Article 5 EC). See also: Article I-11, paragraphs 3 and 4 of the Treaty establishing a Constitution for Europe. There exists an enormous amount of literature on the principle of subsidiarity. Two recent articles are: G. Davies, 'Subsidiarity: The Wrong Idea, In the Wrong Place, At the Wrong Time', *Common Market Law Review*, vol. 43 (2006), pp. 63–85 and E. Herlin-Karnell, 'Subsidiarity in the Area of EU Justice and Home Affairs Law – A Lost Cause?', *European Law Journal*, vol. 15 (2009), pp. 351–361. For more references, see G. Conway, 'Conflicts of Competence Norms in EU Law and the Legal Reasoning of the ECJ', *German Law Journal*, vol. 11 (2010), pp. 966–1005, footnotes 37 and 113.

[23] For this case and interesting exceptions to this procedure of exhaustion, see Van Ooik, o.c., pp. 24–27.

[24] Article 4, paragraph 2 TFEU. See also: Article I-14, paragraph 2 of the Treaty establishing a Constitution for Europe.

[25] Article 4, paragraphs 3 and 4 TFEU. See also: Article I-14, paragraphs 3 and 4 of the Treaty establishing a Constitution for Europe.

of Member States' laws or regulations.' Here, the presumption is that Union and Member States will strengthen each other's action. The Union only complements, stimulates and coordinates the legislation of the Member States.[26] It is not allowed to harmonise legislation of the Member States. The actions of the EU cannot be of such nature that the Member States are no longer able to act normatively. Member States remain authorised to adopt legislation in the areas concerned.[27] Any action of the Member States must, however, be in accordance with the principle of loyal or sincere cooperation.[28] This entails that the Member States are not allowed to act contrary to the interests of the Union. The areas in which the Union has a complementary competence are: protection and improvement of human health; industry; culture; tourism; education, youth, sport and vocational training; civil protection and administrative cooperation.[29]

1.2 Beyond Attributed Powers: The Implied Powers Doctrine

On top of the distribution of explicit competences European law doctrine also considers so-called implied powers. These are so interesting for our inquiry into the competence creep because they show, in an emblematic way, the structure of 'creeping competences'. In this Section, I will take a closer look at the implied powers of the European Union. I will first of all look at the ECJ's case law on implied powers. Yet, before we turn to the European judge, it is important to stress that the doctrine of implied powers was not invented by the ECJ. It finds its origin in American constitutional law where it was developed by the U.S. Supreme Court to increase the power of the Federal Government.[30] Furthermore, implied powers are also widely recognised in the law of international organisations.[31] In the European Union, the ECJ acknowledged the existence of implied powers for the first time in 1956. It then held that: 'Without having recourse to a wide interpretation, it is possible to apply a

---

[26] As Van Ooik puts it: 'In those areas, the "hard core" competences are to be found at national level; the "peripheral" powers are located at EU level.' Cf. Van Ooik, o.c., p. 27.

[27] Yet, Wessel warns us that '[w]hile harmonisation as such may be excluded in relation to these domains, judgements by the Court of Justice may establish a similar effect.' Cf. Wessel, o.c., p. 47.

[28] Article 4, paragraph 3 TEU (ex Article 10 EC). See also: Article I-5, par. 2 of the Treaty establishing a Constitution for Europe.

[29] Article 6 TFEU. See also: Article I-17 of the Treaty establishing a Constitution for Europe.

[30] The doctrine of implied powers was first recognised in 1819, in the famous case of *McCulloch v Maryland*. For a discussion of this case of the U.S. Supreme Court, see: C. Denys, *Impliciete bevoegdheden in de Europese Economische Gemeenschap. Een onderzoek naar de betekenis van 'implied powers'*, Antwerpen: Maklu 1990, pp. 113–117.

[31] For a discussion of the role of implied powers in international law and further references see: K. Skubiszewski, 'Implied Powers of International Organizations', in Y. Dinstein (ed.), *International Law at a Time of Perplexity*, Dordrecht: Kluwer Academic 1989, pp. 855–868 and J. Klabbers, 'Over het leerstuk van de impliciete bevoegdheden in het recht der internationale organisaties', in J.D.M. Steenbergen (ed.), *Ongebogen recht*, Den Haag: Sdu Uitgevers 1998, pp. 1–12.

rule of interpretation generally accepted in both international and national law, according to which, the rules laid down by an international treaty or a law presuppose the rules without which that treaty or law would have no meaning or could not be reasonably and usefully applied.'[32] The institutions of the Union thus possess those powers not mentioned explicitly in the Treaty but that are, nevertheless, necessary for the exercise of an explicitly given competence.

The ECJ went further in other cases. It held for example that although Article 137 EC (now Article 153 TFEU) does not explicitly give the Commission the power to make binding decisions, it nevertheless 'confers a specific task on the Commission [and] it must be accepted, if that provision is not to be rendered wholly ineffective, that it confers on the Commission necessarily and *per se* the powers which are indispensable to carry out that task.'[33] In the same vein, recently the Court stated that even though criminal procedure and criminal law are not areas of Union competence, it may still take measures 'which relate to the criminal law of the Member States which it considers necessary in order to ensure that the rules which it lays down on environmental protection are fully effective.'[34]

It is, however, in the area of external relations that the doctrine of implied powers plays a much bigger role. The foundations were laid in three judgments in the 1970s. In the case of *ERTA*, the ECJ stated that the authority of the Community to enter into international agreements 'arises not only from an express conferment by the Treaty—as is the case with Articles 113 [now Article 207 TFEU] and 114 [now withdrawn] for tariff and trade agreements, and with Article 238 [now Article 217 TFEU] for association agreements —but may equally flow from other provisions of the Treaty and from measures adopted, within the framework of those provisions, by the Community institutions.'[35] This applies especially, the Court says, to those areas where the Community has already exercised *internal* competence. If this is the case, there is a common policy inside the Community. Read in conjunction with the principle of loyal or sincere cooperation, 'it follows that, to the extent to which Community rules are promulgated for the attainment of the objectives of the Treaty, the Member States cannot, outside the framework of the Community institutions, assume obligations which might affect those rules or alter their scope.'[36] Indeed, 'Community powers exclude the possibility of concurrent powers on the part of Member States, since any steps taken outside the framework of the Community

---

[32] Case 8/55, *Fédération Charbonnière de Belgique v High Authority of the European Coal and Steel Community* [1954–56] ECR 245. For a discussion of this case, see: C. Denys, o.c., pp. 119–122.

[33] Cases 281, 283–285, *Germany v Commission* [1987] ECR 3203, par. 28.

[34] Case C-176/03, *Commission v Council* [2005] ECR I-7879, par. 48.

[35] Case 22/70, *Commission v Council (ERTA)* [1971] ECR 263, par. 15–16. This case is also known as *AETR*, the French abbreviation of the Agreement under discussion. Note that these judgments were made when the EU did not yet exist. Hence, I will speak of the Community in this context. As noted earlier, the Treaty of Lisbon abolished the pillars of the Union and gave the EU legal personality (see Article 47 TEU).

[36] Ibid., par. 22.

institutions would be incompatible with the *unity* of the common market and the *uniform application* of Community law.'[37]

In *Kramer*, the ECJ changes its view. It considers that 'it follows from the very duties and powers which Community law has established and assigned to the institutions of the Community on the internal level that the Community has authority to enter into international commitments for the conservation of the resources of the sea.'[38] It is true, the ECJ continues, that when Community institutions have not yet taken actions to fully exercise their powers, the Member States remain competent. However, this power can only be of a transitional nature. Finally, referring once again to the principle of loyal cooperation (now Article 4, paragraph 3 TEU), and Article 116 EC (stating the need of 'common action' after the transition period, now Article 33 TFEU) the Court holds that 'institutions and the Member States will be under a duty to use all the political and legal means at their disposal in order to ensure the participation of the Community in the convention and in other similar agreements.'[39] In this way, the ECJ refines its own decision in *ERTA*. To conclude that an (implied) external competence exists, it is no longer necessary that the corresponding internal competence has actually been exercised. The mere existence of such a power is enough.[40]

The same elements which played major roles in the Court's reasoning in *ERTA* and *Kramer*, featuring the principle of loyal cooperation, reappear in Opinion 1/76. The Court even went further regarding the exclusivity of the EC's external competence by determining that the Community could claim exclusive competence in external relations even where internally no measures were taken yet, in cases where Member States' action could endanger the attainment of a common goal.[41] Furthermore, there is another new element in the considerations of the ECJ. The Agreement concerning the laying-up fund under discussion in the Opinion, also envisaged the establishment of a Fund Tribunal empowered 'to give preliminary rulings (…) [that] may concern not only the validity and interpretation of decisions adopted by the organs of the fund, but also the interpretation of the agreement and the statute.'[42] This was a direct threat to the Court's own jurisdiction, a threat it neutralised immediately. Since the agreement was an act of one of the institutions as meant in Article 177 EC (now Article 267 TFEU) this entailed 'that the Court, within the context of Community legal order, has jurisdiction to give a preliminary ruling on the interpretation of such an agreement. Thus, the question arises whether the provisions relating to the jurisdiction of the Fund Tribunal are compatible with those of the Treaty relating to the jurisdiction of the Court of Justice.'[43] And since 'no one can rule out *a priori* the possibility that the legal organs in question might

---

[37] Ibid., par. 30–31 [My italics, LC].

[38] Joined cases 3, 4 and 6/76, *Kramer* [1976] ECR 1279, par. 30/33.

[39] Ibid., par. 44/45.

[40] See also Denys, o.c., p. 135.

[41] Opinion 1/76 [1977] ECR 741. See in particular par. 10–12.

[42] Ibid., par. 17.

[43] Ibid., par. 18.

arrive at divergent interpretations with consequential effect on legal certainty,'[44] the ECJ could not but 'express certain reservations as regards the compatibility of the structures of the "Fund Tribunal" with the Treaty.'[45]

In Opinion 1/94 concerning the WTO, the ECJ refined the exclusivity of the EC's external competence. The Court held that the case of Opinion 1/76 was special. It concerned an objective that could only be attained with the help of an international agreement. Furthermore, internal rules only made sense after the conclusion of this agreement.[46] Now, the Court stated that 'an internal power to harmonize which has not been exercised in a specific field cannot confer exclusive external competence in that field on the Community.'[47] Even though the ECJ seems to be stricter in this judgment, most recent cases show that it is quite easily willing to conclude that an exclusive competence exists. In one of the so-called 'Open Skies' cases, the ECJ, restating its judgement of *ERTA*, held that an exercised internal Community competence may lead to an exclusive implied external competence. This was the case, '[s]ince those findings imply recognition of an exclusive external competence for the Community in consequence of the adoption of internal measures. It is appropriate to ask whether they also apply in the context of a provision such as Article 84(2) of the Treaty [now Article 100 TFEU], which confers upon the Council the power to decide "whether, to what extent, and by what procedure appropriate provisions may be laid down" for air transport, including, therefore, for its external aspect. If the Member States were free to enter into international commitments affecting the common rules adopted on the basis of Article 84(2) of the Treaty, that would jeopardise the attainment of the objective pursued by those rules, and would thus prevent the Community from fulfilling its task in the defence of the common interest.'[48]

Then, the Court went on to discuss 'under what circumstances the scope of the common rules may be affected or distorted by the international commitments at issue and, therefore, under what circumstances the Community acquires an external competence by reason of the exercise of its internal competence.'[49] It decided on a broad reading of this phrase: 'There is nothing in the Treaty to prevent the institutions arranging, in the common rules laid down by them, concerted action in relation to non-member countries, or to prevent them prescribing the approach to be taken by the Member States in their external dealings.'[50] Recently, the Court reiterated this point in its opinion concerning the signing of the new Lugano Convention. It first held, referring to cases mentioned above, that the EC's competence to conclude international agreements might be shared or exclusive.[51] Then, it took a closer look at the issue of exclusivity. Having pointed to the principle of loyal cooperation, the ECJ stated that

---

[44] Ibid., par. 20.

[45] Ibid., par. 21.

[46] Opinion 1/94 [1994] ECR I-5267, par. 85–86.

[47] Ibid., par. 88.

[48] Case C-476/98, *Commission v Germany* [2002] ECR I-9855, par. 104–105.

[49] Ibid., par. 107.

[50] Ibid., par. 112.

[51] Opinion 1/03 [2006] ECR I-1145, par. 114–116.

what is essential for the decision on the exclusivity of an EC external competence is 'a uniform and consistent application of the Community rules (...). The purpose of the exclusive competence of the Community is primarily to preserve the effectiveness of Community law and the proper functioning of the systems established by its rules, independently of any limits laid down by the provision of the Treaty on which the institutions base the adoption of such rules.'[52] Notice how now Article 3, paragraph 2 TFEU reads as follows: 'The Union shall also have exclusive competence for the conclusion of an international agreement when its conclusion is provided for in a legislative act of the Union or is necessary to enable the Union to exercise its internal competence, or in so far as its conclusion may affect common rules or alter their scope.'

The discussion of these cases leads to a preliminary conclusion. The doctrine of implied powers is a specific interpretation of the Treaty, in particular of those articles governing the division of competences between the European Union and its Member States. It gives the Union some flexibility since it derives unwritten powers from explicitly conferred ones. Furthermore, the considerations of the Court are often similar in the different cases: It links internal and external competences together, and refers to the objectives of the Treaty and the principles of loyal cooperation and effectiveness. Moreover, while recognising the existence of implied powers of the Union, the Court claims to remain within the ambit of the Treaty.

If we take implied powers in the wide formulation, we can also find them in the Treaty itself. I am pointing at the so-called functional provisions: Articles 114 and 352 TFEU (ex Articles 95 and 308 EC).[53] These are functional precisely because they give the Union the power to enact legislation in order to achieve a certain aim. The practical consequence of these articles is that the Union can act in areas where it has no explicit competence.[54] While it is true that in this case one is not dealing with implied powers in the strict sense of the word (there is an explicit provision in the Treaty), the very same logic of effectiveness underlies the functional provisions and the doctrine of implied powers. As a consequence, they have a similar 'creeping' effect on the division of competences.[55] This may also explain why they were the

---

[52] Ibid., par. 128 and 131.

[53] Cf. G. de Búrca & B. de Witte, 'The Delimitation of Powers Between the EU and its Member States', in A. Arnull & D. Wincott (eds.), *Accountability and Legitimacy in the European Union*, Oxford: Oxford University Press 2002, pp. 201–222. In this article, the authors also acknowledge the problematic character of the these two provisions. After a thorough analysis, they argue in favour of reformulation, in stead of pleading for their deletion (as some of the Member States have done).

[54] I. Pernice, *Rethinking the Methods of Dividing and Controlling the Competences of the Union*, Walter Hallstein-Institut für Europäisches Verfassungsrecht Humboldt-Universität zu Berlin, Paper 6/01, Oktober 2001, p. 5. Available at: www.whi-berlin.de/pernice-competencies.htm [visited on 13 October 2009].

[55] On how effectiveness played a crucial role ever since the very early case law on implied powers, see: A. Dashwood and J. Heliskoski, 'The classic authorities revisited' in A. Dashwood and Ch. Hillion (eds.), *The General Law of E.C. External Relations*, London: Sweets & Maxwell 2000, pp. 3–19, at pp. 6–9.

only provisions singled out for revision in the Laeken Declaration.[56] Taking this into account, I treat them here under the heading of 'implied powers'. In the first paragraph of Article 114 TFEU we read: 'Save where otherwise provided in the Treaties, the following provisions shall apply for the achievement of the objectives set out in Article 26. The European Parliament and the Council shall, acting in accordance with the ordinary legislative procedure and after consulting the Economic and Social Committee, adopt the measures for the approximation of the provisions laid down by law, regulation or administrative action in Member States which have as their object the establishment and functioning of the internal market.' This provision gives the Union the power to harmonise the legislation of the Member States. The article has a very wide ambit, since it can be called upon to regulate subjects which are only indirectly concerned with the internal market, and even to resolve distortions of free competition. Currently, it is also used in cases where, previously, Article 352 was applied.[57]

Even though what is now Article 352 TFEU has already been part of the normal system for a long time, its broad formulation gives it a special place in the Treaty. Interestingly, it has been interpreted as 'providing the Community with implied powers.'[58] Article 352, pragraph 1 TFEU runs as follows: 'If action by the Union should prove necessary, within the framework of the policies defined in the Treaties, to attain one of the objectives set out in the Treaties, and the Treaties have not provided the necessary powers, the Council, acting unanimously on a proposal from the Commission and after obtaining the consent of the European Parliament, shall adopt the appropriate measures. Where the measures in question are adopted by the Council in accordance with a special legislative procedure, it shall also act unanimously on a proposal from the Commission and after obtaining the consent of the European Parliament.' This provision has been included to fill in the gaps of

---

[56] Cf. S. Weatherill, 'Competence Creep and Competence Control', in P. Eeckhout and T. Tridimas (eds.), *Yearbook of European Law*, vol. 23 (2004), pp. 1–55, at p. 6: 'The only Treaty provisions explicitly selected by the Laeken agenda for review were the functionally broad Articles 95 and 308 EC. (…) These provisions plainly do not confer an unlimited competence. But they do not tie down legislative action to particular sectors. They instead envisage a broad competence to act in pursuit of the Community's objectives. The limits that are imposed – in short, a tie to market-making under Articles 94 and 95 and a tie to the EC's objectives under Article 308 – are limits that lack precision. And most significant of all they have been driven by a long-standing readiness among the Member States acting unanimously in Council to assert a broad reach to the EC's legislative competence.'

[57] The recent case law concerning (the former) Article 95 EC is very interesting. In the Tobacco Advertising Judgement (Case C-376/98, *Germany v European Parliament and Council* [2000] ECR I-08419), the Court really restricted the use of this article. See for a comment on this judgement: *Common Market Law Review*, vol. 37 (2000), pp. 1301–1305. However, in the Tobacco Manufacturing Directive Case (Case C-491/01, *The Queen and the Secretary of State for Health ex parte British American Tobacco and Imperial Tobacco* [2002] ECR I-11453) the ECJ seems to retreat from its strict interpretation. See also: D. Slater, 'The scope of EC harmonizing powers revisited?', *German Law Journal*, vol. 4 (2003), pp. 137–147.

[58] A. Giardina, 'The Rule of Law and Implied Powers in the European Communities', in: *The Italian Yearbook of International Law. Volume I*, Napoli: Editoriale Scientifica 1975, pp. 99–111, at p. 99.

the present system. Nevertheless, it cannot be used to avoid the Treaty-amending procedure as stated in Article 48 TEU (ex Article 48 EU).[59] Article 352 TFEU may function as a legal basis when there are no specific provisions, or when these are insufficient as regards form or content.[60] Lately, this article has been used less often because the Union was given more competences in specific provisions. Yet, its value for the integration process should not be underestimated. Many Member States regard its existence as one of the main reasons for the limitation of their powers.[61]

1.3 Ensuring that the Law Is Observed? The Mandate of the European Court of Justice

In the debate on Union powers, a special place is assigned to the European Court of Justice. It is not the case that the ECJ is responsible for every instance of 'creeping competences'. Indeed, other EU institutions also play a part in this process, and even the Member States (acting in the Council) contribute to this phenomenon.[62] However, an impartial judiciary is not supposed to take sides in favour of one of the two levels (in this case the EU). Is it not the ECJ's task to protect the Member States against a too ambitious European legislator? Instead, the Court itself has been criticised for interpreting European law extensively in this way, being the main culprit of the 'competence creep'. I will thus focus on the role of the ECJ because it is generally considered as problematic when it comes to limiting EU competences.[63] Furthermore, as I will extensively argue below, its argumentation in cases concerning competences shows the logic behind the 'competence creep'. Before we can judge the legitimacy of the allegations mentioned above, we must acknowledge as a fact that the Court has always played a very important role in the process of European integration. Here, I would like to concentrate on the mandate of the ECJ and the way in which it has taken up the task assigned to it. The obvious starting point

---

[59] Opinion 2/94 [1996] ECR I-1763.

[60] R. Barents & L.J. Brinkhorst, o.c. p. 155. Van Ooik treats this article as a separate category of residual EC/EU competence. He justifies this by pointing to the 'reformulated version' in the European Constitution: Article I-18(1) containing the so-called flexibility clause. This is now Article 352 of the Treaty on the Functioning of the European Union. See: Van Ooik, o.c., pp. 30–33.

[61] Cf. A. von Bogdandy and J. Bast, 'The Vertical Order of Competences', in A. von Bogdandy and J. Bast (eds.), *Principles of European Constitutional Law*, Oxford (etc.): Hart 2006, pp. 335–372, at p. 362: 'For many critics of the Union's order of competences, Art 308 EC is an upsetting thorn in the side. Its abolition has long belonged to the central demands of, for example, representatives of the German *Länder*. Indeed, the Article represents the weakest point in the limiting function of the current division of powers.'

[62] On this topic, see: S. Prechal, S. de Vries and H. van Eijken, o.c.

[63] This has led Joseph Weiler to argue again and again that what the EU needs is a separate 'Constitutional Council' to guard the limits of competences, see e.g. J.H.H. Weiler, 'A Constitution for Europe? Some Hard Choices', *Journal of Common Market Studies*, vol. 40 (2002), pp. 563–580, at pp. 573–574.

for this enterprise is the EC Treaty, and to be more precise, Article 19, paragraph 1 TEU (ex Article 220 EC).[64] After discussing that provision, I will briefly look into the preliminary question procedure and the so-called 'constitutionalisation' of the EC Treaty. Together the topics discussed in this Section give a reasonably good picture of how the ECJ regards its own task.

The first part of the first paragraph of Article 19 TEU says: 'The Court of Justice of the European Union shall include the Court of Justice, the General Court and specialised courts. It shall ensure that in the interpretation and application of the Treaties the law is observed.' Commenting on this article, some scholars link it directly to the issue of competence and note that the ECJ 'is thus required to ensure that the other bodies act within the limits of their respective powers.'[65] Others focus more on the vague nature of the provision and argue that 'the law' should be interpreted as meaning '*more* than Community law in the sense of primary and secondary treaty law.'[66] Furthermore, they stress that the task of the Court is not described anywhere in more detail. This unconditional character of the court's mandate entails two things. First of all, it is the court that is responsible for determining what 'the law' means. This is akin to saying that the notion of law in Article 19 TEU is open. Therefore, in finding the law, the Court may also turn to sources outside Union law. Examples of these other sources are the constitutional traditions of the Member States, international treaties, and even international customary law. In line with this, the second consequence of the formulation of Article 19 TEU is that the Court also decides over the nature and quality of EU law. In this respect, the goals of the Union are important. As we will later see, the Court tends to interpret EU law in a way that enables it to attain the ends of the integration process in an effective way.

That the mandate of the Court is 'relatively open' comes as no surprise when we take into account that the EC Treaty is often described as a *traité cadre*, i.e., a framework treaty in need of further clarification. One could even say that the nature of the Treaty calls for a specific attitude of the Court; the ECJ should be ready to adjudicate with the help of an open treaty, leaving it more room for discretion than an ordinary court.[67] Perhaps this explains why the ECJ can be best described as 'act-

---

[64] Cf. G. de Búrca, 'The European Court of Justice and the Evolution of EU Law', in T.A. Börzel and R.A. Cichowski (eds.), *The State of the European Union: Law, Politics and Society* (vol. 6), Oxford (etc.): Oxford University Press 2003, pp. 48–75, at p. 49: 'It is probably Article 220 (ex-Article 164) that has figured most prominently in the Court's shaping of its own independent sphere of influence over the years. The ECJ used this provision on numerous occasions to define its role broadly.'

[65] L.N. Brown & T. Kennedy, *The Court of Justice of the European Communities* (5th edition), London: Sweet & Maxwell 2000, p. 5.

[66] Cf. R. Barents & L.J. Brinkhorst, o.c., p. 55. [Emphasis in the original] One could also read here: more than 'Union law'.

[67] As Baquero Cruz formulates it: 'The important fact is that the Member States are bound by a Treaty according to which the Court (not national constitutional courts) is the institution responsible with ensuring that the law is observed in its interpretation and application. This means that they have entrusted that institution with the task of resolving those questions left open in the Treaty (among them, the issues of direct effect and supremacy) and in Community legislation which are brought to it in accordance with the various procedures foreseen in the Treaty. This is the system

ing in the dual capacity of a constitutional court and a court providing protection of individual rights', combining technical legal issues with 'the fundamental question of the general orientation, and the system of values which are to apply in the Community.'[68]

The most important power the ECJ possesses in order to perform its task is the ability to receive and answer preliminary questions by national judicial bodies. Indeed, it is not far-fetched to say that the central role of the ECJ in the European legal order is reflected in Article 267 TFEU (ex Article 234 EC), the preliminary reference procedure. This procedure shows how judicial protection in Europe is a responsibility shouldered by the ECJ and national courts, together. In this procedure, national courts may, and highest courts are even obliged to, ask the ECJ for a binding advice on the content and application of EU law in a case at hand. It is the Court's task to provide this information and then send the case back to the national judge. In other words, the decision in the specific case is still taken by the national judge.[69] This means that national courts are the first responsible for the application of EU law in their own national context, making these national courts genuine Union courts. In this respect, the ECJ has formulated demands that national courts and national procedural law should meet in order to secure the effectiveness of Union law. Nevertheless, the preliminary question procedure also makes the ECJ the keeper of the unity of the European legal order. By means of this procedure, the Court is able to intervene almost directly to make sure that Union law is interpreted and applied in a uniform way across the European legal order.

It is exactly this role of the ECJ as the guardian of European legal order that interests us here. The specific way in which the ECJ operates is ultimately retraceable to its own understanding of Article 19 TEU. We have seen that there is an ambiguity in the formulation of this provision. Instead of binding the Court to the Treaties, Article 19 TEU gives the Court some space to determine what the law is. That the ECJ is not too shy to make use of this space can be shown by analysing case law in different fields. One of the best examples remains the case law on the so-called 'constitutionalisation' of Community law.[70] In these cases, the ECJ interpreted the

---

that the Member States agreed upon in the Treaties of Paris and Rome, rejecting other possibilities.' See: J. Baquero Cruz, 'The Changing Constitutional Role of the European Court of Justice', *International Journal of Legal Information*, vol. 34 (2006), pp. 223–245, at pp. 229–230.

[68] U. Everling, 'The Court of Justice As an Decisionmaking Authority', *Michigan Law Review*, vol. 82 (1983–1984), pp. 1294–1310, at p. 1294. Baquero Cruz also approaches the ECJ as a constitutional court. He observes that 'the legal and institutional framework in which the Court operates was always more similar to that of a constitutional and a supreme court than to that of an international court.' See: Baquero Cruz, o.c., p. 227. In this sense, see also: A. Knook, *Europe's Constitutional Court: The Role of the European Court of Justice in the Intertwined Separation of Powers and Division of Powers in the European Union*, Doctoral Thesis, Utrecht University, Utrecht 2009.

[69] Everling, o.c., p. 1299: 'In proceedings for a preliminary ruling under Article 177 of the EEC Treaty [now Article 267 TFEU], the Court is only to answer, in an abstract manner, the question referred to it by the national court, and the national court is to apply the answer to the specific case at hand.'

[70] For a similar process in the context of EU law, see Chap. 5, Section 5 below.

Treaty founding the European Community in a very specific way. Albeit concluded as a normal international treaty, the EC is now 'constitutionalised' as far as the Court is concerned, and the ECJ is regarded as the very agent primarily responsible for this process.[71] What should then be understood by constitutionalisation? The European Community developed from an international organization ruled by a treaty into an entity no longer governed by the rules of international law, but instead by the principles of its own 'constitutional charter'.[72]

To find the first step in the process of constitutionalisation, we need to go back as far as 1962. In the case of *Van Gend en Loos*, the ECJ states that 'the objective of the EEC Treaty, which is to establish a common market, the functioning of which is of direct concern to interested parties in the Community, implies that this Treaty is more than an agreement which creates mutual obligations between the contracting states.'[73] According to the Court, this means that the European Communities form a new legal order to which the Member States have partly ceded their sovereignty. For this reason, the Treaty does not address only the Member States. Unlike ordinary rules of international law, EC rules can directly give rights to, and impose obligations on, the citizens of the Member States.[74] In this way, the Court established that Community law has direct effect: Citizens can directly call upon rules of Community law before their national courts, provided that these are sufficiently clear and precise. The direct effect of Community law, or so the Court says, is a consequence of the Treaty establishing 'a new legal order', and does not depend on what the constitution of a Member State says about the application of international law in its legal order.

The strategy the Court uses in its constitutionalising case law is known as teleological interpretation: Given that the objective (*telos*) of the Treaty is the establishment of a common market, the direct effect of Community law follows as the necessary instrument to attain this aim. Two remarks should be made in this context. Firstly, the *telos* concerns the objective, the end of the *entire* integration process. However, this does not really make things easier: For, what is the ultimate end of European integration?[75] The Court, aware of this difficulty, made it clear that one

---

[71] E. Stein, 'Lawyers, Judges, and the Making of a Transnational Constitution', *American Journal of International Law*, vol. 75 (1981) nr. 1, pp. 1–27 and G.F. Mancini, 'The Making of a Constitution for Europe', *Common Market Law Review*, vol. 26 (1989) nr. 4, pp. 595–614.

[72] For a full enumeration of the constitutional principles, see: F. Snyder, 'The unfinished constitution of the European Union: principles, processes and culture', in: J.H.H. Weiler and M. Wind, *European Constitutionalism Beyond the State*, Cambridge (etc.): Cambridge University Press 2003, pp. 55–73, at p. 62. Interestingly enough, both 'limited powers' and 'implied powers' are included in the list.

[73] Case 26/62, *Van Gend & Loos* [1963] ECR 1.

[74] Ibid.: 'The Community constitutes a new legal order of international law for the benefit of which the states have limited their sovereign rights, albeit within limited fields, and the subjects of which comprise not only Member States but also their nationals. Independently of the legislation of Member States, community law, therefore, not only imposes obligations on individuals, but is also intended to confer upon them rights which become part of their legal heritage.'

[75] Everling, o.c., p. 1305: '[T]he Greek term "telos" in this context signifies the ultimate objective and the deeper purpose of the entire process of European integration. But what is the "telos" of the Community today? Is it still that of the founders, if even they were agreed in that respect?'

objective, namely the common market, had been at the very heart of the integration project.[76] Here, my second remark cuts in. This concept has been replaced by that of the internal market. Therefore, one may now speak of the 'internal market logic'. In the case of *Flaminio Costa v E.N.E.L.*, the Court used this argumentation. It stated that the EC Treaty constituted its 'own legal order', incorporated in those of the Member Sates.[77] Since Community legislation springs from an 'independent source', it binds both the Members States and their citizens. This entails that the former are not allowed to adopt legislation contrary to Community law.[78] This doctrine is now known as the primacy of EC law, another key concept of European constitutional law.

Following Article 263 TFEU (ex Article 230 EC), the actions of the EU institutions also fall under the jurisdiction of the Court.[79] It was in 1986, in the case of *Les Verts*, that the Court explicitly stated the consequences of this. It is worthwhile to quote its argument in full: 'It must first be emphasized in this regard that the European Economic Community is a community based on the rule of law, inasmuch as neither its Member States nor its institutions can avoid a review of the question whether the measures adopted by them are in conformity with the basic constitutional charter, the Treaty. In particular, in Articles 173 [now Article 263 TFEU] and 184 [now Article 277 TFEU], on the one hand, and in Article 177 [now Article 267 TFEU], on the other, the Treaty established a complete system of legal remedies and procedures designed to permit the Court of Justice to review the legality of measures adopted by institutions.'[80] This legality check is, first and foremost, a competence check. The Court will find out whether an institution's actions were within the borders of its competence. Now we may say that the European Union, being a legal community, a legal order with its own constitutional charter, respects the principle of protection by an independent and impartial judiciary. The legal recognition of the Charter of Fundamental Rights of the European Union in the Treaty of Lisbon is surely the next step.[81]

---

[76] Ibid.: 'The Common Market constitutes the starting point for the entire integration process and all attempts at more far-reaching economic and political progress stem from it. Running like a red thread through the whole of the Court's case law is the idea that this core of the Community must remain sacrosanct.'

[77] Case 6/64, *Costa v E.N.E.L.* [1964] ECR 585: 'By contrast with ordinary international treaties, the EEC Treaty has created its own legal system which, on the entry into force of the Treaty, became an integral part of the legal systems of the Member States and which their courts are bound to apply.'

[78] Ibid.: 'It follows from all these observations that the law stemming from the Treaty could not, because of its special and original nature, be overridden by domestic legal provisions, however framed, without being deprived of its character of community law, and without the legal basis of the community itself being called into question.'

[79] Article 263 of the Treaty on the Functioning of the European Union.

[80] Case 294/83, *Parti Ecologiste 'Les Verts' v. Parliament* [1986] ECR 1339, par. 23. The Court repeated its characterisation of the Treaty as the constitutional charter of the community in Opinion 1/91 [1991] ECR I-6079. Here, the court also implicitly refers to its own task as securing the 'homogeneity of the rules of law'.

[81] See Article 6, paragraph 1 TEU.

1.4   Competences and Authority

When we discussed the division of competences at the beginning of this chapter, we distinguished only a limited number of exclusive Union competences. However, after the last sections, one might conclude 'that on the basis of the principle of implied powers, the duty of genuine cooperation (Article 10 EC) and above all the "internal market logic" as interpreted by the Court of Justice, competences have been or can be transferred to the Community and the Union in a manner not strictly complying with the narrow boundaries of the attribution doctrine. (...) In other words: There seems to be more exclusivity than meets the eye.'[82] This is one of the reasons of the infamous competence creep: Although the Treaties themself are rather reluctant when it comes to assigning exclusive competences to the EU, one way or another, the Union obtained them, anyway. And a closer look at the Treaties has taught us that by acknowledging both the principle of conferred powers and 'implied power' clauses like Article 352 TFEU and Article 3, paragraph 2 TFEU, it has codified, rather than resolved, the strain between restricting Union powers and allowing some flexibility, i.e., ultimately between two different ways of conceiving of Union competences.

One speaks of creeping competences precisely because it is unclear what the limits of Union powers are. There is, moreover, another dimension of this problem. What we encounter here is that 'the institutional question of *who gets to decide this question* as the final legal arbiter is as important as, or even more important than, the material legal question of *what* are the actual substantive limits.'[83] These two related problems are at the legal heart of the competence creep. Together they show what is ultimately at stake in the issue of competences in European law: Who has the authority to make rules, and who has the authority to decide this question?

With regard to the substantive problem, it is important to bear in mind that, all the talk of constitutionalisation notwithstanding, what is now the European Union was founded as a normal international organisation. That also explains the centrality of the principle of attributed powers: This is actually the default situation for international organisations. In the case of the EC, the principle of conferred powers was so obvious to the founders of the Community that they did not even include it in the EC Treaty. It only obtained its place in the Treaties as a result of the amendments made by the Maastricht Treaty. In that sense, the situation can be roughly described as follows: In order not to act *ultra vires*, any legislative Union action must be based on a prior legal basis in the Treaties. Now, the problem is that implied powers question this simple picture. Therefore, they rake up the quarrel on *Kompetenz-Kompetenz*: 'Both national and European constitutional law assume, in the internal logic of their respective legal systems, the role of higher law. In this way, there is

---

[82] Wessel, o.c., p. 49.

[83] J.H.H. Weiler, A.-M., Slaughter, A. Stone Sweet, 'Prologue – The European Courts of Justice', in: A.-M. Slaughter, A. Stone Sweet and J.H.H. Weiler, *The European Court and National Courts – Doctrine and Jurisprudence. Legal Change in Its Social Context*, Oxford: Hart 1998, pp. v-xiv, at p. vii.

no agreement as to the 'kompetenz/kompetenz' between national legal orders and the EU legal order.'[84]

To put a finger on the problem, let us take the example of implied powers once again. Even though implied powers have become a doctrinal classic in international law, they have never been completely accepted. The strain between recognising them and adhering strictly to attributed powers, between flexibility and containment, can be seen as 'the tension between sovereignty and community in a different guise.'[85] In other words, we are dealing with the question how to understand the relationship between Member States and European Union. Do the Member States remain fully in control, consequently making their will decisive in determining the powers of the Union? Or does the Union constitute a separate subject of international law, possessing a will of its own? This is exactly what implied powers are all about: the *ultimate commonality* of the market, the *final unity* of the European legal order. Or, what amounts to the same, at stake here is the *autonomy* of European Union law, or the celebrated *sui generis* character, i.e., the very nature of Union law. This is what makes them worthy of closer scrutiny. Though they emerge under various names in scholarly reflections on EU law, in essence, they harbour the problem of the competence creep.

One of the criticisms often raised against implied powers is that acknowledging them would amount to the sort of instrumentalism that can be summarised under the formula 'the end justifies the means'. This criticism is directly connected with the rationale underlying the principle of conferred powers: The competences of an international organisation are the instruments through which its aims should be achieved. True enough, effectiveness is a guiding principle for the interpretation of treaties.[86] As a consequence, the authority of international organisations is to be understood primarily in that key: International organisations have authority to the extent that they can effectively achieve their ends. The criterion of effectiveness would then point to the idea that law is first and foremost an instrument to reach policy goals. In the case of international organisations, these goals are the very reasons why the international organisation was founded in the first place. These objectives are often enumerated in one of the first articles of the founding treaty, and described in rather vague terms. This, then, is what the principle of conferred powers is all about: It marks the line between the powers needed for the attainment of the goals and those that are additional, and thus (from this viewpoint) unnecessary and even dangerous. Where the organisation may validly act by using the first category of powers, as soon as it claims powers belonging to the second category,

---

[84] M. Poiares Maduro, 'Europe and the constitution: what if this is as good as it gets?', in: J.H.H. Weiler and M. Wind, *European Constitutionalism Beyond the State*, Cambridge (etc.): Cambridge University Press 2003, pp. 74–102, at p. 77.

[85] J. Klabbers, *An Introduction to International Institutional Law*, Cambridge (etc.): Cambridge University Press 2002, p. 6.

[86] P. Malanczuk, *Akehurst's Modern Introduction to International Law*, London [etc.]: Routledge 1997, p. 367: 'There is a presumption of interpretation in international law that a treaty should be interpreted so as to give full effect to its purposes.'

its acts are *ultra vires*.[87] However, supporters of implied powers will point to the flexibility organisations need in order to meet their objectives. Choosing in favour for or against implied powers would then amount to making a political decision on whether international organisations are something good.[88]

And yet, it would be too simple to solve the legal problem by reducing it to a political choice. Their differences notwithstanding, supporters of implied powers and strict adherents to conferred powers share a basic presupposition. For, whether one starts from the principle of conferred powers or from the doctrine of implied powers, the competences of international organisations are seen as instrumental, or strictly functional, *by both sides*. Instrumentalism is thus not only hiding in a flexible interpretation of Union powers. Also, a strict reading of the principle of conferral leads to an instrumental view of law. Beneath the doctrinal surface, the problem is how to understand *the relationship between law and politics*? I will take my cue from the philosophy of Gustav Radbruch to explain this point. In the vocabulary of the neo-Kantian philosopher, this issue is connected with the conceptual element in the idea of law called 'legal expediency' (*Zweckmäßigkeit*), which concerns the purpose-oriented character of law. It is indeed from politics, Radbruch argues, that law receives its purpose.[89] In other words, the discussions in everyday politics are always about which purposes law should serve and which content it should consequently have. From the viewpoint of legal expediency, law appears as a political artefact. Legal expediency unveils the political nature of law, and in that sense it asks the question of the relationship between law and politics. This is one of the central questions in the debate on implied powers and, more generally, on creeping competences.

1.5   Legal Power and Integration: Rereading the Maastricht Decision

Even when it seems that we have drifted far away from our goal of analysing the competence creep of the European Union, we have actually only paved the way for a philosophical thesis on the problem of the competence creep. I will illustrate my point by discussing a case that quite literary shook the foundations of European law.[90] Seldom was the critique on the European Union, for assigning itself more

---

[87] Cf. Giardina, o.c., p. 101: 'The constituent Treaty of an organization should, in other words, be taken as a parametre for the legality of the organization's acts.'

[88] Cf. J. Klabbers, *An Introduction to International Institutional Law*, pp. 40–41.

[89] Cf. G. Radbruch, *Legal Philosophy*, in: *The Legal Philosophies of Lask, Radbruch, and Dabin*, translated by K. Wilk, Cambridge (Mass.): Harvard University Press 1950, pp. 47–226, Section 7. According to Radbruch, law's purpose is defined by starting from one of three kinds of values: individual, collective or work values. These values are connected with three different worldviews and three different political positions.

[90] Cf. J. Baquero Cruz, 'The Legacy of the Maastricht-Urteil and the Pluralist Movement', *European Law Journal*, vol. 14 (2008), pp. 389–422. This article gives an overview of the practical and theoretical consequences of the judgement.

and more powers, so severe and so profound as in the Maastricht decision of the *Bundesverfassungsgericht*, the German Federal Constitutional Court (FCC). Since it would take too long to give a full account of the reasoning of the Maastricht-judgement, I would like to concentrate on what can be called the very heart of the decision: the distinction between a 'community or federation of states' and a 'state', its presuppositions and consequences. In this distinction, the two dimensions of the debate on competences meet.

With the word 'state', the FCC refers to a nation-state, i.e., a state that is based on one nation whose people regard themselves as a unity in virtue of an allegedly shared culture, history and (even) destiny. In this sense, the FCC believes the Federal Republic of Germany to be a state. Furthermore, even though it does not mention this explicitly, the Court also regards the other Member States of the European Union as states in this specific sense of the word. In contradistinction to them, the European Union is a so-called 'federation of States'. This characterization has several consequences. First of all, the German Court proclaims that the Member States remain the *Herren der Verträge*, the Masters of the Treaties. It is not so much the EU that can bind the Member States but, on the contrary, the Member States as creators and, therefore, masters—the German *Herr* also has the meaning of chief or even Lord—of the Union are able to exercise their authority over it. What it boils down to is that the Member States retain the competence to withdraw from the Union. Considering that at that time the Treaties lacked an article on withdrawal or secession, this might seem a fine example of legal boasting. However, the political impact of this statement should not be underestimated, especially not now that it comes from the highest legal authority and the *constitutional* court of one of the most influential Member States. Furthermore, the Treaty of Lisbon has actually introduced articles on withdrawal from the Union.[91]

A second consequence of the Constitutional Court's characterisation is that it retains for itself the power to subject EU law to an examination of lawfulness. This means that the final authority over the validity of Union law in Germany resides with the FCC instead of the ECJ. In the same way, the Constitutional Court argues that the ultimate ground of validity of EU law in Germany is the German transposition law.[92] This is in blatant contradiction to the *acquis communautaire* that stipulates that Union law enters the legal orders of the Member States directly and without transposition. The FCC, however, is of the opinion that EU law owes its validity to German (i.e., national) law. As a consequence, Germany remains a sovereign state, as do the other Member States. And it is precisely at this point that the Constitutional Court strikes the EU legal order at its heart. As sovereign states, the Member States have not given up their sovereign rights—as the European Court of Justice has claimed—but, rather, they have instituted the European Union to jointly exercise part of their sovereignty. In other words, the European Union, being a federation of states, can only claim legitimacy for its actions through the Member

---

[91] See Article 50 TEU.

[92] Extracts from Brunner et al. v. The European Union Treaty, *Common Market Law Review*, vol. 31 (1994), pp. 251–262 at p. 258.

States and their parliaments. The autonomous legal order that it claims to be is ultimately dependent on its Member States for legitimacy.

This has major implications for one of the most critical issues in the legal development of the European Union, to wit, democracy. The FCC conceives of democracy as popular sovereignty in the sense that a democracy always presupposes a single people, a *demos*. In its own words: 'Each of the peoples of the individual States is the starting point for a state power relating to that people.'[93] The democracy principle entails that taking care of governmental tasks and the exercise of governmental competences is ultimately imputable to, and justifiable before, the people: 'Democracy, if it is not to remain a merely formal principle of accountability, is dependent on the presence of certain pre-legal conditions, such as a continuous free debate between opposing social forces, interests and ideas, in which political goals also become clarified and change course, and out of which comes a public opinion which forms the beginnings of political intentions.'[94] The FCC believes that these conditions are not present in the EU.[95]

The principled argument is somewhat like this. In a democracy, the people is sovereign. This means that every governmental act obtains legitimacy because it can ultimately be traced back to the people as the source of all authority. In other words, the people is the ultimate foundation of the legal order, its final ground and centre of imputation. Everything then boils down to the question of how the FCC understands this role of the people. What is probably both the most enigmatic and the most important passage of the Maastricht decision concerns exactly this issue: 'The States need sufficiently important spheres of activity of their own in which the people of each can develop and articulate itself in a process of political will-formation which it legitimises and controls, in order thus *to give legal expression* to what binds the people together (to a greater or lesser degree of homogeneity) spiritually, socially and politically. From all that, it follows that functions and powers of substantial importance must remain for the German Bundestag.'[96]

Here, we see how the FCC conceives of the people: It is a pre-legal entity, a 'spiritual' or cultural (the German word is *geistig*), social and political whole. In other words, prior to entering into legal relationships, the people is a political unity with its own identity that distinguishes it from others. Whatever law can mean, somehow it has to reflect this identity, e.g., articulating, protecting, deploying, refining it. To express its identity in a political process, the people ought to retain certain legal means also in a supra-national context. These means are the so-called 'functions and powers of substantial importance' for the German parliament, i.e., certain legislative competences. The argument of the constitutional court ultimately leads to a plea for the preservation of national competences *vis-à-vis* the Union. This is not so

---

[93] Ibid., p. 257.

[94] Ibid., p. 256.

[95] For an influential critique of this 'No Demos-thesis', see: J.H.H. Weiler, 'Does Europe Need a Constitution? Demos, Telos and the German Maastricht Decision', *European Law Journal*, vol. 1 (1995), pp. 219–258.

[96] Extracts from Brunner et al. v. The European Union Treaty, p. 257 [My italics, LC].

strange when we consider that the concept of competence is the legal institution of authority. Moreover, it is exactly in the domain of competences that the distinction between a 'state' and a 'federation of states' becomes clear.

The European Union, a federation of states, receives its competences from its Member States. Those of the Member States, on the other hand, are obtained by attribution, by original ascription. Here, the German constitutional court takes up the question of *Kompetenz-Kompetenz*.[97] In each of the Member States, the people directly legitimises the competences of the government. As the basis of the legal order and source of all authority, the people possesses *Kompetenz-Kompetenz*, i.e., the power to change the limits of its own competences (and, thus, to increase them). At several places in its judgement, the FCC argues, however, that the European Union lacks this *Kompetenz-Kompetenz*. As a consequence, the European Union only has those competences explicitly given to it by the Member States. An increase of the competences of the European Union can only be achieved by a revision of the Treaties. In this respect, the FCC stresses the importance of the principles of conferred powers, subsidiarity and proportionality. It even goes so far as to say that any attempt of institutions of the European Union to augment their competences, is an *ultra vires* act that cannot bind the Member States. Therefore, the German Constitutional Court explicitly rejects the doctrines of Article 308 EC as residual competence, *effet utile* and implied powers as developed by the European Court of Justice.

Now, what can we conclude after having discussed this case? It is only fair to admit that the German Constitutional Court has a point. The picture of a European Union that, with the help of an overactive Court of Justice, encroaches on national powers is something to worry about. Indeed, creeping competences are creepy. They will lead to a complete erosion of the principle of conferred powers. However, what about the alternative the FCC envisions? It basically proposes a very strict reading of the principle of conferred powers. Retracing the powers of the European Union to the Member States, and claiming that they remain the 'Masters of the Treaty', leads the FCC to the interpretation that any given competences can be demanded back at any time. The German Constitutional Court seems to say that whoever has the power to give, also holds the power to take back. In this case, the Member States have given power to the EU and thus they can also ask it back at the moment the Union does not meet their demands.

Yet, is this position tenable? Is this how the principle of conferred powers should be read? Surely, the result of this reading is that we can no longer make sense of the integration process. With this interpretation of the principle of conferral, the whole *acquis communautaire* is put at stake, and it is left to the constitutional courts of the Member States to decide over its future. Can we still speak of a future for European integration in this way? The reason why this last question should be answered negatively lies in the institutional nature of the integration process. Put simply, the bottom line is that one cannot disengage oneself from what one bound oneself to. Of course, it is always possible to get out, especially now that the new EU Treaty

---

[97] For more on the debate on *Kompetenz-Kompetenz*, see: A. Arnull, *The European Union and its Court of Justice* (Second Edition), Oxford (etc.): Oxford University Press 2006, pp. 255–261.

as amended by the Treaty of Lisbon explicitly includes the possibility to step out of the European Union.[98] However, this is not what the German Constitutional Court is after. The FCC wants Germany to stay within the EU, albeit only on the conditions that it itself has formulated and only if it can constantly assess whether or not Union legislation remains within its boundaries. This is impossible, I allege, because this is not how institutions work. One cannot stay within an institution (e.g., marriage, the integration process) while continuously assessing the functionality of that institution. The consequence would be that what is *acquis* today might be declared *ultra vires* tomorrow. In that case, the *acquis communautaire* would no longer be able to function as the bond that keeps the Member States together, since no one can trust it. Should we then conclude that whatever one chooses, in favour or against creeping competences, the principle of conferred powers and the *acquis communautaire* loose? I propose to explore a third way. What we encounter in this dilemma is a phenomenon inherent in the concept of legal power itself, a phenomenon we cannot begin to understand without delving deeper into the very foundations of legal power. The next chapter will be the first step in this investigation.

1.6   Conclusion

This chapter presented the legal problem central to this book: 'creeping competences'. After having described the present division of competences between European Union and Member States, I focussed on implied powers as an emblematic case of this phenomenon. Subsequently, I turned to the ECJ and, in particular, to its broadly formulated mandate to clarify the special role this institution plays in the debate on powers of the EU. Then, I showed that the issue of legal competence in EU law is ultimately connected with the problem of the authority of the Union. In this authority problem, a material and an institutional dimension were distinguished. These come together in the infamous Maastricht decision of the German Federal Constitutional Court. This decision demonstrates that the questions regarding competences and authority in the European Union ask for an inquiry into the very foundations of the concept of legal power itself.

---

[98] Article 50 of the Treaty on European Union.

Chapter 2
Paradigms of Constitution-Making, or Two Tales of One Dualism

The question of legal competence, i.e., the question of the (limits to) powers of the European Union is often the elephant in the room one prefers not to talk about as discussions quickly run into deadlock. Two camps stand opposed to each other in a dispute that seems unsolvable, since one is forced to take one of two sides, or so it appears. Either, one starts from the position of the Member States and is inclined to defend a rigorous interpretation of the principle of conferred powers, repudiating implied powers as inadmissible, or, the benchmark is the Union as an independent legal entity, and in that case, a doctrine like implied powers is welcomed as an essential means to obtain much desired flexibility. *Tertium non datur*, any attempt to bridge the difference seems jinxed from the start, with the *acquis communautaire* as the dupe.

It is a basic assumption of this book that any attempt to reach a solution has to start from a much deeper understanding of what is at stake in the attribution of legal competence. I will work from the hypothesis that the basic issue in discussions on creeping competences is that of the relationship between constituent (constituting) and constitutional (constituted) power. This distinction has proven to be central to discussions on democracy, the rule of law and the relationship between law and politics. This chapter will make some first steps in the analysis of the conceptual framework that the question of competence brings into play. First of all, I will show how the question of competence brings us to the heart of constitutional theory. Section 2.2 will focus on theories of permanent revolution and their ideas on constituent power. The third section will describe how constitutionalism denies the political roots of law. In the fourth section, I will demonstrate that what is at stake in both traditions of constitutional theory is the struggle with one and the same dualism. In the course of the discussion, I will have ample opportunity to show how this dualism developed in the history of constitutional thinking.

L. Corrias, *The Passivity of Law,*
DOI 10.1007/978-94-007-1034-4_2, © Springer Science+Business Media B.V. 2011

2.1 Competence and Constitution

Competences are not a marginal problem for a European Union claiming to be a constitutional legal order. On the contrary, there is an unbreakable bond between the claim of constitutionality and competences, backed up by strong traditions of legal thinking in Europe. To sustain this claim, I would like to look first at how the concept of legal competence is understood in analytical legal philosophy. In the analytical tradition of legal thinking scholars agree that the legal concept of competence refers to the power to change legal relations.[1] These legal relations are central to Hohfeld's analysis of legal concepts. In his famous *Fundamental Legal Conceptions as Applied in Juridical Reasoning*, he expounds 'the "lowest common denominators" in terms of which all legal problems can be stated.'[2] For him, these common denominators should be expressed in terms of legal relations.[3] Hohfeld thinks of competence as 'the (legal) power to effect the particular change of legal relations that is involved in the problem.'[4] A power correlates with a liability of others to respect the exercise of power. An example may explain this: 'To say that A has a power entails that he can by his voluntary act change the legal relations of some other person, B, who has the correlative liability; and that it is not true that A has a disability as against B's legal relations, correlating with an immunity of B.'[5] Competence norms are thus those norms that confer on a person the power to change legal relations.[6] Not complying with a competence norm does not lead to a sanction (as not complying with other norms does). In case of a lack of competence, the supposed legal act is invalid. In other words: 'If we do not comply with such rules [i.e., legal power-conferring rules, LC], the result is not a sanction or a punishment, for it is not breach or violation of any obligation, nor an offense, but nullity.'[7]

Another important issue is whether or not competence norms qualify as norms properly speaking.[8] According to Kelsen, this is not the case since legal norms should be seen as 'the primary norm which stipulates the sanction.'[9] Competence norms are only derived from these 'real' norms. Hart strongly criticizes this view. According to him, competence norms have a completely different function in social

---

[1] See: G. Conway, 'Conflicts of Competence Norms in EU Law and the Legal Reasoning of the ECJ', *German Law Journal*, vol. 11 (2010), pp. 966–1005, footnote 42, at p. 973 for references.

[2] W.N. Hohfeld, *Fundamental Legal Conceptions as Applied in Judicial Reasoning and Other Legal Essays* (ed. W.W. Cook), New Haven: Yale University Press 1923, p. 6.

[3] Cf. J.W. Harris, *Legal Philosophies* (2nd edition), London (etc.): Butterworths 1997, p. 84.

[4] Hohfeld, o.c., p. 51.

[5] Harris, o.c., p. 84.

[6] Cf. Conway, o.c., p. 975.

[7] E. Bulygin, 'On Norms of Competence', *Law & Philosophy*, vol. 11 (1992), pp. 201–216, at p. 208.

[8] Cf. Ibid, pp. 204–207 and Conway, o.c., pp. 974–975. See also: T. Spaak, 'Norms that Confer Competence', *Ratio Juris: An International Journal of Jurisprudence and Philosophy of Law*, vol. 16 (2003), pp. 89–104, at pp. 95–97.

[9] H. Kelsen, *General Theory of Law and State*, New York: Russel & Russel 1961, p. 61.

life and thus can not be reduced to other norms. In the private sphere, they constitute 'an additional element introduced by the law into social life over and above that of coercive control.'[10] Also in the public sphere there is a crucial difference: 'Those who exercise these powers to make authoritative enactments and orders use these rules in a form of purposive activity utterly different from performance of duty or submission to coercive control.'[11] He concludes then that '[t]o represent such rules as mere aspects or fragments of the rules of duty is, even more than in the private sphere, to obscure the distinctive characteristics of law and of the activities possible within its framework.'[12]

In his work on norms that confer competence, Torben Spaak takes the position that norms are prescriptions in the sense of Georg Hendrik von Wright.[13] This entails that 'the primary *function* of norms is to *guide human behavior by giving reasons for action.*'[14] Yet, competence norms do not do this. They are norms conferring a duty on legal officials 'to recognize as legally valid certain changes of legal positions brought about in a certain way in a certain situation by a certain category of persons.'[15] Not unlike technical norms, they merely 'indicate the necessary means to a given end.'[16] As a consequence, he comes to the conclusion 'that competence norms do not guide human behavior by giving reasons for action, and that, consequently, we should not recognize them as genuine norms.'[17] Now, Conway makes an illuminating comment on this position:

> Here, there seems a regress as to the exact origin of constitutional competence norms, which perhaps ultimately is determined by brute politics, rather than legal theory. A norm creates a power or competence, but the norm creating the power or competence presupposes a power or norm to create such competence conferral, and so on. Competence norms thus need to be interpreted in light of the constitutional framework determining what the 'origins' and 'ends' are of competence. In other words, there is a chain of validity, one norm creates another norm and each of these norms has to be interpreted.[18]

As Conway rightly points out, at this moment the issue of competences touches upon fundamental issues in constitutional theory. More concretely, one needs to think of the crucial question of 'a constitutional anchoring of competence norms, which can be related to the principle of conferral in EU law.'[19] And a little further he connects that to the idea of 'the will of the law-maker or constituent power.'[20]

---

[10] H.L.A. Hart, *The Concept of Law* (2nd edition), Oxford (etc.): Oxford University Press 1994, p. 41.

[11] Ibid.

[12] Ibid.

[13] T. Spaak, o.c., p. 92.

[14] Ibid., p. 93 [Italics in the original].

[15] Ibid., p. 94.

[16] Ibid., p. 99.

[17] Ibid.

[18] G. Conway, o.c., p. 976.

[19] Ibid.

[20] Ibid.

This ties in with what we have seen in the previous chapter: The FCC holds that the people is the bearer of *Kompetenz-Kompetenz*. With this characterisation, the FCC assigns to the people the classical role of constituent power.[21] The people as constituent power is the subject of the constitution, whereas the powers of the state (legislative, executive and judiciary) are the constituted powers. For their legitimacy, the latter are dependent on the people as constituent power. This must be understood in the sense that the people, being the subject of political power, gives the institutions of the state their restricted powers, their competences. This shows the fundamental significance of the issue of competence as a constitutional theme.

Now, note that the FCC links the issue of legal competence directly with 'what binds the people together'. Here is the central passage of the Maastricht decision one more time: 'The States need sufficiently important spheres of activity of their own in which the people of each can develop and articulate itself in a process of political will-formation which it legitimises and controls, in order thus *to give legal expression* to what binds the people together (to a greater or lesser degree of homogeneity) spiritually, socially and politically. From all that, it follows that functions and powers of substantial importance must remain for the German Bundestag.'[22] Competences, the FCC holds, have everything to do with the identity of the people. That would be a rather unrevealing observation, were it not for its sequel. On closer reading, and more importantly, it also holds that competences have to do with expressing this identity, and with expressing it in a mode called law. This threefold clue will turn out to open more gates in old castle Europe than one may expect. But, before we are able to appreciate this, we should begin by realising where the gates and the gatekeepers are, i.e., what well-established theories guard the topic of political identity and constitutional law in the legal cultures with which we are familiar.

I propose to look at two traditions of constitutional theory, in particular. These traditions approach the topic of constitution-making in distinct, even opposed ways.[23] The two traditions differ in what they think a constitution should do, and what its functions and purposes are. Another way of separating them is by connecting each with its own place of birth: either America and France, or Germany and Great Britain.[24] Cutting across the great divide between common law and civil law, there is a revolutionary model that can be distinguished from an evolutionary model. Starting with the former, one can speak of the theory of constituent power as a French-American tradition because it emerged with the revolutions in those

---

[21] Cf. H.K. Lindahl, 'European Integration: Popular Sovereignty and a Politics of Boundaries', *European Law Journal*, vol. 6 (2000), pp. 239–256.

[22] Extracts from Brunner et al. v. The European Union Treaty, *Common Market Law Review*, vol. 31 (1994), pp. 251–262 at p. 257 [My italics, LC].

[23] I will follow the distinction made in: H. Arendt, *On Revolution*, London: Penguin 1973 [1963].

[24] Cf. Ch. Möllers, 'Pouvoir Constituant-Constitution-Constitutionalisation', in: A. von Bogdandy and J. Bast, *Principles of European Constitutional Law*, Oxford (etc.): Hart 2006, pp. 183–226. Möllers follows the distinction made by Arendt, but assigns to each of the traditions its geographical place.

countries.[25] It focuses on the founding of a new order, and combines this with a radically democratic appeal. Although the French revolution chronologically followed the one at the opposite side of the ocean, it has always had more theoretical allure.[26] One of the reasons might be that founding a new order through a new constitution has always been connected with the name of the French revolutionary Sieyès, who theorized the law-making potential of the revolution at great length.

2.2 Constituent Power and the Primacy of Politics: Sieyès and His Legacy

The theory of constituent power is utterly modern, precisely by being connected with the revolutions in America and France.[27] In antiquity, the concept of revolution was unknown. Of course, there were plenty of regime changes. However, these were considered to be the next stage of an inescapable cycle. Revolutions, as we can learn from Hannah Arendt, cannot be understood with the help of this framework. Their pretension to be the start of something radically new does not register. Against the backdrop of an inalterable scheme of dominion, regime changes just reverse the charges in an ongoing battle, bringing no change to what the battle is about. Theoretically, 'revolutions are the only political events which confront us directly and inevitably with the problem of beginning.'[28] The growing dominance of Christian over ancient thinking, and the subsequent replacement of the cyclical with a rectilinear model of time, gradually provided the conceptual space for the kind of claim revolutions typically make. So, revolution is modern precisely because the concept is 'inextricably bound up with the notion that the course of history suddenly begins anew, that an entirely new story, a story never known or told before, is about to unfold, was unknown to the two great revolutions at the end of the Eighteenth Century.'[29]

If beginning is the first big idea connected with the concept of revolution, freedom is the second one. The new beginning the revolution seeks is a new beginning *in freedom*.[30] Freedom should be understood here as a political attribute; Man could

---

[25] The connection between these two revolutions becomes clear from the life and writings of Thomas Paine. Cf. C.H. McIlwain, *Constitutionalism: Ancient and Modern*, Indianapolis: Liberty Fund 2008, p. 8.

[26] Cf. Arendt, o.c., for example, at p. 24 and pp. 94–95. Arendt fundamentally disagrees with this evaluation. One of the aims of her book is to theoretically rehabilitate the American Revolution.

[27] Arendt, o.c., p. 12.

[28] Ibid., p. 21. See also p. 34 where she speaks of 'the experience of man's faculty to begin something new.'

[29] Ibid., p. 28.

[30] Ibid., p. 29: 'Crucial, then, to any understanding of revolutions in the modern age is that the idea of freedom and the experience of a new beginning should coincide.' See also Möllers, o.c., p. 186: 'Because the constitution must ignore and abolish already existing political power structures, it must make individual freedom its systematic reference point.'

only be free living with others in a polity. Yet, and this is crucial, this is not possible under any kind of political regime. Indeed, the revolutionary tradition goes hand in hand with a demand for a polity in which man could be truly free, yet bound in relationships to all others in that polity. In other words, a revolution heralds the foundation of a republic.[31] As a consequence, the conceptual space provided by Christianity turned against the provider. Machiavelli is important in this respect because he is considered to be the first who envisioned the foundation of a new and completely secular order. This order was supposed to be 'independent of the teachings of the Church, in particular, and of moral standards, transcending the sphere of human affairs, in general.'[32] However, the founding of a new order could not be done but by imposing a new authority by law. This new authority only counted as *authority* if it could, one way or another, link up with what was already authoritative. As we will see, it is this problem that will continue to haunt the revolutionary theory of constitution-making. The birth of a new legal order cannot be justified without referring (to a minimal degree) to the authorities overthrown.[33] They have to be pictured as the wrong agents at the right place. The revolution would lose its stakes if the place would vanish together with its occupants.

To understand the full significance of revolution as a political phenomenon, and its theoretical repercussions for the notion of constitution, one cannot but turn to France at the end of the Eighteenth Century. It is indeed the French Revolution that has offered the blueprint to all subsequent revolutionary movements.[34] It is here that the concept of revolution is understood for the first time as an irresistible movement, a wave to which we had better surrender, or else it will knock us down completely. Most of all, its theoretical influence resides in the new philosophy of history it offered. This culminated in the thought of Hegel, who conceptualised the movement of history as both necessary and dialectical. While these characteristics seem obvious within a cyclical model of time, they are not, if one speaks on the basis of a rectilinear model. They can only be explained as a direct account of how the various stages of the French Revolution were experienced.[35]

This is where the concepts of constituent and constituted power cut in. Although these notions are usually traced back to the work of Jean-Jacques Rousseau, it is the name of Emmanuel Joseph Sieyès that is indissolubly connected with them. Extracting bits and pieces from Rousseau where it seemed convenient, yet deviating from him at crucial points, the French abbot and revolutionary, Sieyès, formulated what is

---

[31] This also has consequences for the concept of constitution. Cf. Möllers, o.c., p. 186: 'With this, constitution becomes an exclusive concept: Certain forms of order are now no longer labelled as faulty or wrong constitutions: Rather, their claim to be constitutions at all, is denied.'

[32] Arendt, o.c., p. 36.

[33] Arendt, o.c., pp. 38–39 and p. 155.

[34] Ibid., p. 50.

[35] Ibid., p. 55: '[T]he fact that necessity as an inherent characteristic of history should survive the modern break in the cycle of eternal recurrences and make its reappearance in a movement that was essentially rectilinear, and hence did not revolve back to what was known before, but stretched out into an unknown future, this fact owes its existence not to theoretical speculation but to political experience and the course of real events.'

considered to be the established view concerning the relationship between constituent and constituted power.[36] In his famous political pamphlet '*Qu'est-ce que le Tiers état?*', he devised his theory of constituent power in order to provide an alternative for the divine authority that the French kings claimed for themselves. Indeed, they alleged that their powers derived from a *droit divin*, and pointed to a higher, godly source to legitimise their authority.[37] One could call this conceptual account of the intertwinements between political and godly authority a kind of political theology.

Sieyès opposed this *droit divin*, and held firmly that the people, rather than the monarch, is the supreme source of authority.[38] This means that the theory of the relationship between constituent and constituted power is closely linked to the principle of democracy.[39] Indeed, in a democracy, all power flows from the people as a matter of principle. This entails that the people is considered to be the author of the constitution, the political force that gives the constitution.[40] In other words, the people is the subject of constituent power without being itself constituted by law. Then, there are the powers called into being by the constitution: the legislature, the executive power and the judiciary. These are so-called constituted or constitutional powers. According to Sieyès, constituent and constituted power should be understood as strictly separated. In this model, there is a clear primacy of the constituent power.[41] As one can see, in the view of Sieyès, constituted powers are subordinate to the constituent power because their power ultimately depends on that of the people as the constituent or sovereign power of a democratic state. Their power is only an emanation of the constituent power of the people. The power of the state organs only exists due to, and is limited by, the constitution (the law). State organs are bearers of constituted power; this is legal power, or competence. The people is the ultimate source of all law and legitimacy and, as such, is independent. In a democracy,

---

[36] It is, actually, quite difficult to find any textual evidence for the claim that Rousseau invented the concepts of constituent and constituted power. In this respect, see: J.-J. Rousseau, 'The Social Contract', in: *The Social Contract and Other Later Political Writings*, ed. and trans. V. Gourevitch, Cambridge: Cambridge University Press 1997 [1762], pp. 39–152, at p. 49, where Rousseau states that 'before examining the act by which a people elects a king, it would be well to examine the act by which a people is a people. For this act, being necessarily prior to the other, is the true foundation of society.'

[37] Arendt, o.c., p. 156: '[T]he absolute monarch (…) also incarnated on earth a divine origin in which law and power coincided. His will, because it supposedly represented God's will on earth, was the source of both law and power, and it was this identical origin that made law powerful and power legitimate.'

[38] E.J. Sieyès, *What is the Third Estate?*, London: Pall Mall Press 1963, p. 126: 'The national will […] never needs anything but its own existence to be legal. It is the source of all legality.'

[39] Cf. A. Negri, *Insurgencies. Constituent Power and the Modern State*, Minneapolis (etc.): University of Minnesota Press 1999, p. 1: 'To speak of constituent power is to speak of democracy.' I will come back to Negri's theory later in this section.

[40] E.J. Sieyès, o.c., p. 119: 'If we have no constitution, it must be made, and only the nation has the right to make it.'

[41] In the words of the German phenomenologist Waldenfels: There is 'a preference in the difference'. Cf. B. Waldenfels, *Vielstimmigkeit der Rede: Studien zur Phänomenologie des Fremden 4*, Frankfurt am Mein: Suhrkamp 1999, p. 197.

the people is the sun illuminating everything. Accordingly, the people as constituent power is conceived of as some kind of god: one and undividable, transcendent, omnipotent and therefore able to create from a void (*creatio ex nihilo*). This means that one could say that Sieyès replaced the religious political theology of the *droit divin* with the secular political theology of the sovereign people.[42]

Now, the problem for Sieyès is how people can grow into 'the people', i.e., how a mere plurality of people can come to see themselves as a whole and refer to this whole as a unity. To solve this problem, Sieyès introduces the basic concept of the nation. The nation is the unifying point of identity to which all individuals relate. The legal expression of the nation takes place through the constitution and the other laws. At the same time, Sieyès's theory reads as a chronological tale of the birth of the legal order. The act of giving the constitution is the start, the origin of the legal order. That is why Sieyès holds that the nation's existence precedes everything: '[t]he nation is prior to everything. It is the source of everything. Its will is always legal; (...).'[43] Strictly speaking, one should even say that the nation is pre-legal: '[P]rior to, and above the nation, there is only *natural law*.'[44] For this reason, the nation is independent from the formal bonds of positive law created by the constitution. Moreover, the nation is not even allowed to bind itself to a positive form. The nation is independent of all forms. Sieyès can, therefore, say that it remains in a state of nature.[45] This means that the nation is, and remains absent from, the legal stage. Precisely for this reason, the nation needs to be represented in the legal order. This is the task of the representative body: to replace the nation and act in its place.[46] That explains why the constitutional forms posed by the nation bind this body.

It is not difficult to discern the dualistic relationship in this scheme of reasoning between the nation (constituent power) on the one hand, and state organs (constituted power) on the other. First, there is the nation: omnipotent, independent, unbound, the 'formless forming' subject of the constitution.[47] Precisely by stating that the nation cannot leave the state of nature, Sieyès emphasises that there is an absolute (and not merely a relative) difference between the nation as constituent power and the organs of the state.[48] The latter only exist after, and as an effect of, the creative labour of the nation. The powers of the state are dependent on the nation, bound by

---

[42] E.-W. Böckenförde, 'Die verfassunggebende Gewalt des Volkes – Ein Grenzbegriff des Verfassungsrechts', in: *Staat, Verfassung, Demokratie. Studien zur Verfassungstheorie und zum Verfassungsrecht*, Frankfurt am Main: Suhrkamp 1991, pp. 90–112, at p. 95. I will analyse Böckenförde's theory in the next section.

[43] E.J. Sieyès, o.c., p. 124. See also Arendt, o.c., p. 163.

[44] Sieyès, o.c., p. 124 [Italics in the original].

[45] Ibid, pp. 127–128: 'We must conceive the nations of the world as being like men living outside society or "in a state of nature", as it is called.'

[46] Sieyès, o.c., p. 137: 'If it is to accomplish its task, the representative body must always be the substitute for the nation, itself.'

[47] Cf. C. Schmitt, *Verfassungslehre*, Berlin: Duncker & Humblot 1970 [1928], p. 79 and following. The theory of Schmitt will be discussed below in Sect. 2.4.

[48] Cf. Arendt, o.c., pp. 19–20: 'For, the hypothesis of a state of nature implies the existence of a beginning that is separated from everything following it as though by an unbridgeable chasm.'

the constitutional ties it formulated. One could thus go further than Sieyès himself, and say that *all* state powers (not just the representative body) in all their actions represent the nation. Representation should be understood here as substitution: The powers in the state replace the nation (that cannot leave the state of nature). This dualistic scheme of Sieyès has direct consequences for the concept of (legal) competence. As mentioned above, unlike the nation, the state organs do not have unlimited power. State organs possess competences: power created and limited by law. Because all actions of the state organs have to take place within the boundaries of given competences, one might say that representing the nation occurs through these competences. Exercising a competence can then be viewed as representing (replacing, rendering present again) the nation, as a legal representation of its pre-legal identity.

According to Sieyès, the constitution of the legal order is a truly creative act: The nation creates the legal order *ex nihilo*. Indeed, in the fifth chapter of his pamphlet, Sieyès maintains that the nation exists independent of, and prior to, this act of constitution. Later, however, he says that the nation is equal to the total number of inhabitants, thus persuading his audience that the nation is an empirical entity rather than a construct of political discourse.[49] Yet, the equation seems to be highly problematic. If we define the nation in terms of inhabitants, our very first question should be inhabitants *whereof*? Sieyès seems to suggest that for an answer one can always point to a territorial border. The territory already makes clear whom the inhabitants, together forming the nation, are. But, quite apart from the problem of borders in a non-territorial sense, this will just push the question one step further back. In virtue of what else than a preceding nation, can a river or a mountain range count as a border, thus constituting a territory? Inversely, if a border precedes the nation, i.e., if it is indeed constitutive for its existence, how is Sieyès able to insist that the nation is formless and completely independent? The formation of a political community, Sieyès argues, begins with isolated citizens wanting to unite. In other words, as Rousseau before him, Sieyès starts from a contractual model. Consequently, Sieyès faces the very same problem as the man from Geneva.[50] Contrary to Sieyès however, Rousseau acknowledges this problem when he writes that 'men would have to be prior to laws what they ought to become by means of them.'[51] In other words, the consequence should turn into the cause. The contractual model presupposes that one knows who the contracting parties are. But how is one supposed to know this? Of course, one could refer to another contract to settle this issue. However, one merely whisks the problem away, without solving it. Namely, the new contract would pose the very same question of the contracting parties. To put it briefly, one is caught in an infinite regress.[52]

---

[49] Sieyès, o.c., p. 133: 'Where is the nation to be found? Where it is; in the 40,000 parishes which embrace the whole territory, all its inhabitants and every element of the commonwealth; indisputably, the nation lies there.'

[50] See also Arendt, o.c., pp. 183–184.

[51] Rousseau, o.c., p. 71.

[52] If one does choose not to presuppose a contract before the contract, the argument of Sieyès would still run into one of the other two logical problems as defined by Albert in his Münchhausen Trilemma—*petitio principii* or mere dogmatism.

Sieyès's theory is thus incoherent and cannot help us to understand the problem of competences described in the previous chapter. Does this mean that all theories of constituent power are to be discarded? Are there not more sophisticated theories around? Let us turn to a contemporary elaboration of constituent power in order to investigate this. Although he criticises Sieyès in some respects, the Italian political theorist, Antonio Negri, tries to breathe new life into the concept of constituent power vested in the people in order to make it usable for contemporary politics. Negri aims at sketching a radical theory of constituent power, in the sense of 'democracy as a theory of absolute government.'[53] He explicitly distinguishes this approach from any kind of constitutionalism: Constituent power cannot be grasped by constitutionalism because the latter is essentially a theory of limited government. In other words, for Negri, constituent power and constituted power are not only strictly separated concepts, but also concepts diametrically opposed to one another. Any attempt at reconciliation is, therefore, completely futile and even dangerous: It risks eliminating constituent power, and this 'might nullify the very meaning of the juridical system and the democratic relation that must characterize its horizon.'[54] A legal approach to constituent power fails hopelessly.[55] Negri explicitly states and holds on to a dualistic approach: 'if, in the history of democracy and democratic constitutions, *the dualism between constituent power and constituted power* has never produced a synthesis, we must focus precisely on this negativity, on this lack of synthesis, in order to try to understand constituent power.'[56]

The way in which Negri subsequently proceeds to define constituent power calls to mind the omnipotent, formless, forming subject of Sieyès: 'Constituent power is defined, emerging from the vortex of the void, from the abyss of the absence of determinations, as a totally open need. (...) Constituent power is this force that, in the absence of finalities, is projected out as an all-powerful and always more expansive tendency.'[57] Negri passionately emphasises the radical nature of constituent power as being 'an act of choice, the precise determination that opens a horizon, the radical apparatus of something that does not yet exist, and whose conditions of existence imply that the creative act does not lose its characteristics in the act of creating.'[58] Although he explicitly rejects the equation of constituent power with the institution of power, Negri, nevertheless, holds that constituent power is inti-

---

[53] Negri, o.c., p. 2.

[54] Ibid., p. 3.

[55] Ibid., p. 10: 'Whether it is transcendent, immanent or coextensive, the relationship that juridical theory (and through it the constituted arrangement) wants to impose on constituent power works in the direction of neutralization, mystification, or, really, the attribution of senselessness.'

[56] Ibid., p. 11 [My italics, LC].

[57] Ibid., p. 14. At p. 16, he states: 'The radical quality of the constituent principle is absolute. It comes from a void and constitutes everything.' At p. 23 he speaks of an 'originary productivity'.

[58] Ibid., p. 22.

mately connected with community.[59] His understanding of constituent power is a revolutionary one.[60]

To develop his own theory, Negri rereads the history of political thinking. He traces the concept of constituent power back to the *praxis* of revolution as described by Machiavelli (absolute democracy), Harrington (counter power and the egalitarian appeal), the American Constitutional movement (the spatial expression of freedom), the French Revolution (the temporal dimension of an ever unfinished constitution), Communism (the role of the commune and the Party as living labour), to end with a meditation on constituent power as an alternative for modernity: the multitude (inspired primarily by the work of Spinoza and Sartre). Negri's alternative consists in understanding constituent power as the revolutionary and purely creative power of the multitude. It is the power that continuously breaks open the bounds of what is constituted. In this way, it becomes the source of a radically new future, an always open politics and genuine liberty.[61] Furthermore, this brings with it an open ethics and what Negri calls a 'non-philosophy' of history.

With his concept of the multitude, Negri places his theory explicitly beyond Modernity. Modernity, in his reading, is 'the negation of any possibility that the multitude may express itself as subjectivity.'[62] That is to say, Modernity has preformatted the category of 'subjectivity' in such a way that it can only contain a unified, i.e., bounded, tamed, and therefore, lamed subject. But isn't subjectivity a palimpsest of older categories that are less restrictive and, thus, less oppressive? It is exactly this question of the subjectivity of constituent power that Negri answers with the notion of *multitudo*. This multitude always remains open, ever resistant to any definitive formation.[63] It is a new ontological category, the key to a new concept of rationality: a boundless, uninterrupted movement of individuals regarding each other as equals and, thus, releasing their unequal respective resources to the benefit of all.[64] This constituent power leads, first of all, to a new understanding of rationality, both critically destroying obstacles to, and constructing forms of, co-operation.

---

[59] Ibid., p. 23: 'The desire for community is the spirit and soul of constituent power—the desire for a community that is as thoroughly real as it is absent, the trajectory and motor of a movement whose essential determination is the demand of being, repeated, pressing on an absence.'

[60] Ibid, p. 23.

[61] Negri points to the crisis of constituent power and that '[i]t presents itself as the continual interruption of the constitutive rhythm and, as revolutionary becoming with respect to political constructions and constituted being,' as such it 'reveals the incommensurability of the expression of the strength of the multitude.' Ibid., p. 318.

[62] Ibid., p. 325.

[63] Ibid., p. 327: 'The subject is a continual oscillation of strength, a continual reconfiguring of the actual possibility of strength's becoming a world. The subject is the point on which the constitution of strength establishes itself. (…) Constituent power is a creative strength of being, that is, of concrete figures of reality, values, institutions, and logics of the order of reality. Constituent power constitutes society and identifies the social and the political in an ontological nexus.'

[64] Ibid, p. 331: '[T]he multitude is an infinite multiplicity of free and creative singularities. (…) Constituent power takes shape not as reduction to one of the singularities but as the place of their intertwining and expansion.'

Secondly, and without a doubt more importantly for Negri, it leads to a new way of understanding the political. Indeed, according to Negri, it leads to the necessary and actual definition of the political.[65] This concept of the political, so Negri ends his argument, is that of continued revolution.

However poetic and often persuasive Negri is, the question remains whether he is ultimately able to offer a true alternative for what he calls the legal neutralisation of constituent power. Since his argument is developed on a fundamental level, this question concerns the very bedrock of his theory. That which he calls his 'real metaphysical approach' resides in 'recognizing that every formation of community and its duration are the continual product of the strength of singularities.'[66] This sentence on one of the very last pages of the book is clearly formulated as some kind of conclusion. However, is its meaning really so obvious? How is it possible to come from the strength of a *multiplicity* of individuals to the *unity* that the word 'community' undeniably implies? How does one transform the multitude into a 'we', a first person plural? Negri does not answer this question. To understand what the problem is, we should return once more to the first chapter of his book. Reading carefully, one realises that Negri's reason for opposing theories of constitutionalism is that they replace absolute democracy with some kind of indirect democracy. In other words, constitutionalism neutralises the constituent power by the legal doctrine of representation. This doctrine wants us to believe that the people remains the supreme power, although a constitutive assembly represents it by absorbing every action people can take in the political arena. Subsequently, it is this assembly that gives the constitution by which the powers of the state come into being. Negri's criticism supposes that the notion of representation is a legal trick to muzzle constituent power.[67] It supposes, hence, that there is no necessary connection between political power and representation: Absolute power can exist without representation.

The question, now, is whether this position is tenable. Without a doubt, Negri has a point when he warns us about a too rigid conception of constituted power, one that would freeze the *status quo* as it is, without a possibility of change. Also, he has a point in warning us about forms of representation that undercut all participation. Against these accounts, Negri is right to show that constituent power is not something that can be institutionalised once and for all. Yet, he seems to go too far

---

[65] Ibid., p. 333: '[C]onstituent power is the definition of any possible paradigm of the political. The political has no definition unless it takes its point of departure from the concept of constituent power. [...] In the constituent definition of the political, community is decided and reconstructed everyday, and violence is part of this decision and reconstruction. (...) Ontologically, we are faced with the multitude of singularities and the creative work of strength. The political is the site of this interweaving insofar as it presents itself as creative process.'

[66] Ibid., p. 334.

[67] Negri, o.c., p. 3: 'The paradigm is split: To originary, commissionary constituent power is opposed constituent power proper, in its assembly form; finally, constituted power is opposed to both. In this way, constituent power is absorbed into the mechanism of representation. (...) [T]he idea of constituent power is juridically preformed, whereas it was claimed that it would generate the law; it is in fact absorbed in the notion of political representation, whereas it was supposed to legitimize this notion.'

in his criticism. Negri claims that 'constituent power is a subject',[68] and that it is the multitude that embodies subjectivity without any form of representation. But then he writes: 'It is our task to accelerate this strength and recognize its necessity in the love of time.'[69] One thing is sure: This is not the radical plurality of a multitude. Negri distinguishes a vanguard and attributes it a power of acceleration over the constituent power. Furthermore, it is interesting to see that Negri implicitly acknowledges the need of a representative movement: How else is one to understand the reference to a 'we', a first person plural, in these very last lines of the book?[70] As a consequence, also Negri's theory of constituent power is ultimately incoherent. It cannot do without the concept of representation that it explicitly rejects.

2.3 Tamed Power: Constitutionalism and the Case for Limited Government

Perhaps the second constitutional tradition is more helpful for our investigation into the problem of competences and authority. As mentioned above, this line of thought on constitutions has mostly been developed in Germany and Great Britain, where law is regarded in an evolutionary, rather than a revolutionary, perspective. Instead of overthrowing the *status quo* by a new order, this perspective on the constitution regards it primarily as a gradually emerging convention limiting the powers of the state. In fact, it comes close to what in the previous section was called constitutionalism. In this section, I will briefly analyse the tradition of constitutionalism. I will pay special attention to what distinguishes these theories from those of constituent power.

We can find an early expression of modern constitutionalism in the work of Henry St. John Bolingbroke. His famous definition of a constitution holds: 'By constitution, we mean, whenever we speak with propriety and exactness, that assemblage of laws, institutions and customs, derived from certain fixed principles of reason, directed to certain fixed objects of the common good, that compose the general system, according to which the community hath agreed to be governed.'[71] This definition, having much in common with ideas that can already be found in the work of Ancient writers, regards certain laws as 'constitutional' because of their superior character and binding authority. These were not the fruit of a radical beginning, as in the tradition of constituent power. To the contrary, they were handed over from the past in the form of institutions.[72] Even though constitutionalism appears

---

[68] Negri, o.c., p. 324.

[69] Negri, o.c., p. 336.

[70] For a similar critique, see: B. van Roermund, 'Constituerende macht, soevereiniteit en representatie', *Tijdschrift voor Filosofie*, vol. 64 (2002), pp. 509–532.

[71] Bolingbroke, H. St. John, *A Dissertation upon Parties* (1733–34), in: *The Works of Lord Bolingbroke* (1841), II, p. 81, quoted in: C.H. McIlwain, *Constitutionalism: Ancient and Modern*, Indianapolis: Liberty Fund 2008, p. 9.

[72] Cf. C.H. McIlwain, o.c., p. 14.

in different guises over time, it keeps one essential idea, which is the limitation of government.[73]

In a contemporary article on the political foundations of constitutionalism, we can find the following description of what a constitution is supposed to do: 'A constitution *constitutes* a political entity, establishes its fundamental *structure*, and defines the *limits* within which power can be exercised politically.'[74] Accordingly, the constitution has three functions: constitutive, formative and limiting. The first purpose comes to the fore when we ask more precisely what it means 'to constitute'. The answer is that 'constituting a polity is the act of giving origin to a political entity and of sanctioning its nature and primary end', in other words, 'the constitution defines a people and its way of life.'[75] When it is the constitution that gives origin to a political entity, this means that no political entity exists prior to the constitution. In other words, contrary to the theory of Sieyès, constitutionalism seems to date the birth of the people at the same moment as (and not *preceding to*) the birth of the constitution. The constitution is, as it were, a speech act calling the legal order into existence in virtue of certain conventions of the polity; it is not an act that aims at overthrowing the conventions it feeds on.

When we look at the second purpose of the constitution, the two traditions are also mutually opposed. A constitution's second purpose 'is that it gives *form* to the institutions and procedures of governance (in its broadest sense, comprising the legislative, administrative and judicial functions) of a political community.' These make up 'the functional division of competences and powers within the community according to certain objectives and values.'[76] The formative function, assigned by Sieyès to the nation as a formless former, is supposed here to be exercised by the constitution. Since no people exists prior to the constitution, constitutionalism cannot assume it as the sovereign creator of the polity. The constitution takes over this function: It is the constitution that is forming. One could, therefore, say that constitutionalism denies the extra-legal origin of the legal order. As a result, constitutionalisation can only mean a process whereby the legal order as it exists transforms into a more intense version of itself.

Yet, this does not mean that the constitution has lost its function as form. The last purpose—limitation—reflects this: '[T]he third main purpose of the constitution is to limit the exercise of power.'[77] Liberal thought has usually taken this notion of limitation in a negative way as a 'firewall' against the sphere of government

---

[73] Ibid., p. 19: '[I]n all its successive phases, constitutionalism has one essential quality: it is a legal limitation on government; it is the antithesis of arbitrary rule; its opposite is despotic government, the government of will instead of law.' See also: G.F.M. van der Tang, *Grondwetsbegrip en grondwetsidee*, Gouda: Quint 1998, Sect. 3.4.

[74] D. Castiglione, 'The Political Theory of the Constitution', in: R. Bellamy and D. Castiglione (eds.), *Constitutionalism in Transformation: European and Theoretical Perspectives*, Oxford (etc.): Blackwell 1996, pp. 5–23 at p. 9–10 [Italics in the original].

[75] Ibid., p. 10.

[76] Ibid. [Italics in the original].

[77] Ibid.

action.[78] However, these limitations are also factual, and follow directly from the constitutive function. According to the tradition of constitutionalism, the creation of the polity is already its limitation since it names certain ways in which power can be exercised in a 'political' way, hereby factually excluding others. This means that the constitutive limitations 'guarantee that there are areas of activity and social relationships not directly touched by politics itself, insofar as they fall outside either its scope or its reach,' because 'the definition of the "political" guarantees that political power is limited insofar as its normal workings are made regular and predictable.'[79] Nevertheless, both negative and constitutive limitations 'represent the attempt to de-personalize political power.'[80] Concerning the last point, the traditions of constituent power and that of constitutionalism agree with one another: The constitution *limits* political power. However, they fundamentally disagree as to the appraisal of this limitation. Whereas constitutionalism defends it as one of the three main purposes of any constitution, the theory originally devised by Sieyès regards any attempt of limiting the sovereign power of the nation as problematic. Formulated differently, agreement exists on the need to distinguish a political sphere from a legal one. Disagreement concerns the way in which politics and law relate.

It is exactly this last topic that forms 'the classical *topoi* of the relationship between the "government of laws" and the "government of man" (...) [which] captures the essence of discussions about constitutionalism.'[81] For our purposes, it is important what conclusion on the nature of political power we should draw from this time-honoured theory.[82] In this view, power appears as essentially limited: '[P]olitical power is not absolute both because, in its normal administration, it is limited by the laws, and because it is *political* in nature—a power, that is, exercised on the basis of the principle of (relative) equality.'[83] This vision of political power differs fundamentally from what we have seen in the tradition of constituent power. Indeed, according to the latter view, the power of the nation was the absolute source of all power. Of course, one could discard this problem by pointing to the *pre-political* nature of the nation as constituent power. However, this merely hides the difficulty, rather than offers a veritable solution. The problem, it seems to me, is that constitutionalism always already starts from a notion of power that is limited, rather than absolute. Political power is limited because it is supposed to be based on equality as a matter of principle. By explicitly limiting political power, the constitution

---

[78] Cf. Arendt, o.c., p. 143: 'the liberties which the laws of constitutional government guarantee are all of a negative character (...) a safeguard against government.'

[79] Castiglione, o.c., p. 11.

[80] Ibid.

[81] Ibid. [Italics in the original].

[82] Aristotle starts his political thinking from the perspective of a *polis* devised of free and equal citizens. Equality was a criterion of justice: an equal distribution is a just distribution for it gives to each his due (*suum cuique tribuere*). Accordingly, *politeia* (usually translated as 'constitution') was to reflect the equality of citizens as a politically just regime. The constitution corresponded to the ultimate purpose (*telos*) of political life. Cf. Castiglione, o.c., pp. 11–14.

[83] Ibid., p. 14.

(as one of its main functions) reiterates the point. So power is limited... because it is constitutional power, i.e., power exercised according to limiting principles. The limitation of power, so precious to all theories of constitutionalism, is only possible if one *presupposes* that political power is limited in the first place. It is exactly this presupposition that the theories of constituent power attack. Just as do the theories of constituent power, the theory of constitutionalism ultimately runs into circularity.

This circle returns in a specifically legal perspective on the issue. The famous German constitutional lawyer and legal theorist, Ernst-Wolfgang Böckenförde, wrote about the concept of constituent power as being a concept at the borders of constitutional law.[84] For him, as a constitutional lawyer, the question raised by the concept of constituent power is, first and foremost, why a positive constitution would have a higher authority than ordinary laws. This higher value does not reside in the constitution itself, but rather, in a *pre-constitutional* factor: The special power or authority that gave it. It is this special power, Böckenförde states, that is called constituent power ever since the French Revolution. The question of constituent power concerns, therefore, the origin and basis of legitimacy of the constitution. This query takes us to the very borders of constitutional law because it inquires after the constitution itself, and more. This 'more', Böckenförde argues, entails that this topic transcends the scope of positive law. Note, however, that the 'more' goes beyond positive law for reasons different from those that Negri submitted in the previous section. It is not the plural subjectivity of 'the multitude' growing to permanent revolution, but rather, the plural objectivity of the facts that have to be taken into account in any legal order. Whereas the ground (or foundation) of law is a part of law and, therefore, an object for scholarly legal discipline, no legal order can allow itself not to link up with what is given without suffering in authority: 'The connection between law and what is given pre-legally, the problem of the missing link between norms and facts, appears imperatively in the case of the constitution.'[85]

Even though he recognises other ways of approaching the question, Böckenförde wants to stress that in his constitutional law-approach, the concept of constituent power has the function of legitimising the normative validity of the constitution, on the one hand, and stabilising this validity, on the other. In order to obtain these aims, Böckenförde dismisses both what he calls 'the empty legitimacy of Kelsen' (who allegedly cut norms loose from facts) and the ideal legitimacy of natural law theories (which advocate continuity between positive norms and norms of reason). One should recognise the power giving the constitution as a political player, i.e., as a political force (*Kraft*). Consequently, he comes to the following definition: 'The constituent power is that (political) power and authority that is able to give, support and nullify the constitution in its normative claim to validity. It is not identical to the

---

[84] E.-W. Böckenförde, 'Die verfassunggebende Gewalt des Volkes – Ein Grenzbegriff des Verfassungsrechts', in: *Staat, Verfassung, Demokratie. Studien zur Verfassungstheorie und zum Verfassungsrecht*, Frankfurt am Main: Suhrkamp 1991, pp. 90–112.

[85] Ibid., pp. 91–92: 'Die Verknüpfung des Rechts mit vorrechtlichen Gegebenheiten, das Problem des missing link zwischen Normativität und Faktizität kommt daher bei der Verfassung unabweisbar zum Vorschein.'

constituted state powers, but precedes it. However, when [the constituent power] expresses itself, it works on these [state] powers and, depending on the form of the expression, also in them.'[86]

This characterisation is close to that of Sieyès, and Böckenförde seems to follow the French revolutionary on other points, also. His is a sophisticated defence of constitutionalism, taking the opposite position into account. But under the surface, Böckenförde consistently returns to the basic tenets underlying his constitutionalist position. For example, he agrees that the question of who should be the bearer (or subject) of constituent power is a strange one. Precisely because it is a democratic and revolutionary concept, both in origin and in content, there can be but one possible subject: the people. However, the next question is: What does 'people' mean in this context? Following Sieyès, Böckenförde understands the people as a nation. This is a people in the *political* sense: 'the group of human beings (politically converging and delimitating itself) that is aware of itself as a political entity that matters and that enters history acting as one.'[87]

From the point of view of constitutional law, however, the higher authority of the constituent power is not only a blessing, but also a problem. Since the constituent power of the people precedes and transcends the positive constitution, it cannot be bound by this constitution. Constituent power retains 'an original, immediate and elementary character.'[88] Although it seems inviting to dismiss constituent power (and the whims of politics) altogether, Böckenförde explicitly rejects this possibility as a fiction. The constituent power of the people remains available as a political force. Moreover, he argues that, without the continuous support of political and legal convictions of a particular society for the fundamental traits of the constitution, it becomes eroded. This may lead to civil uprisings or to total apathy.

Contrary to what Sieyès teaches, Böckenförde emphasises that the problem with the concept of constituent power is that it confronts constitutional law with opposite demands. On the one hand, it gives an opportunity to ground the higher authority of the constitution, but then one should keep the *connection* between the constituent power of the people and the positive constitution. On the other hand, the pre-normative fluctuations of constituent power are a threat to the stability of the constitutional order and, therefore, a *detachment* is needed. How does one deal with this problem? How is one to keep the legitimising quality of constituent power without exposing oneself to its political force? Böckenförde sees here an important task for constitutional law, even though he acknowledges that this goal cannot ever be attained completely. The assignment of constitutional law is 'to somewhat re-

---

[86] Ibid., p. 94: 'Verfassunggebende Gewalt ist diejenige (politische) Kraft und Autorität, die in der Lage ist, die Verfassung in ihrem normativen Geltungsanspruch hervorzubringen, zu tragen und aufzuheben. Sie ist nicht mit der verfaßten Staatsgewalt identisch, sondern liegt ihr voraus. Sie wirkt aber, wenn sie sich äußert, auf diese ein und je nach ihrer Äußerungsform auch in sie hinein.'

[87] Ibid., p. 96: 'die (politisch sich zusammenfindende und abgrenzende) Gruppe von Menschen, die sich ihrer selbst als politische Größe bewußt ist und als solche handelnd in die Geschichte eintritt.'

[88] Ibid., p. 99: 'einen originären, unmittelbaren, auch elementaren Character.'

strict the never excludable actions of the constituent power of the people. With the right precautions one could make sure that its expressions, when they appear, lead to procedures especially prepared for this purpose, where they are picked up and made valid by their channelling. In this way, they [the expressions, LC] would retain their possibility of actualisation.'[89] Böckenförde enumerates three different ways in which this could be done. The first possibility is a distinction and demarcation between constituent power and the constituted powers. This entails some classical legal-conceptual work. The second way would be to develop democratic procedures to articulate and regiment the expressions of the constituent power. Yet, most of the time, these expressions are negative and remain rather vague. One should, therefore, try to convert them into clear designs and executable orders; examples are a constitutional convention and a referendum about a specific proposal to change the constitution.

Furthermore, there is a third way to restrain the constituent power that, nevertheless, aims at leaving the door open for influence of the unordered people *in the framework of* the constitution. To understand what Böckenförde means by this, it is essential to grasp his distinction between the unorganised people and the organised people, and how the two relate: 'It is only when the people acts as an organised entity, in the form of active citizenry, that the unorganised people of the constituent power also somehow takes part and is present. In state-political reality, it is possible to legally distinguish between the people as organ and the people as sovereign. However, it is impossible to separate them, as if they were two different real entities; in the end, they are both the same "people".'[90] As an example of this inseparability, Böckenförde points to procedures of direct constitution-making.

In the final analysis, Böckenförde tries to answer the question whether, and in which sense, positive law can bind constituent power. He starts by observing that in democratic theory no such prior legal bond can exist. However, he proceeds by rejecting the view that constituent power is a random and arbitrary force. He has two different arguments for this move, one conceptual and one ethical. To start with the former, for Böckenförde the concept of constituent power entails the will for a constitution. Since a constitution cannot mean absolute power, the concept of constituent power already entails the delimitation of power. However, if we scrutinize this argument, it turns out to be a *petitio principii*. Böckenförde claims that constituent power already means limited power because it is the will to make a constitution. But the only way to say that constituent power is limited power is to

---

[89] Ibid., p. 100: 'Die niemals ausschließbaren Aktionen der verfassunggebenden Gewalt des Volkes können irgendwie eingegrenzt und es kann durch geeignete Vorkehrungen erreicht werden, daß ihre Äußerungen, wenn sie hervortreten, in dafür bereitgestellte Verfahren einmünden, dadurch aufgefangen werden und sich kanalisiert zur Geltung bringen, in dieser Weise aber auch die Möglichkeit der Aktualisierung haben.'

[90] Ibid., p. 104: 'Denn immer dann, wenn das Volk als organisierte Größe, in Form der Aktivbürgerschaft, handelnd auftritt, ist auch das unorganisierte Volk des pouvoir constituant irgendwie beteiligt und mit anwesend. In der staatlich-politischen Wirklichkeit lassen sich Volk als Organ und Volk als Souverän zwar juridisch unterscheiden; sie lassen sich aber nicht voneinander abtrennen, als ob sie zwei verschiedene reale Größen wären; beide sind letztlich dasselbe >>Volk<<.'

presuppose that it is the will to make a constitution. Yet, this is exactly the question. Negri, for example, would never agree with the view that constituent power entails the will to make a constitution. According to him, any form of constitutionalism is immediately an act of treason towards the constituent power. Furthermore, it does not follow from Böckenförde's earlier definition of the nation: If it were already an organised entity before the constitution, why would it need a constitution at all? For what reason would it limit its force?

Let us turn to Böckenförde's second argument for a limited conception of constituent power. In this framework, his reasoning is that constituent power can be limited either from the outside by non-positive law, or from the inside. Human rights are called upon in our day to form this limitation. Böckenförde proposes to understand this limitation not in the sense of positive law imposed on constituent power (which would be self-contradictory) but rather as a demand that remains dependent on recognition by the bearer of constituent power: 'This demand can only be legally claimable if it complies with it. For the concrete legal validity, it boils down again to the recognition and positive conversion of the bearer of constituent power, itself.'[91] Following Hermann Heller, Böckenförde regards this as an *ethical* limitation. He will also refer to it as the 'spirit' of a people.[92] This entails that it cannot be seen as a legally claimable right. But this seems to beg the question. Presupposing an ethical limitation prior to the legal limitation amounts to presupposing a constitution *behind* the constitution. In other words, it is again a limitation before the limitation appears, without it being argued for.

2.4 Law, State and Democracy: Rereading the Schmitt-Kelsen Debate

A direct confrontation between a supporter of the primacy of politics and a defender of constitutionalism can be found in a discussion on the legal-political foundations of the Weimar Republic. Just after the First World War, confronted with the failing of the Weimar Constitution, Carl Schmitt and Hans Kelsen engaged in a debate. Their polemic did not just concern the legitimacy of this constitution; it also forced them to take a stance towards the underlying issues concerning the relationship between law and politics. The political background of the debate made the contributors defend their own position with ever-sharper arguments, letting their views come to the fore in their most radical form. Furthermore, the debate had

---

[91] Ibid., pp. 109–110: 'deren rechtliche Einforderbarkeit davon abhängt, daß er ihr entspricht, so kommt es für die konkrete rechtliche Geltung wieder auf die Anerkennung und positive Umsetzung durch den Träger der verfassunggebenden Gewalt selbst an.'

[92] Ibid., p. 111: 'Worauf es ankommt, ist also, daß in einem Volk dann, wenn es sich als verfassunggebende Gewalt betätigt, ein lebendiges Rechtsbewußtsein, wirksame Ordnungsideen und ein ethisch-politischer Gestaltungswille vorhanden sind, kurz, daß es einen >>Geist<< in sich trägt, der sich in Institutionen, Regeln und Verfahren ausformen kann und auch ausformt.'

dramatic consequences, both on a personal and on an ideological level. Whereas Kelsen chose to flee to the United States, Schmitt flirted with National Socialism. It also makes clear that it is too easy to equate the view that proclaims the primacy of politics with a revolutionary tradition, as Arendt does. The Weimar Republic shows that this position has defenders among conservative (Von Savigny, Schmitt) and progressive thinkers (Heller and Luxemburg). In the same vein, the tradition of constitutionalism has supporters on the left (Kelsen, Habermas) and on the right (Burke). In the following pages, I will reread the discussion between Schmitt and Kelsen.[93] I will first discuss their views on the relationship between parliament and democracy, and subsequently, their opinions on the relationship between law and state. Finally, I will draw some conclusions concerning the way legal doctrine understands the concept of competence.

According to Carl Schmitt, the failure of the Weimar Constitution shows that there is a contradiction between parliamentarism and democracy. By disconnecting the two concepts, Schmitt does not only claim that they can exist separately, but also opens the possibility for dictatorship as a legitimate alternative for a parliamentary democracy under certain circumstances.[94] To understand this last move, we need to focus on Schmitt's concept of democracy. For Schmitt, democracy is equal to the principle of popular sovereignty: The people are both the rulers and the ruled.[95] With regard to the concept of people, Schmitt holds that it is a political unity.[96] As such, it precedes the legal order: The political unity of the people is presupposed in every legally binding decision. Day-to-day politics can only take place after an act of self-inclusion drawing a border between 'we' and 'them', 'inside' and 'outside', 'friend' and 'enemy'. The drawing of this border is the institution of the community. The unity of the people, Schmitt argues, resides in equality understood as homogeneity.[97] This homogeneity is at the very heart of democracy, for, '[t]he democratic identity of governed and governing arises from that.'[98] Because of this homogene-

---

[93] For my interpretation of the debate between Schmitt and Kelsen, I am much indepted to Hans Lindahl, see: H. Lindahl, 'Constituent Power and Reflexive Identity: Towards an Ontology of Collective Selfhood', in M. Loughlin and N. Walker (eds.), *The Paradox of Constitutionalism: Constituent Power and Constitutional Form*, Oxford (etc.): Oxford University Press 2007, pp. 9–24.

[94] See: C. Schmitt, *The Crisis of Parliamentary Democracy*, trans. E. Kennedy, Cambridge, Mass.: MIT Press 1985, in particular the 'Preface to the Second Edition (1926): On the Contradiction between Parliamentarism and Democracy', p. 16–17. See also C. Schmitt, *Verfassungslehre*, Berlin: Duncker & Humblot 1970 [1928], p. 237: 'Eine Diktatur insbesondere ist nur auf demokratischer Grundlage möglich.'

[95] C. Schmitt, *Verfassungslehre*, p. 234: 'Demokratie (…) ist Identität von Herrscher und Beherrschten, Regierenden und Regierten, Befehlenden und Gehorchenden.'

[96] This becomes clear in the following definition of democracy: 'Demokratie ist eine dem Prinzip der Identität (nämlich des konkret vorhandenen Volkes mit sich selbst als politische Einheit) entsprechende Staatsform.' Cf. C. Schmitt, *Verfassungslehre*, p. 223.

[97] Ibid., p. 226: 'Die spezifische Staatsform der Demokratie kann nur auf einen spezifischen und substanziellen Begriff der Gleichheit begründet werden.' Schmitt speaks of homogeneity at p. 235 and p. 238. See also p. 34, where he states that: 'Die demokratische Gleichheit ist wesentlich Gleichartigkeit, und zwar Gleichartigkeit des Volkes.'

[98] C. Schmitt, *The Crisis of Parliamentary Democracy*, p. 14.

ity, citizens are equals; strangers are excluded as being unequal. In Schmitt's words: 'Every actual democracy rests on the principle that not only are equals equal, but unequals will not be treated equally. Democracy requires, therefore, first homogeneity and second—if the need arises—elimination or eradication of heterogeneity.'[99]

It is important to take into account that, for Schmitt, the people *qua* agent is a *real* entity. Only as a real entity can the people interfere in the course of political events and be the bearer of sovereignty, the subject of constituent power.[100] Schmitt claims that, in this respect, the concept of 'the people' takes over from God. Whereas in the Middle Ages, God was sovereign in virtue of His omnipotence, in Modernity, the people is considered to be 'a mortal God', to quote Hobbes's famous phrase, and thus, unlimited in power. This thesis fits into Schmitt's broader contention of a political theology: The modern concepts of law and politics are the secularised versions of theological notions.[101] It is only against this background that we can understand what Schmitt has to say about sovereignty. For Schmitt, sovereignty entails the fundamental decision regarding the people as a whole; it is the political decision *par excellence*.[102] It draws the line between homogeneity and heterogeneity, between who is inside (a friend) and who is outside (an enemy).[103] The consequence of this definition is of the utmost interest to our own inquiry because it concerns competence as legal power. According to Schmitt, sovereignty cannot be legal power because it is the power to create legal powers. In other words, sovereignty precedes competence because the people (as a political unity) precedes the legal order (as a legal unity, an order of competences). By calling it *Kompetenz-Kompetenz*, one only begs the question.

As an analogy of the power of God, the sovereign power of the people is without limits. This is intimately connected with the state of exception. Sovereignty, as the highest power, comes to the fore in the state of exception because then the usual limits on state powers (competences) are suspended: 'The precondition as well as the content of jurisdictional competence in such a case must necessarily be unlimited.'[104] In the state of exception, exceptional powers are needed because what is at stake is the very existence of the people in its unity, i.e., in its homogeneity.[105] This means, first of all, that the state of exception is not something that

---

[99] Ibid., p. 9.

[100] C. Schmitt, *Verfassungslehre*, p. 223: 'Das Volk ist Träger der verfassunggebenden Gewalt und gibt sich selbst seine Verfassung.' At p. 236 Schmitt stresses: 'Staatsgewalt und Regierung gehen in der Demokratie vom Volke aus.'

[101] Cf. C. Schmitt, *Political Theology. Four Chapters on the Concept of Sovereignty*, The University of Chicago Press 1985, p. 36.

[102] Ibid., p. 6: 'The decision on the exception is a decision in the true sense of the word.'

[103] C. Schmitt, *The Crisis of Parliamentary Democracy*, p. 11: 'Until now there has never been a democracy that did not recognize the concept "foreign" and that could have realized the equality of all men.' The distinction between 'friend' and 'enemy' is central to C. Schmitt, *The Concept of the Political*, trans. G. Schwab, Chicago: The University of Chicago Press 1996 [1932].

[104] C. Schmitt, *Political Theology*, p. 7.

[105] Ibid., p. 6: 'The exception, which is not codified in the existing legal order, can at best be characterized as a case of extreme peril, a danger to the existence of the state, or the like.'

happens only rarely. Every time the unity of the people is in danger, this calls for a sovereign decision, a decision on who is equal and who is unequal.[106] This is a decision that draws the border between 'we' and 'them'. The second consequence is a paradoxical one. When Schmitt characterises the sovereign decision as a decision on the state of exception, it is this state that defines normality, and not the other way around. It is the exception that constitutes what is normal; the normal case exists only by the grace of the exception.[107]

If what is decided upon in the case of exception is the homogeneity, the ultimate unity of the people, this brings us back to the question of democracy. With his account of the sovereign decision, Schmitt has given us a particular reading of the principle of popular sovereignty. Indeed, for Schmitt, the people being at the same time rulers and ruled means that the laws in a democracy represent the concrete homogeneity of the people, the people as a unity.[108] Representing should be understood as *copying*: The people is only sovereign when the laws that rule it are a copy of its particular and concrete homogeneity.[109] The question that immediately arises is whether parliament is able to perform this task? Schmitt's answer is negative, as democracy and parliament are incompatible in the final analysis.

Schmitt argues that the incompatibility between democracy and parliament is essentially one between homogeneity and diversity. We have seen how he connects homogeneity with the concrete unity of the people. Diversity, on the other hand, is linked to the characteristically liberal idea of parliament.[110] According to Schmitt, liberalism is a position that starts from the individual, and thus, from selfishness and a plurality of opinions.[111] This is completely at odds with democracy, where the homogeneity between citizens relates them to each other in solidarity. Therefore, he speaks of an 'inescapable contradiction of liberal individualism and democratic

---

[106] C. Schmitt, *Verfassungslehre*, p. 227: 'Der demokratische Begriff der Gleichheit ist ein politischer Begriff und nimmt, wie jeder echte politische Begriff, auf die Möglichkeit einer Unterscheidung Bezug.'

[107] C. Schmitt, *Political Theology*, p. 15: 'The exception is more interesting than the rule. The rule proves nothing; the exception proves everything: It confirms not only the rule, but also its existence which derives only from the exception.'

[108] C. Schmitt, *Verfassungslehre*, p. 235: 'repräsentiert werden nicht die Regierenden, sondern die politische Einheit als Ganzes.'

[109] Schmitt stresses this concrete character of equality, in *The Crisis of Parliamentary Democracy*, p. 9: 'The question of equality is (...) about the substance of equality. It can be found in certain physical and moral qualities, as for example, in civic virtue, in *arete*, the classical democracy of *vertus* (*vertu*). (...) Since the Nineteenth Century, it has existed above all in membership in a particular nation, in national homogeneity. Equality is only interesting and valuable politically so long as it has substance, and for that reason, at least the possibility and the risk of inequality.'

[110] C. Schmitt, *The Crisis of Parliamentary Democracy*, p. 8: 'The belief in parliamentarism, in government by discussion, belongs to the intellectual world of liberalism. It does not belong to democracy.'

[111] Ibid., p. 4: 'But worse, and destroying almost every hope, in a few states parliamentarism has already produced a situation in which all public business has become an object of spoils and compromise for the parties and their followers, and politics, far from being the concern of an elite, has become the despised business of a rather dubious class of persons.'

homogeneity.'[112] Liberalism should be connected with civil society where man appears as a private person and not as a citizen. As persons, everyone is equal. However, Schmitt warns us that '[t]he equality of all persons as persons is not democracy but a certain kind of liberalism, not a state form but an individualistic-humanitarian ethics and *Weltanschauung*.'[113] So, 'private person' is not a political category. This becomes clear when we focus on the individual rights advocated by classical liberalism: These were supposed to secure that the individual retains a domain in which he is free in the sense of *free from* governmental interference. This negative freedom is the product of a chasm between state and civil society, a chasm that works at the expense of the common good and the political state. In contradistinction to the liberal freedoms, Schmitt, therefore, points to the importance of positive political rights. To wrap up the argument, Schmitt rejects parliament because of its liberal nature. Liberalism denies the truly political content of democracy as a decision about what makes the people. Because of its reduction of human relations to relations between selfish individuals, the liberal institution of parliament is unable to represent the people as a unity. Paradoxical as it may seem, for Schmitt parliament is not democratically legitimised.[114]

Schmitt also understands the relationship between state and law in a dualistic way. According to him, the much-praised 'democratic *Rechtsstaat*' breaks down in two distinct components. On the one hand, there is a political component: Democracy. On the other hand, there is a liberal-legal component: The *Rechtsstaat*, the civil constitutional state that is based on individualism.[115] In the state, this element comes to the fore in the recognition of individual rights and the separation of powers.[116] Schmitt argues that these components are not just different, but are even at odds with one another. The civil constitutional state reduces power to competence.[117] In this way, Schmitt argues, it is responsible for the elimination of the political element from the legal order, thus letting it slip away into the darker spheres of sheer power.[118] Because Schmitt sees an undeniable link between democracy and

---

[112] Ibid., p. 17. See also p. 2, where he mentions that 'the distinction between liberal parliamentary ideas and mass democratic ideas cannot remain unnoticed any longer.'

[113] Ibid., p. 13.

[114] Ibid., p. 15: 'As democracy, modern mass democracy attempts to realize an identity of governed and governing, and thus it confronts parliament as an inconceivable and outmoded institution. If democratic identity is taken seriously, then in an emergency, no other constitutional institution can withstand the sole criterion of the people's will, however it is expressed. Against the will of the people especially, an institution based on discussion by independent representatives has no autonomous justification for its existence, even less so because the belief in discussion is not democratic but originally liberal.'

[115] C. Schmitt, *Verfassungslehre*, p. 125: 'Die moderne bürgerlich-rechtsstaatliche Verfassung entspricht in ihren Prinzipien dem Verfassungsideal des bürgerlichen Individualismus.'

[116] Ibid., p. 127: 'Grundrechte und Gewaltenteilung bezeichnen demnach den wesentlichen Inhalt des rechtsstaatlichen Bestandteils der modernen Verfassung.'

[117] Ibid., p. 126: 'die (prinzipiell begrenzte) staatliche Macht wird geteilt und in einem System umschriebener Kompetenzen erfaßt.'

[118] Ibid.p. 125: 'Das Politische kann nicht vom Staat – der politischen Einheit eines Volkes – getrennt werden, und das Staatsrecht entpolitisieren, hieße nichts anderes als das Staatsrecht entstaatlichen.'

the political, the constitutional state is a threat to democracy understood as popular sovereignty. Contrary to the idea of *Rechtsstaat*, Schmitt's own vision of the state is characterised by its independent existence. For him, the state is equal to the constitution (*Verfassung*). Therefore, what is at stake in the constitution is the independent political existence of the state.[119] Note that this differs from a strictly legal concept of the constitution. For (constitutional) lawyers, the constitution is, first of all, a set of basic legal rules on the organisation of public power which calls the state into existence as a *legal* entity. Schmitt fundamentally disagrees with this view. Any constitution in the legal (normative) sense presupposes a unity, the unity of a *political* will belonging to a people.[120] The constitution, in the theory of Schmitt, is the political decision of a people concerning its independent existence, its existence as a separate unity. So, a political unity precedes the legal order.[121] That a political order must precede the legal order means that the genesis of the legal order is a political act, the act of the people giving the constitution.[122] This act is thus preceded by the decision on the political organisation of a people. Note that Schmitt speaks of a decision to organise, which entails that the people already exists before this decision. There is already a separation between 'we' and 'them', between friends and enemies, before any law can be enacted. Schmitt claims that this is a natural distinction based on the people as an organic unity.[123] As such, this forms the foundation of the legal order, the political form that precedes it.[124] It is this absolute foundation that the legal order copies.

The consequence of Schmitt's thoughts on constitutions is a view radically opposed to the *Rechtsstaat,* and its reduction of power to competence. Against this no-

---

[119] Cf. C. Schmitt, *Verfassungslehre*, p. 4, where Schmitt speaks of the *Verfassung* as 'den konkreten einzelnen Staat (…) in seiner konkreten politischen Existenz. (…) [D]er Staat ist Verfassung, d. h. ein seinsmäßig vorhandener Zustand, ein *status* von Einheit und Ordnung. Der Staat würde aufhören zu existieren, wenn diese Verfassung, d. h. diese Einheit und Ordnung aufhörte. Die Verfassung ist seine "Seele", sein konkretes Leben und seine individuelle Existenz.'

[120] Ibid., p. 9: 'In Wahrheit gilt eine Verfassung, weil sie von einer verfassunggebenden Gewalt (d. h. Macht oder Autorität) ausgeht und durch deren Willen gesetzt ist. Das Wort "Wille" bezeichnet im Gegensatz zu bloßen Normen eine seinsmäßige Größe als den Ursprung eines Sollens. Der Wille ist existenziell vorhanden, seine Macht oder Autorität liegt in seinem Sein.'

[121] Ibid., p. 10: 'Der Begriff der Rechtsordnung enthält zwei völlig verschiedene Elemente: das normative Element des Rechts und das seinsmäßige Element der konkreten Ordnung. Die Einheit und Ordnung liegt in der politischen Existenz des Staates, nicht in Gesetzen, Regeln und irgendwelchen Normativitäten.'

[122] Ibid., p. 238: 'Das Volk ist in der Demokratie Subjekt der verfassunggebenden Gewalt. Jede Verfassung beruht nach demokratischer Auffassung auch in ihrem rechtstaatlichen Bestandteil auf der konkreten politischen Entscheidung des politisch handlungsfähigen Volkes. Jede demokratische Verfassung setzt ein solches handlungsfähiges Volk voraus.'

[123] C. Schmitt, *Political Theology*, p. 49: 'The unity that a people represents does not possess this decisionist character; it is an organic unity, and with national consciousness, the ideas of the state originated as an organic whole.'

[124] C. Schmitt, *Verfassungslehre*, p. 200: 'Die Prinzipien der bürgerlichen Freiheit können wohl einen Staat modifizieren und temperieren, aber nicht aus sich heraus eine politische Form begründen.'

tion of legal power, Schmitt holds that competences ultimately depend on power in the strong sense of the word, i.e., political power. In other words, the power to give the constitution, i.e., constituent power, is the source of all legal power. It would be a mistake, however, to place this political act *par excellence* only at the beginning of the legal order. It is the sovereign decision that we described above: Not only every time the state is in crisis, but also every time its political unity is at stake, however trifle the issue might be, this asks for a political decision. This is the state of exception, as distinct from the state of emergency. In these cases, one can witness how legal power depends on political power.[125] Then, the sovereign appears, the one 'who decides on the exception,'[126] the one who has the power to suspend the normal legal order *in toto*, the order of competences.[127] This brings Schmitt to a distinction between two concepts of law. The concept of law that belongs to the constitutional state stresses its rationality. Yet, this rationality presupposes the irrationality of what Schmitt calls the democratic-political concept of law. The latter is a concrete act of will of the sovereign people. Schmitt refutes the sovereignty of law as proclaimed by the *Rechtsstaat*, by pointing to democracy as the political sovereignty of the people.

The starting point of Kelsen's argument is radically opposed to that of Schmitt. The Austrian lawyer, first of all, stresses the connection between democracy and parliament.[128] Yes, their fate is inextricably linked.[129] Even though his definition of democracy seems almost identical to the one of Schmitt—identity of rulers and ruled—it differs on a decisive point.[130] This becomes clear when we look at the concept of 'people'. Where Schmitt stresses the homogeneity of the people, its *real* unity, Kelsen tries to question it. Where Schmitt chooses equality as the basic characteristic of democracy, for Kelsen it resides in freedom.[131] Where Schmitt says

---

[125] C. Schmitt, *Political Theology*, p. 13: 'The exception reveals most clearly the essence of the state's authority.'

[126] Ibid., p. 5.

[127] Ibid., p. 12: 'What characterizes an exception is principally unlimited authority, which means the suspension of the entire existing order.'

[128] Cf. H. Kelsen, 'On the Essence and Value of Democracy', trans. B. Cooper and S. Hemetsberger, in: A.J. Jacobson and B. Schlink (eds.), *Weimar: A Jurisprudence of Crisis*, Berkeley (etc.): University of California Press 2002 [1929], pp. 84–109, at p. 92: 'Modern democracy is based upon political parties, whose significance increases the more the democratic principle is implemented. Considering this fact, one can understand the tendency—though still weak—to anchor political parties *in the constitution* and give legal form to what they have de facto long since become: organs forming the will of the state.' [Italics in the original].

[129] Ibid., p. 95–96: 'Within the democratic parliamentary republic, the problem of parliamentarism becomes a fateful question. The existence of modern democracy depends on whether parliament is a workable tool to solve the social problems of our time. (…) Thus a decision about parliamentarism is at the same time a decision about democracy.'

[130] How close Kelsen's definition is to that of Schmitt becomes clear from the following quotation: 'Democracy is the identity of the leader and the led, of the subject and the object of rule; it means the rule of the people over the people.' Cf. H. Kelsen, 'On the Essence and Value of Democracy', p. 89.

[131] With regard to democracy, Kelsen states: 'Politically free is he who is subject to a legal order in the creation of which he participates. An individual is free if what he "ought to" do according

that the people is a political (pre-legal) concept, Kelsen stresses that it is a legal notion. For a better understanding of this last claim, one should keep in mind what has been said above about the relationship between the people and democracy. In a democracy, the people is both subject and object of legislative ruling. Kelsen admits that as ruled, as the object of rules, the people is indeed a unity: a unity of norms, a unity of several actions. So, the unity of the people is the unity of a legal order. The people is a normative, i.e., a *legal* unity.[132]

Things are different with regard to the people as the subject of rules. Kelsen points to the fact that the number of citizens really actively engaged in norm creation is much smaller than that of those ruled. The group of 'norm creators' is limited to the voters.[133] The difference between the people as rulers and the people as ruled is shown by the existence of political parties. One may regard these as the embodiment of the plurality of the people. So, the people as rulers is the sum total of voters, a factual disunity. On the other hand, the people as being ruled corresponds to a legal unity. This is the unity of a legal order. In other words, since we are always already born in an existing legal order, Kelsen argues, the people as a legal unity always already exists. *Pace* Schmitt, political unity is formed by the legal act drawing the borders of the polity.

Kelsen's point against Schmitt is relevant on yet another level. Above, I have demonstrated how Schmitt puts emphasis on the conceptual and even temporal primacy of constituent power. Kelsen remarks that '[u]sually, an individual is born into a community constituted by a pre-existing social order.'[134] That is to say, Kelsen, by showing how we always already find ourselves within an existing legal order, in a sense, points out how there is a primacy of the constituted order. Far from being problematic, it is this constituted state that forms the condition for all acts of constitution. According to Kelsen, the reason why I, as an individual, participate in politics is to change the existing (constituted) condition into one that suits me more, into a condition with which I could agree.[135] Important in his theory is *the difference* between the normative unity of the people, on the one hand, and its factual disunity on the other.[136] Precisely because of this difference, he can understand the factual disunity as

---

to the social order coincides with what he "wills to" do. Democracy means that the "will" which is represented in the legal order of the State is identical with the wills of the subjects.' See: Cf. H. Kelsen, *General Theory of Law and State*, New York: Russel & Russel 1961, p. 284.

[132] H. Kelsen, 'On the Essence and Value of Democracy', p. 90: 'Only in a *normative* sense can one speak of a unity. (...) Fundamentally, only a *legal* element can be conceived more or less precisely as the unity of the people: the *unity* of the *state's legal order*, which rules the behavior of the human beings subject to its norms.' [Italics in the original].

[133] Ibid., p. 91: 'Participation in creating the will of the community is the content of so-called *political rights*. Even in an extreme democracy, the people as embodiment of those with political rights represents only a small segment of those obligated by the state order, of the people as object of rule.' [Italics in the original].

[134] H. Kelsen, *General Theory of Law and State*, p. 286.

[135] Ibid.: 'The problem, thus, can be narrowed down to the question how an existing order can be changed.'

[136] Cf. H. Kelsen, 'On the Essence and Value of Democracy', p. 90: '[T]he unity of the people is only (...) the object of rule. As ruling *subject*, human beings are recognised only to the extent that

a continuous discussion about how to achieve unity. In a situation of unity, rulers and ruled would actually coincide; every member of a polity could agree with the laws. This would be a state of true political freedom in the sense of self-determination.[137]

One could discard these ideas as utopian or unreal, but then one misses Kelsen's point. He stresses that democracy is exactly this tension between an ideal unity and a factual disunity. This makes his theory an important argument against totalitarian regimes. While claiming the unity of the people to be really available, these regimes try to deny the tension and look away from it. Against these attempts, Kelsen is able to point to the continuous tension within democracy. Moreover, the tension helps to explain the value of majority rule. This rule reflects the conviction that the people is factually a plurality. Thus, it denies the totalitarian claim. Furthermore, it offers the minority the easiest way to become a majority.[138] Kelsen's view on parliament is an immediate result of his views on democracy. Since the unity of the people is a fiction, parliament as the representation of that unity can also only be a fiction. This fiction resides in the difference between the unity and the disunity of the people. It makes that the acts of parliament are but a compromise between the different groups within society, a compromise about the content of laws.[139] Democracy is a method for Kelsen; it is only a form of social order. It says nothing whatsoever about the content of the rules. Parliament is the exemplary (however not the only) place where the discussion about the content can take place, the place where a unity can be formed of the plurality of opinions and interests.

Kelsen also disagrees with Schmitt when it comes to the relationship between law and state. Contrary to Schmitt's dualism of law and state, the Austrian lawyer defends the position that law and state are one and the same.[140] Therefore, Kelsen

---

they participate in *creating* the state order. And it is precisely this function, crucial for the idea of democracy, which includes the "people" in the norm-creating process and at the same time reveals the unavoidable distance between this "people" and the "people" understood as the embodiment of those subject to norms.' [Italics in the original].

[137] H. Kelsen, *General Theory of Law and State*, p. 285: 'The ideal of self-determination requires that the social order shall be created by the unanimous decision of all its subjects, and that it shall remain in force only as long as it enjoys the approval of all.'

[138] Ibid., p. 286: 'The idea underlying the principle of majority is that the social order shall be in concordance with as many subjects as possible, and in discordance with as few as possible. Since political freedom means agreement between the individual will and the collective will expressed in the social order, it is the principle of simple majority which secures the highest degree of political freedom that is possible within society.' For an interesting elaboration of this Kelsenian approach to democracy with regard to the freedom of speech, see: Q.L. Hong, *The Legal Inclusion of Extremist Speech*, Nijmegen: Wolf Legal Publishers 2005.

[139] H. Kelsen, *General Theory of Law and State*, p. 287–288: 'The will of the community, in a democracy, is always created through a running discussion between majority and minority, through free consideration of arguments for and against a certain regulation of a subject matter. (…) Free discussion between majority and minority is essential to democracy because this is the way to create an atmosphere favourable to a compromise between majority and minority; and, compromise is a part of democracy's very nature. (…) It is precisely because of this tendency towards compromise that democracy is an approximation to the ideal of complete self-determination.'

[140] Ibid., p. 182: 'However this dualism [of law and State, LC] is theoretically indefensible. The State as a legal community is not something apart from its legal order, any more than the corpora-

holds that every state is a legal order. The order or unity of the state consists of a plurality of human actions. However, the only human actions relevant in this regard are those that can actually be imputed to the state. In order to distinguish state actions from other human action, Kelsen observes that state actions are essentially representative. That is to say, state actions are never imputed to the subject performing them but always to someone else.[141] For Kelsen, the state is this point of imputation, the point that makes it possible to understand all these actions as a unity.[142] 'Unity' here should not be taken to mean that all actions are performed from one central point, but performances by various agents are authoritatively judged from some final point by whether they make sense as a whole. It means that they aim at systematic coherence: The idea is that each norm hangs together with all other norms so that its application brings the whole legal order to bear on the case in question. Thus, what a norm prescribes amounts to this whole. In other words, a state action can only be qualified as such when it coheres with all enforceable (i.e., legal) norms.[143] Indeed, for Kelsen, the state is a normative legal order, to wit an order that regulates human behaviour by means of norms.[144] The will of the state is, then, nothing else than the content of the legal norms.[145]

Kelsen's monism offers a strong argument against the invocation of a state of exception to exceed the boundaries of given competences. Since Kelsen stresses

---

tion is distinct from its constitutive order.' See also p. 189: 'There is only a juristic concept of the State: the State as—centralised—legal order.'

[141] Ibid., pp. 186–187: 'What is the criterion by which those relations of domination that constitute the State are distinguished from those which do not? (...) The one who commands "in the name of the State." How then do we distinguish between commands "in the name of the State", and other commands? Hardly otherwise than by means of the legal order which constitutes the State. Commands "in the name of the State" are such as are issued in accordance with an order whose validity the sociologist must presuppose when he distinguishes between commands which are acts of State, and commands which do not have this character.'

[142] Ibid., p. 191: 'The judgment by which we refer a human action to the State, as to an invisible person, means an imputation of a human action to the State. The problem of the State is a problem of imputation. The State is, so to speak, a common point into which various human actions are projected, a common point of imputation for different human actions. The individuals whose actions are considered to be actions of the State, whose actions are imputed to the State, are designed "organs" of the State. Not every individual, however, is capable of performing an act of the State, and only some actions by those capable are acts of the State.'

[143] Kelsen stresses that the legal order is a special kind of social order, not merely because of its normative nature, but because its norms are being enforced by coercion: A legal order is a *Zwangsordnung*. Cf. H. Kelsen, 'Das Wesen des Staates', in: H. Klacatsky, R. Marcić and H. Schambeck (eds.), *Die Wiener Rechtstheoretische Schule*, Wien (etc.): Europa Verlag 1968, pp. 1713–1728, at p. 1723. See also: H. Kelsen, 'Law, State, and Justice in the Pure Theory of Law', in: *What is Justice? Justice, Law, and Politics in the Mirror of Science. Collected Essays by Hans Kelsen*, Berkeley (etc.): University of California Press 1971, pp. 288–302 at p. 289.

[144] H. Kelsen, *General Theory of Law and State*, p. 182: 'The term "community" designates only the fact that the mutual behaviour of certain individuals is regulated by a normative order.'

[145] As a consequence, Kelsen argues, sociology presupposes this legal notion when it wants to say something about behaviour in a certain society. Thus, for Kelsen there is no distinction between the legal order and society, either. Cf. H. Kelsen, *General Theory of Law and State*, p. 188–189.

that law and state are one and the same, an action against the law is *eo ipso* an action against the state. This has an important consequence for the relationship between state power and legal power: Only the exercise of competence, i.e., the use of power within the limits of the law, counts as an act of state authority.[146] Consequently, exceeding competences for the sake of the state is impossible.[147] The full extent of Kelsen's thoughts on competence becomes clear when we understand legal powers in connection with the positivity of law.[148] Competences are powers given and restrained by positive law, i.e., human law, and therefore essentially contingent on competences already attributed. Thus, competences, like other aspects of the legal order, are predicated on the majority vote of the moment as it comes through in legislation, even in constitutional legislation. To realise this order in its contingency, while giving the minority the institutional chance to become the majority, is what democracy is all about. In that respect, democracy and *Rechtsstaat* are conceptually connected: Both show that the existing order is not a necessity. The monism of law and state that Kelsen defends as an alternative against the dualistic account of Schmitt, ultimately means that every state is a *Rechtsstaat*, a constitutional legal order in the sense discussed above.

However, Schmitt also has a point against Kelsen. Even though Kelsen rejects Schmitt's dualism, and defends a monism of law and state, his theory hides its own dualism. Kelsen can only equate law and state by *implicitly* defending a dualism of law and politics. Schmitt's critique would be that, in this way, Kelsen does not take politics seriously. For Kelsen, politics falls completely outside the domain of law. This position is, however, not tenable since the positivity of law (something Kelsen explicitly defends) is linked to it being a political artefact. Even without defending a primacy of politics over law, one cannot deny that the connection between law and politics is much closer than Kelsen wants us to believe.

2.5 The Dualistic View and the Competence Creep

Now that I have analysed both the theory of constituent power and the tradition of constitutionalism, the conclusion is that, notwithstanding their importance as far as they go, both end up in a *petitio principii*. Authors like Sieyès and Schmitt presuppose the existence of the nation before the existence of the state. The tradition of constitutionalism, in its turn, presupposes that power is already limited before the

---

[146] Ibid., p. 190: 'Power in a social or political sense implies authority and a relation of superior to inferior.'

[147] Ibid., p. 192: 'An action is an act of the State insofar as it is an execution of the legal order.' See also H. Kelsen, 'Das Wesen des Staates', p. 1721: 'Nur der normativ qualifizierte Tatbestand ist Staatsakt, nur in ihm handelt der *Staat*. Und darum gibt es – im Bereiche des Sozialen – ein Phänomen, das im Bereiche der Natur gänzlich ausgeschlossen ist: die Nichtigkeit, den nichtigen Staatsakt.' [Italics in the original].

[148] H. Kelsen, 'Law, State, and Justice in the Pure Theory of Law', p. 296–297: '"Positive" law means that a law is created by acts of human beings which take place in time and space (…)'.

constitution. That is why Kelsen reduces all state power to legal power, thereby ditching the political dimension of law. Above, I have, most of all, stressed the differences between the traditions. However, these differences are possible only because they share a common presupposition: the dualism between constituent and constituted power. Böckenförde hints at this dualism when he speaks of the distinction between unordered and ordered people, and between *Sein* (the domain of 'is', or facts) and *Sollen* (the domain of 'ought', or norms).[149] One may speak of a dualism precisely because a distinction is made between two separate domains. These are politics and law, absolute power and limited power, presence and absence, formless forming and form, *Geist* and expression, original and representation. The two traditions of constitution-making both take this dualism for granted in their discussions. Furthermore, their differences can be understood as different conceptualisations of it. Whereas the theory of constituent power stresses the political moment, constitutionalism steers away from the political roots of law and puts all hope on constituted powers. In other words, the traditions *mirror* each other. The theory of constituent power reads the dualism from the viewpoint of a sovereign constituent power; constitutionalism turns this view around by taking its vantage point from constituted power. So, both traditions emphasise opposite poles of one and the same dualism.[150]

Let us now return to the problem of the competence creep in the European Union. In the previous chapter, we have seen how the European Court of Justice, a legal institution, formulated the doctrine of implied powers. It did this while claiming that it only recognised powers already given in the Treaty. In other words, according to the ECJ, its recognition of implied powers was an act of applying the law. At the same time, however, I have shown the *creative* nature of this act: After the recognition of the existence of implied competence, the European legislator had more powers than before. Now the question is whether the dualistic theories of constituent power and those of constitutionalism can make sense of this.

Both traditions of constitution-making regard legal power as essentially limited, power under law. This is a consequence of a strict separation of law and politics. From the viewpoint of the theory of constituent power, the creativity of the judge, as exercised in the recognition of implied powers, is inadmissible. What happens in the cases on implied powers is that the judge takes a political decision, the decision of where the limits of powers lie. This is the *Kompetenz-Kompetenz*, the power of sovereignty. This power belongs to the people as constituent power, not to one of the constituted powers. Even if the people would have to be represented, certainly it should not be by the most undemocratic power in the state, the judicial branch. When we start from the tradition of constitutionalism, we will also reject the doc-

---

[149] E.-W. Böckenförde, o.c., pp. 104–112.

[150] Cf. Möllers, o.c., p. 193: 'Order-founding and power-shaping constitutional traditions do not principally contradict one another; (...) western legal systems have long been familiar with the antagonism of two forms of law: one driven by politics and one that arose autonomously. This dualism, which gives courts the scope to create law, and legislatures the general power to correct the courts, is also necessary for the adequate functioning of the legal and political systems.'

trine of implied powers as developed by the ECJ. The punch line here is again that the powers given to state organs are *legal* powers and, therefore, essentially limited. In the case of the European Union, they are even enumerated in the Treaty. Any change in this system can only occur through the *political* process of Treaty revision. It cannot happen by an act of the Court of Justice. By appropriating the power to assign the Union more competences, the ECJ has overstepped the boundaries of its own powers.

The two traditions of constitution-making discussed in this chapter come to the same conclusion regarding the implied powers doctrine of the ECJ. Emphasising the limited nature of legal power and the separation of law and politics, both traditions would reject the actions of the ECJ. However, because of their own inconsistencies they fail to offer a viable alternative. This brings us back to where we started: How are we to make sense of the competence creep? I suggest digging deeper into the nature of legal competence. My assumption is that the doctrine of implied powers questions exactly the limited nature of legal power and, therefore, the dualism of law and politics underlying it. It asks us to rethink both, and that is exactly what we will do in the next chapters.

2.6   Conclusion

In this chapter, I first showed that the question of legal competence is a fundamental issue of constitutional theory. Then, I sketched the views of two opposing traditions of constitutional thinking. Both traditions, theories of constituent power and the tradition of constitutionalism, ultimately fall prey to circular reasoning. This also goes for the positions taken by Carl Schmitt and Hans Kelsen in their discussion on law, state and democracy. The cause of these problems is that they both take for granted the dualism between constituent power and constituted power. They differ as to which pole of the dichotomy receives primacy over the other. However, neither can make sense of the doctrine of implied powers. In the end, this means that the simple conception of competence as power under law is not tenable, and that a better understanding of competence can only be obtained by rethinking the relationship between constituent and constituted power beyond the dualistic view.

Chapter 3
Rethinking Constituent Power: A Chiastic Alternative

The discussion on the creeping competences of the European Union, in particular the doctrine of implied powers examined in the first chapter, led to an inquiry into constitution-making. In the previous chapter, I showed that the existing theories of constitution-making are basically dualistic. For this reason, they cannot shed light on the phenomenon of implied powers. To escape from this deadlock, I propose to rethink constitution-making by devising an alternative theory of the relationship between constituent and constituted power. In order to do this, the legal-political problem of constituent power will be traced to its philosophical foundations. As I will shortly argue, this involves the question of creation in the legal-political sphere. My argument will show that the detour by philosophy will eventually pay out, and help to obtain a better understanding of the competence creep. In this chapter, my aim is thus to give a first outline of an alternative theory of the constitution of legal order. I will develop a theory of 'constitution as expression', taking my cue from the work of Maurice Merleau-Ponty. As I will argue in Sect. 3.2, this implies conceiving of creative expression as metamorphosis. Subsequently, I will show how Merleau-Ponty develops this as a theory of what he calls 'institution'. Right here, I should add that 'institution' in Merleau-Ponty's work is the philosophically equivalent term for the double-edged legal term 'constitution', dovetailing in constituent and constitutional power. To avoid conceptual problems, and to link up with the vocabulary of legal and political philosophy, I will keep speaking of 'constitution'.[1] The particular concept of constitution developed here catches the relationship between constituent and constituted power as a chiastic one. This has important consequences for historicity, meaning in history and, finally, constitution-making. I

---

[1] It should be stressed, however, that for Merleau-Ponty there is an important difference between 'constitution' and 'institution'. For him 'constitution' is still connected with a philosophy of consciousness, i.e. with a theory of sense-giving that takes its cue from a subject. The notion of 'institution' is actually meant to radicalize his own early thought and to complement the concept of 'constitution'. What is crucially different in 'institution' when compared to 'constitution' is the temporal, historical and intersubjective dimension of sense. Later, he will connect this to the dimension of 'objective ideality'. For an overview of the importance of the notion of 'institution' for Merleau-Ponty's oeuvre, see R. Vallier, 'Institution. The Significance of Merleau-Ponty's 1954 Course at the Collège de France', *Chiasmi International*, no. 7 (2005), pp. 281–303.

L. Corrias, *The Passivity of Law,*
DOI 10.1007/978-94-007-1034-4_3, © Springer Science+Business Media B.V. 2011

will deal with these issues in the last sections of this chapter. Yet, first of all, the introductory section will look into the dualistic theories of constituent power, once more, and disclose their implicit ontology of creation.

3.1   Constituent Power: An Ontology of Creation

As we have seen above, the concept of legal power is directly linked with the relationship between constituent and constituted power. With these notions, constitutional thinking captures what it means to give the constitution, i.e., what it entails to found or establish the legal order. In the theories described in the previous chapter, the concept of constitution was connected to a model in which creation is understood in a dualistic way. In this section, let me rephrase these theories in order to show their underlying ontology. As we have seen, the dualistic theories on constitution-making can take either of two forms. In one version, the external world is seen as nothing more than a self-projection by a constituting subject. The object does not exist independently of a subject: Rather, it is only a protrusion of the constituting subject. According to this view, creation is a magical act that lets something be where there was nothing before: 'Being is wrested from nothingness; from the void emerges the universe. There is a supreme actor who acts, who actualizes, who creates; and a world which is actualized, which is created.'[2] This form of creation is called *creatio ex nihilo,* and it is central to theories of constituent power. What happens in the act of creation is the pure actualisation, or 'exteriorisation', of an idea by a supreme actor, present at the moment of the creation. We have seen that this actor takes different forms: the nation of Sieyès, the multitude of Negri, and Schmitt's sovereign. Notwithstanding the differences, the ground model underlying these theories remains one and the same: What is created is the product of a supreme creator. Consequently, reality (in this case the legal order) appears as guided by (*pro-ducere*) a pre-given force. The second version of a dualistic conception of creation turns this model around by replacing creation from a void with its complete opposite. Instead of making something out of nothing, what occurs in the act of creation is a mere copying of a pre-given reality. Speaking in terms of artistic creation: Theories upholding this view would perceive a painting of a tree as imitation or copy of the original tree with regard to some specific aspect of it. In other words, creation from a void regards the process of creation as pure subjectivity, pure activity, pure presence; creation as copying, on the other hand, would stand for pure objectivity, pure passivity and pure absence. This second version of a dualistic model of constitution-making is what we have encountered in the theories of constitutionalism. One way or another, constitutionalism holds the view that the legal

---

[2] D.C. Mullen, *Beyond Subjectivity and Representation: Perception, Expression, and Creation in Nietzsche, Heidegger and Merleau-Ponty,* Lanham (etc.): University Press of America 1999, p. 65. To illustrate this point, Mullen calls into mind the Biblical sense of creation: 'And God created the heavens and the earth.'

constitution merely copies a pre-given state of affairs. Above, we have described this as 'a constitution behind the constitution'.

As we have already seen in the previous chapter, both models amount to the same dualism between constituent and constitutional power. Now, we are able to give the deeper reason for this. On an ontological level, both presuppose a pre-existing reality of which the created object is merely a place-holder. It exhaustively represents either the mind of the maker in the world out there, or a particular in the world out there in the mind of the maker. Therefore, both theories can be caught under the name of representationalism. What binds them together is that both start from this cleft between mind and maker: A dualistic ontology and, consequently, a dualistic conception of the process of creation. Creation as representation presupposes a fissure, an unsurpassable gap between the creator and the created in which the process of creation disappears. This view cannot avoid the pitfalls of Western metaphysics, i.e., its tendency to think in strict dichotomies like 'subjectivity and objectivity, activity and passivity, presence and absence.'[3] The creator is the subjective pole, active and present in the act of creation. The created, on the other hand, is but the object of the process, purely passive and absent from the act of creation. For this reason, neither of the representationalist theories takes seriously the creation of something meaningful. What is created is nothing more than a representation of a creator that gave it meaning. It is either an actualisation of a meaningful idea in the mind of the creator, or the copy of a meaningful reality out there. Therefore what is created cannot be meaningful for anyone but its creator, nor can it be meaningful by itself. Furthermore, what it is, its identity, can only be derived from an original meaning given to it. It follows that the identity of what is created is fixed, once and for all, on its day of birth; it can only infinitely repeat this identity.

As regards this ontology, there is one last issue of importance. Since the act of constitution-making is not only found in the legal sphere, constitution in the legal-political sense of the word, as the establishment of the legal order, is closely linked to constitution in other fields of experience and action. The reason for this is that legal constitution is only one example of a more general phenomenon. This is the constitution of meaning by ordering, or indeed, simply the process of 'making sense'. This structure of ordering concerns the constitution of meaning, the creation of something meaningful. While meaning is not found ready-made in the world, nor completely invented, ordering always has something of the creation of a work of art.[4] So, legal constitution-making is a form of ordering; it makes a social order appear as a meaningful whole, and discards what falls outside of it as not-meaningful, so what emerges is '*a regulated* (i.e., nonarbitrary) *connection of one thing and*

---

[3] Ibid.

[4] Cf. B. Waldenfels, *Order in the Twilight*, trans. D. J. Parent, Athens, Ohio: Ohio University Press 1996, p. 107: 'If a cognitive and practical order lies ready-made neither in things nor prior to things, then it must be produced or invented. Insofar as productive imagination is at work in this, we can speak of an *artistic* moment calling for a *poetics* of cognition and action.' [Italics in the original]

another.'[5] Following Merleau-Ponty, I will argue that this should be understood as a process of expression. In this context, the notion of expression and constitution that I will develop hereafter should be understood on an ontological level. At this level, there is not yet a strict distinction between the different fields in which constitution occurs. In other words, without claiming to be exhaustive in any way, I will argue that at this level, language, painting, law, and even bodily gestures and perception are comparable. There is no question of analogy here. Rather, following Merleau-Ponty, I will argue that expression or constitution has a similar ontological ground structure in all these different domains.[6] What I will try to show in this and later chapters is how several aspects of this ontology have interesting consequences for the issue of constitution-making in general, and the problem of creeping competences in the EU legal order, in particular.

I take my cue from the ontology Merleau-Ponty has developed in the last years before his death. At first sight, the choice for Merleau-Ponty is not obvious. Indeed, in his rich oeuvre he has never explicitly dealt with legal problems. Nor did he develop an explicit political philosophy, in spite of his many interventions in the political debates of his time. However, his philosophical work can be seen as one of the most radical attempts in Western philosophy to overcome dualistic thinking. Merleau-Ponty's work will thus be used in order to overcome dualistic thinking as I have encountered it in the two main traditions of constitution-making discussed in the previous chapter. His ontological work is especially interesting since it was developed from a phenomenological approach that took its cue from perception and a radical questioning of what expression means.[7] It is not so strange to regard law as a form of expression. Recall the following key consideration in the German Federal Constitutional Court's judgment on the Treaty of Maastricht, where it expounds its view on the role legislation plays in a national state: 'The States need sufficiently important spheres of activity of their own in which the people of each can develop and articulate itself in a process of political will-formation which it legitimises and controls, in order thus *to give legal expression* to what binds the people together (to a greater or lesser degree of homogeneity) spiritually, socially and politically. From all that, it follows that functions and powers of substantial importance must remain for the German Bundestag.'[8] In these lines, the Constitutional Court gives

---

[5] Ibid., p. 1. [Italics in the original]

[6] Cf. M. Merleau-Ponty, *The Prose of the World*, trans. J. O'Neill, Evanston, Ill.: Northwestern University Press 1964, p. 85/M. Merleau-Ponty, *La prose du monde*, Paris: Gallimard 1969, p. 120: '[T]he phenomenon of expression, which gathers itself step by step and launches itself again through the mystery of rationality. We would undoubtedly recover the true sense of the concept of history if we acquired the habit of modelling it on the example of the arts and the languages. The close connection between each expression and every other within a single order instituted by the first act of expression effects the junction of the individual and the universal.' Hereafter, this book will be referred to as PW, with first the English pages, then the French ones.

[7] Cf. R. Barbaras, *De l'être du phénomène. Sur l'ontologie de Merleau-Ponty*, Grenoble: Éditions Jérôme Millon 2001, pp. 80–88.

[8] Extracts from Brunner et al. v. The European Union Treaty, *Common Market Law Review*, vol. 31 (1994), pp. 251–262 at p. 257. [My italics, LC]

its view on what legislation, in general, and the constitution, in particular, mean in a modern democracy. Law is recognised as a fundamental expression of 'what binds the people together'. Yet, as we have seen in the first chapter of our inquiry, the German Federal Constitutional Court starts from two presuppositions that we regard as untenable. First of all, it regards law and politics as separate domains. Secondly, it reduces legal expression to a form of representation of the pre-given political unity. It is my aim to give an alternative reading of what expression in a legal-political sphere might entail.

In a certain sense, this tradition of regarding the legal-political sphere as essential to an understanding of man is a very old one. As is well known, Aristotle calls man a '*zoion politikon*', designating him in this way as a being that can only exist with others in a polity.[9] In other words, one could argue that Aristotle already recognises that it is through the constitution of a polity that man gives full meaning to his existence. Or, to turn the argument around, that only in the *polis* does man express his being fully. Constitution-making is, in such a view, the way *par excellence* to give meaning to his life, indeed to express what it means to be man. In Aristotle, this is directly linked with man's faculty for language.[10] Language and politics appear thus as the primordial fields in which man gives meaning to his life. It is in this tradition that I would like to interpret Merleau-Ponty's thoughts on expression. On the primordial level of expression, speech and politics are ways in which meaning is given to the world. Merleau-Ponty's concept of expression has a structure that blurs the strict dualistic dichotomies in which the present theories of constitution-making remain trapped. In the following section, we will further examine this structure of expression by looking into examples from different fields. With Aristotle's lessons in mind, it will not come as a surprise that we will first look into the domain of language.

3.2   Expression: Creation as Metamorphosis

According to Merleau-Ponty, expression goes beyond a dualistic account of creation by introducing it as a form of transgressing established meaningfulness, i.e., as metamorphosis.[11] If there is creation in expression, it is because of a twist that engages an established pattern of meaning only to push it over the edge of its establishment. With the concept of metamorphosis, he intends to introduce an ontology

---

[9] Aristotle, *Politics*, trans. E. Barker, Oxford (etc.): Oxford University Press 1995, 1253, p. 10.

[10] Ibid., p. 11.

[11] Cf. PW, p. 68/p. 95: 'There is a triple resumption through which he continues while going beyond, conserves while destroying, interprets through deviation, and infuses a new meaning into what nevertheless called for and anticipated it. It is not simply a metamorphosis in the fairy tale sense of a miracle or magic, violence, or aggression. It is not an absolute creation in an absolute solitude. It is also a response to what the world, the past, and previous works demanded of him, namely, accomplishment and fraternity.' For creation as transgression in the work of Merleau-Ponty, see A. Delcò, *Merleau-Ponty et l'expérience de la création. Du paradigme au schème*, Presses Universitaires de France: Paris 2005, pp. 121–127.

different from the one described as dualistic. The latter was called dualistic because it involves a world where the subject and object of creation, creator and created, are strictly divided over two poles, and where creation is the magic trick to bridge the gap between the two. As a consequence, the identity of the created is fixed, once and for all, at the moment of creation. Metamorphosis, on the other hand, involves 'a liable world of flux and transformation.'[12] It does not settle for the moment of creation being clouded in mystery. What the notion of metamorphosis tries to catch is exactly what happens in the act *between* creator and created, to grasp creation itself, because 'there is metamorphosis only in between.'[13] Metamorphosis goes beyond the strict categories of dualistic thought by a movement similar to what in philosophy has been called deconstruction: 'Metamorphosis breaks down categories by breaching them.'[14]

Literature offers plenty of examples of this phenomenon. From these tales, we can learn things that are of interest for our inquiry, because they show three distinctive features of what Merleau-Ponty calls metamorphosis. First of all, metamorphosis is a change that cannot be understood in strictly biological terms. The change does not simply consist in going from one stage of a cycle to the next one, but it is rather a *rupture* of a cycle. Secondly, metamorphosis always involves the transgression of a border. This border cannot normally be transgressed because it delimitates identity. Note, and this is the third point, that the metamorphosis is paradoxical: The creation of something new, nevertheless, claims to be no creation at all. Exactly what is finally at stake in different stories of metamorphosis is identity: How can something new come into being that is yet the same? It is not so much a transformation of an entity into something else, but rather an unfolding of what is already there, always already implied. In other words, what we are dealing with is 'a self that really changes while really remaining the same thing.'[15] What does this mean for the concept of expression? Expression is creation as metamorphosis. It is a form of (re)ordering that has the structure of what Merleau-Ponty has called (borrowing the term from Malraux) a 'coherent deformation'.[16] It is a deformation, since a real change occurs. And yet, this change is coherent because the new form is presented as an unveiling of the self. This paradox can also be formulated as follows: We are dealing with a 'creation that is at the same time an adequation, the only way to obtain an adequation.'[17]

---

[12] C. Walker Bynum, *Metamorphosis and Identity*, New York: Zone Books 2001, p. 30.

[13] Ibid.

[14] Ibid., p. 31.

[15] Walker Bynum, o.c., p. 166.

[16] Cf. M. Merleau-Ponty, *Signs*, trans. R.C. McCleary, Evanston, Ill.: Northwestern University Press 1964, p. 54/M. Merleau-Ponty, *Signes*, Paris: Gallimard 2001 [1960], pp. 87–88: 'There is signification when we submit the data of the world to a "coherent deformation".' Hereafter, this book will be referred to as S, with first the English pages, then the French ones.

[17] M. Merleau-Ponty, *The Visible and the Invisible*, trans. A. Lingis, Evanston, Ill.: Northwestern University Press 1968, p. 197/M. Merleau-Ponty, *Le visible et l'invisible*, Paris: Gallimard 2003 [1964], p. 248. Hereafter, this book will be referred to as VI, with first the English pages, then the French ones.

Here the distinction between speaking speech and spoken speech enters the scene. Although Merleau-Ponty introduced these concepts in the field of language, we should not forget that they are part of his general theory of expression. In different guises, the notions of speaking speech and spoken speech will keep playing a pivotal role in his entire oeuvre.[18] As to the nature of this distinction, it is important to stress, first of all, that it concerns two ways in which the expressive force of language emerges. In reality, speaking speech and spoken speech always go hand-in-hand: They are internally related to one another.[19] Speaking speech and spoken speech are thus two poles of an analytical distinction, not opposite categories for empirical data. While it is possible to give examples of transgression and metamorphosis, it is impossible to give examples of pure acts of speaking speech or spoken speech.

Spoken speech is the established use of language in which the common meanings of words are used. Unsurprisingly, these common meanings are roughly equal to the ones we may find in the dictionary. These meanings are 'sedimented'. This concept derives from geology where it is used to describe the process of formation or accumulation of sediment in layers. Sedimentation has two key characteristics: duration and fertility. The first characteristic points to the past: Sedimentation forms a history, it allows for the past to be understood as a meaningful whole. In other words, duration means that sedimentation both takes time and gives time. Fertility refers to the future: Sedimentation opens the possibility for meaningfulness in the future. Note that this is done in one and the same occurrence: Forming a meaningful past and opening the possibility of a meaningful future are two sides of the same coin. The same movement that forms the past makes the future possible. To understand this, consider the silt of the Nile River. It was this silt, deposited by annual floods along the banks, which created the rich and fertile soil that enabled and sustained the rise of civilization in Ancient Egypt. In the same way, sedimented meanings form the soil that nourishes new speech acts. These sedimented meanings form the given material of the past that is at the disposal of the whole community of speakers, ready to be taken up in future speech acts. They are what appears as 'given' for a 'coherent deformation'.

Speaking speech, on the other hand, is the use of language that transgresses the ordinary, sedimented meanings, carrying them over into new vernaculars. One may find speaking speech in slang, in advertising, and of course in poetry. Its creativity notwithstanding, speaking speech is not a creation from a void. Rather, what happens in speaking speech is a rearrangement of the existing that makes old words say new things. To illustrate expression as transgression or metamorphosis, let us

---

[18] The concepts are particularly important in the posthumously published works PW and VI. In this respect, I completely disagree with the interpretation given by Schmidt. Not only does he interpret this distinction wrongly (it has nothing to do with Heidegger's distinction between *Rede* and *Gerede*), he also underestimates its importance in the whole oeuvre of Merleau-Ponty. See J. Schmidt, *Maurice Merleau-Ponty: between phenomenology and structuralism*, London: Macmillan 1985, p. 115.

[19] Cf. J. Slatman, *L'expression au-delà de la représentation. Sur l'*aisthêsis *et l'esthétique chez Merleau-Ponty*, s.n., Wageningen 2001, pp. 130–131.

look at the following example. E.E. Cummings starts one of his poems with the following lines:

> love is more thicker than forget
> more thinner than recall[20]

Here, the word 'more' is used in combination with the comparative degree ('thicker' and 'thinner'). Usually, 'more' combined with a positive degree is enough to form the comparative degree. For instance, 'more comprehensible' is the comparative degree of 'comprehensible'. The comparative degree of other words is formed by adding the suffix '-er' to the positive degree. Thus, 'thicker' and 'thinner' are the comparative degrees of 'thick' and 'thin', respectively. In this case, from a purely grammatical point of view, just 'thicker' and 'thinner' without the word 'more' would have been enough. From the perspective of the readers, going from a positive degree to a comparative degree, we are accustomed to take one step only. This is exactly why the combination of 'more' with a comparative degree is so surprising. We, the readers, thinking that we are done after one step, are forced to take yet another one. The combinations 'more thicker' and 'more thinner' are suggestive of a specific superlative degree formed by a double comparative, i.e., a superlative that will never reach the final point that is characteristic of superlatives. In a sense, the most-left comparative ('more') becomes the denial of what a comparative is: It transgresses the comparative. We are taken to a realm beyond conventional expression, and only here are we able to make sense of the nature of love. The combinations 'more thicker' and 'more thinner' contain its whole mystery: Grammatically tautological, they are used to stress the exceeding nature of love.

As I have mentioned above, the notion of 'speech' in this context is not bound up with language in the lexical sense. Since language is only one area of expression, let me take another example of metamorphosis from the field of architecture. In the beginning of the 1980s, the most famous museum of Paris, the Louvre, was in need of renovation.[21] The New York architect, Ieoh Ming Pei, had the task of transforming the royal palace into a building for the people without loosing its monumentality. Built on the remains of an earlier castle, the Louvre had been a palace for the French royal family since 1559, only to be exchanged for Versailles by Louis XIV, fleeing Paris. After its abandonment by the kings, the Louvre was home to several academies and artists. From 1793 onwards, the building has served as a museum. Without disrespecting its past, the Louvre now had to be prepared for the future. This was the assignment for which Pei was hired. The architect chose the ancient form of the pyramid for the entrance, making it the emblem of the new Louvre.[22] The pyramid

---

[20] 'love is more thicker than forget', first published in: E.E. Cummings, *50 Poems*, Duell, Sloan and Pearce 1940.

[21] J. Tietz, *Geschiedenis van de architectuur in de 20e eeuw*, vertaling J. B. Kanon en D. Antoons, Könneman: Keulen 1999, p. 91. For a more detailed account of the renovation of the Louvre, see: M. Laclotte (ed.), *Le nouveau visage du Louvre. Numéro spécial de la Revue du Louvre et des Musées de France*, Paris: Conseil des Musées Nationaux 1989.

[22] Cf. I.M. Pei, cited in: S. Cotté, *I.M. Pei, l'architecte des musées*, in: M. Laclotte (ed.), *Le nouveau visage du Louvre*, pp. 13–15, at p. 14: 'Le Louvre est né en tant que Palais et, à ce titre, les

is not only a geometrical symbol of majesty, but it also stands for closure and death. As the grave of the ancient Egyptian pharaohs, it was constructed as a last resting place. Using the pyramid, Pei, however, changed the closed and detached form of the Egyptians into an open one by the use of glass. From a building closed and inaccessible, it transforms into an entrance that, together with the richly illuminated subterranean halls, sends out a message of hospitality.[23] Once a place that wanted ordinary people to stay out, that rejected them, the pyramid now attracts us and tells us to come and enter and enjoy our time inside, to feel welcome to visit, again and again.[24] The Louvre, once the 'hiding-place' for the rulers, has become democratic. With its glass skin, the pyramid allows a glance at the genealogy of power. From a place for kings only, it has become a place for all kinds of people, a place, indeed, where we mortals may dwell.[25] The innovation reached in this way is paradigmatic for metamorphosis. Something new is not formed by a creation from a void. Rather, one of architecture's oldest forms is reanimated by a change of its material. Pei created something new by turning around the old; he brought about the metamorphosis of the pyramid, and with it, of the Louvre. This is creation as transgression.

My third and last example of metamorphosis is taken from the history of European integration. It is reflected in the declaration of 9 May 1950, of the French minister of foreign affairs, Robert Schumann, which is generally acknowledged as one of the founding documents of the process of European integration. This declaration proposed to bring under a common command, a High Authority, the coal and steel production of France and Germany. Also, here we witness that there is no question of a creation from a void: 'Europe will not be made all at once, or according to a single plan. It will be built through concrete achievements which first create a de facto solidarity.'[26] The uniting of Europe is, thus, not a *creatio ex nihilo*. Rather, this 'first step in the federation of Europe' is a speaking speech that builds on a unity *presupposed* in this act of uniting. This proposition is formed by the reference to the name, 'Europe'. Schumann is well aware that real and lasting peace on the old continent needs more than just efforts from Germany and France. Therefore, he is eager to stress that the 'organization [is] open to the participation of the other countries of Europe.' The unit*ing* of Europe appears as merely a metamorphosis of what is already (in a minimal sense) a unit*ed* Europe.[27] This is the spoken speech

---

hommes d'État et les architects, au cours des siècles, l'ont enrichi de significations symboliques. Mais maintenant il a changé d'affection. La rupture de la function autorise l'invention d'une nouvelle forme symbolique. La pyramide deviendra l'emblème de cette nouvelle fonction.'

[23] M. Laclotte, o.c., p. 5: 'l'impression d'ouverture, de générosité dans l'accueil.'

[24] Ibid.: 'Non, il faut que le public s'attarde, revienne, et qu'on lui donne le goût de revenir.'

[25] Ibid., p. 12: 'le Louvre ne sera pas seulement une attraction touristique, ni le plus prestigieux des conservatoires, mais un lieu de vie.'

[26] Robert Schumann, Declaration of 9 May 1950, available at http://europa.eu/abc/symbols/9-may/decl_en.htm [visited on 18 October 2009]. The phrases within quotation marks in this one and the following paragraph are taken from this website.

[27] Cf. H. Lindahl, 'European Integration: Popular Sovereignty and a Politics of Boundaries', *European Law Journal*, vol. 6 (2002), pp. 239–256. Lindahl does not refer to Schumann but points to a similar structure in the preamble of the EC Treaty.

that makes another Europe, that of Robert Schumann, possible. Integration is, thus, a process that thrives on a unity assumed to be always already there. A new step in the integration process takes up this established meaningful whole, Europe, to take it further, bringing it into a new dimension.

These examples show that the relationship between speaking speech and spoken speech is one of mutual dependency. Let us return to the example of the Louvre pyramid. I characterised this pyramid as a transgression of 'given' meaning. Pei's innovation, the glass pyramid, took its cue from the existing form of the pyramid and took it one step further by the use of glass for its surface. However, one should not forget that Pei's extensive use of glass was only possible because of the introduction of glass as an architectonic material. It might be hard to imagine, but before 1850, glass played only a marginal role in architecture. Crystal Palace, Joseph Paxton's masterpiece of 1851, totally built out of glass, iron and wood, was a true revolution.[28] Indeed, the Crystal Palace was the inauguration of a new architectural world, a world in which glass had to be taken seriously as a building material. The Louvre's glass pyramid was only possible because Pei could draw water from the well dug by Paxton, while Paxton himself could only be revolutionary because he drew on all those others who, step by step, introduced glass in architecture. But, Pei also drew on the established in a more artistic sense. His design 'responded to the desperate need to integrate the museum into the fabric of the city and transform the Louvre's main courtyard from a dismal parking lot to a grand public gathering place.'[29]

This shows that, as I said above, expression is not a *creatio ex nihilo,* but rather, an act that takes up the old and reorders it so that it says new things. The poem of Cummings, and the pyramid of Pei are cases in point, and also the Schumann declaration made this clear. There can be no expression without already established meanings; therefore, speaking speech is dependent on spoken speech. Furthermore, another reason exists why one ought to speak about a relationship of dependency. In order to survive and sediment, an act of expression needs to be taken up again and again. Thus, it is only by gradually sedimenting that speaking speech gains creative force. This means that, to some extent, such creativity can only be acknowledged in hindsight. To continue with the example: Glass as a building material only survived because of its success with different architects such as Taut, Gropius and Meyer, Johnson and Mies von der Rohe. Their efforts made buildings like Pei's pyramid, or Gehry's Dancing House in Prague possible. Initially, also Pei's pyramid was 'derided as a violation of the museum's classical integrity. But two decades later, it is one of the top tourist attractions in Paris, attracting some 8.5 million annual visitors.'[30]

Remember, however, that neither speaking speech nor spoken speech exist in pure form. As I have pointed out in the poem of Cummings, even poetry's creativeness is not a kind of pure creation, but rather, a transgression of ordinary language.

---

[28] Tietz, o.c., p. 7–9.

[29] K. Carbone, 'Viva Le Louvre! At 20, I.M. Pei's Controversial Pyramid Defies Critics', available at: http://www.fastcompany.com/blog/ken-carbone/yes-less/viva-le-louvre-20-im-peis-controversial-pyramid-defies-critics [visited on 29 October 2009].

[30] Ibid.

Every act of expression is always more or less speaking *and* spoken.[31] This means that the difference between speaking speech and spoken speech is relative rather than privative. Nevertheless, it would be a mistake to say that all speech acts are simply a mix of speaking speech and spoken speech. Rather, speaking speech is the speaking *of* the spoken; it is born in the margins of conventional speech, in its periphery.[32] Call to mind the fertility of the sedimentation process: What is sedimented opens up the possibility of meaning *in the future*. Sedimented meanings are ready to be taken up in new speech acts, ready to be used to say new things.[33] Spoken speech is not something absolute, untouchable like an eternal truth. Far from being problematic, this is exactly what makes true creativity possible, and even necessary. The whole of sedimented meanings is not something that has always existed. Meaning must have been instituted once, to become established. Now, this act of establishing meaning is truly creative; it is an act of speaking speech. In other words, spoken speech can never be absolutely spoken, precisely because it can never exhaust its own origin in speaking speech. As every order of meanings was once established by an act of speaking speech, it is impossible for spoken speech to deny its own contingency and, therefore, it will have to recapture its status as *spoken,* again and again. Indeed, spoken speech, in order to remain spoken, is dependent on new speech acts. Else, it will become a dead letter. At the same time, spoken speech retains a nucleus of creativity because of the structure of expression itself: Making something new possible by reshuffling established meaningfulness, by a 'coherent deformation'. On the one hand, there is no such thing as pure repetition, nor can there be something absolutely and completely new.[34] On the other hand, it is impossible that something is said once and for all. This is exactly why spoken speech is also dependent on speaking speech.

Speaking speech and spoken speech being mutually dependent, we cannot say which one comes first. Therefore—and this is particularly relevant in the context of constitution-making—Merleau-Ponty characterises the relationship between speaking speech and spoken speech as one of *Fundierung*: 'The founding term, or originator (…) is primary in the sense that the originated is presented as a determinate or explicit form of the originator, which prevents the latter from reabsorbing

---

[31] PW, p. 38 footnote/p. 54 footnote: 'Each act of speech repeats all the others, that is why there are no absolute limits between languages. Sedimentation and reactivation.'

[32] A. Delcò, o.c., p. 121. Merleau-Ponty also calls it 'an oblique action', M. Merleau-Ponty, *Un inédit de Maurice Merleau-Ponty*, in: *Parcours deux 1951–1961*, Verdier: Lagrasse 2000, pp. 36–48, at p. 44.

[33] PW, pp. 28–29/p. 41: 'For speech, understood in this way, the idea of a *finished expression* is chimerical: such an idea is what we call successful communication. But successful communication occurs only if the listener, instead of following the verbal chain link by link, on his own account, resumes the other's linguistic gesticulation and carries it further.' [Italics in the original]

[34] Cf. B. Waldenfels, 'Das Paradox des Ausdrucks', in: *Deutsch-französische Gedankengänge*, Frankfurt am Main: Suhrkamp 1995, pp. 105–123 at p. 110: 'Das Ausdrucksgeschehen kann sich den beiden Extremen einer puren Innovation oder einer puren Repetititon mehr oder weniger annähern, aber erreichen kann es diese nicht. (…) Die rein creative Rede hätte *nichts* zu sagen, die rein repetitive Rede hätte nichts zu *sagen*.' [Italics in the original]

the former, and yet the originator is not primary in the empiricist sense, and the originated is not simply derived from it, since it is through the originated that the originator is made manifest.'[35] What does this mean for creative expression? Speaking speech might be called primary, since it is such an act that has made an order of speech possible in the first place. Spoken speech is a determinate form of speaking speech, to wit, that part that is established. Hence speaking speech can be called the originator, and spoken speech would then be the originated. Yet, speaking speech does not exist in a pure form, but only as the speaking *of* the spoken, and one cannot understand spoken speech as a simple deduction from an act of speaking speech. The originator is thus derived from what it originates. This is what the concept of 'coherent deformation' amounts to.

We encounter a paradox here. Merleau-Ponty tells us that this is the paradox of expression itself.[36] A new act of creative expression is dependent on other acts that will take it up so that it can sediment and become part of the whole of meanings. A speech act introducing new meanings should, therefore, always take up already established meanings if it wants to be understood. It should present itself as '*coherent* deformation'. In other words: A new speech act can only be speaking, in the sense of creative expression, if it poses itself as spoken.[37] The success of a creative act depends on how convincingly it does this. A new meaning needs to be accepted in order to last and become established. And, in order to be accepted, one should appeal to the language that is spoken until then. Whether or not a new act of creative expression will take root and sediment can, however, only be determined in retrospect, to wit, only for so far it has been taken up by other speech acts. This is the *Nachträglichkeit* of creative expression.[38] In other words, a new speech act will always refer to an 'existing' corpus of established meaningfulness, and pose itself as only a continuation of what was already there. Yet, because of the retroactive force, the reference to this whole always comes too early. It is only an anticipation of a new possible meaning that could be given to this whole and it is reading something in the established whole that has never been there. The reference is, therefore, to 'a past which has never been a present.'[39] On the other hand, what counts as meaningful is also dependent on new acts of creative expression that take it up in order that it can sediment and remain 'spoken'. In order to register as speech and remain meaningful, a new act of creative expression should thus pose itself as 'speaking'

---

[35] M. Merleau-Ponty, *Phenomenology of Perception*, trans. C. Smith, London and New York: Routledge 2003, p. 458/M. Merleau-Ponty, *Phénoménologie de la perception*, Paris: Gallimard 1945, p. 451. Hereafter, this book will be referred to as PP, with first the English pages, then the French ones.

[36] PP, p. 452/pp. 445–446 and PW, p. 35/p. 51.

[37] PW, p. 144/p. 201: 'In basing signification upon speech, we wish to say it is essential to signification never to appear except as the sequel to a discourse already under way. (…) [I]t is the achievement of each word not only to be the expression of *this here* but also to surrender itself entirely as a fragment of universal discourse, to announce a system of interpretation.' [Italics in the original]

[38] Cf. B. Waldenfels, 'Das Paradox des Ausdrucks', pp. 116–117.

[39] PP, p. 282/p. 280: 'a kind of original past, a past which has never been a present.'

to a minimal degree, continuing given meaning. It should present itself as a 'coherent *deformation*'. Here, then, is the paradox of creative expression: There is only deformation through coherence, while there is only coherence through deformation.

From now on, borrowing another concept of Merleau-Ponty, I will call the intertwined relationship between speaking speech and spoken speech, *chiastic*. The chiasm is a trope used by Merleau-Ponty in his latest works to describe the ontological interrelatedness between ourselves and the world, as it perspires, in particular, in the body.[40] In the next chapter, I will pay more attention to this. I would like to use the concept of chiasm because it implies an interval between its two poles without falling back into the kind of dualism that reduces one pole to the other in the final analysis: Subject to object, or object to subject, mind to body or body to mind, the creator to the created or the created to the creator. This is precisely what distinguishes the relationship between speaking speech and spoken speech from a dualism: Speaking speech and spoken speech cannot be reduced to one another, in other words they can never fully coincide.[41] There is no question of reduction in this relationship, as both are irreducible parts of one and the same coin of expression. Furthermore, it is this very interval that allows for expression to be possible, time and again. If a dualism can be imagined as two circles that can ultimately be joined together, forming one circle, the interval in the chiasm prevents a final coincidence. Speaking speech and spoken speech are bound to each other, but will never be one and the same, like the two foci of an ellipse. Let us now see how the philosophy of expression leads to a reflection on historicity.

3.3   Expression and Historicity

The philosophy of expression described in the previous section can be summarised as follows. First of all, speaking speech and spoken speech are mutually dependent. Secondly, neither speaking speech nor spoken speech exists in a pure form. Hence, the distinction is relative, rather than privative. Thirdly, speaking speech and spoken speech are in a paradoxical relation to one another, and it is in this relationship that the process of metamorphosis ('coherent deformation') of meaning occurs. In other words, meaning arises between acts of expression, through sedimentation. Fourthly, speaking speech and spoken speech cannot coincide. Their relationship is chiastic. In this section, we will take another step in our inquiry into creative expression by regarding it as a process of meaning emerging *in time*. In this way, the theme of expression of meaning is linked to that of historicity. What does it mean to say that meaning unfolds in time? Taking his cue from expression in the art of painting, Merleau-Ponty makes a distinction between two answers to this question. The first form of historicity that I will discuss is that of the Museum.

---

[40] Cf. VI, Chap. 4. The Intertwining—The Chiasm.
[41] Cf. B. Waldenfels, *Verfremdung der Moderne. Phänomenologische Grenzgänge*, Göttingen: Wallstein Verlag 2001, p. 18.

It is hardly surprising to say that the Museum provides us with a view of the history of painting. Or even that we base 'our consciousness of painting as painting' on the Museum.[42] But how are paintings (or other works of art) presented to us in a Museum? Usually, the paintings in a Museum are offered to us in an orderly way. This suggests a degree of unity between certain painters. It intimates that these painters and their works are comparable. Ordering the history of painting, the Museum offers us a systematic overview of the unity of painting. So far so good, one might say. Museums perform an important function as places where works of art from all over the world are collected and presented in an orderly way. Yet, Merleau-Ponty is critical of exactly this aspect of the Museum. The question he asks is, from which perspective do paintings appear as unified in a Museum? The Museum can only find this unity *retrospectively*, by showing us 'dead productions' in its 'mournful light'.[43] The works of art in a Museum are presented out of their context of birth, i.e., far away from the artists' labour.[44] Merleau-Ponty calls the historicity of the Museum, therefore, a historicity of death. The Museum is a *necropolis*.[45]

There is, however, another way of approaching the historicity of painting, and it carries another way of connecting the unity of painting in its wake. This is the historicity of life that takes its cue from the labour of painting itself, the task that all painters feel called to perform. It is this historicity of life that precedes and enables the historicity of the Museum.[46] What are the characteristics of this historicity of life? In the previous section, we have characterised expression as metamorphosis. Now, this notion of metamorphosis also contains a dimension of a response. This does not only refer to the singular way in which a painter answers to the world (to what gives itself as 'to be painted') but also to the past, and thus to other works, and works of other's. Merleau-Ponty argues that every single work of art founds, or constitutes, a fertile field in which other works can obtain meaning. Paintings are comparable to each other on this deeper level because they are bound by the single task of painting, and obtain meaning in a lateral way; meaning comes about in the reference of paintings to each other. It is this moment of constitution, in all its singularity, that forms the key for a new understanding of the past, and that takes it up in order to keep it available for the future. Speaking of the painter, Merleau-Ponty puts it like this: 'It is thus that the world as soon as he has seen it, his first attempts at painting, and the whole past of painting all deliver up a *tradition* to the painter – *that is*, Husserl remarks, *the power to forget origins* and to give to the past, not a survival, which is the hypocritical form of forgetfulness, but a new life, which is the noble form of

---

[42] S, p. 62/p. 100.

[43] Ibid.

[44] Ibid., p. 63/p. 101: 'The Museum kills the vehemence of painting.'

[45] This characterisation of the Museum makes an interesting comparison between Merleau-Ponty's and Foucault's archaeological approaches possible, see: L. Lawlor, *Thinking through French Philosphy: The Being of the Question*, Bloomington: Indiana University Press 2003, Chap. 2.

[46] S, p. 62/p. 100: 'But painting exists first of all in each painter who works, and it is there in a pure state, whereas the Museum compromises it with the somber pleasures of retrospection.'

memory.'[47] While the Museum stores works of arts so that they may survive, it does so for a price: It forgets the living work of painting. But the painter is someone 'who each morning finds in the shape of things the same questioning and the same call he never stops responding to.'[48] His work, his devotion to the task of painting, is not guided by some kind of spirit of painting, nor is it a complete jump into the obscure. In the dialogue between the world and the painter, the latter's work is oriented: 'It is always only a question of advancing the line of the already opened furrow.'[49] In this labour of the painter, ploughing further in the fertile furrows of the past, we may find the historicity of life: 'the historicity which lives in the painter at work when with a single gesture he links the tradition that he recaptures and the tradition that he founds.'[50] Meaning is caught here in its movement, not as a spirit in the air, nor as a simple copy of a pre-given reality. What we have found is the importance of the singular expressive gesture: 'The meaning of the expressive gesture upon which we have based the unity of painting is, in principle, a meaning in genesis.'[51]

This characterisation of expression as meaning-in-genesis has an important consequence. Because expressive acts are not simply factual actions but have a meaning, each one of them 'inaugurates an order and founds an institution or a tradition.'[52] The proper realm of expression is not so much the realm of events (the purely factual) but, rather, of advents. Merleau-Ponty takes the distinction between events and advents from Ricoeur, and proposes 'to consider the order of culture or meaning an original order of *advent*, which should not be derived from that of mere events, if they exist, or treated as simply the effect of extraordinary conjunctions.'[53] Merleau-Ponty stresses that he does not want to introduce a spirit of painting, after all. Rather, what he points at is the intrinsic meaningfulness of expressive gestures, starting from the most simple movements of our body.[54] In other words, he points to 'a unity of human style' that holds all painters and all their works together.[55] It is exactly this that makes paintings comparable.[56] While Merleau-Ponty uses the French word 'style', it is important to stress that he does not refer to style in the

---

[47] S, p. 59/p. 95. [Italics in the original]

[48] Ibid., p. 58/p. 94.

[49] Ibid.

[50] Ibid., p. 63/p. 101.

[51] Ibid., p. 69/p. 112.

[52] Ibid., p. 67/p. 108.

[53] Ibid., p. 68/p. 109. Cf. P. Ricoeur, 'Husserl et le sens de l'histoire', *Revue de métaphysique et de morale*, 1949 (3–4), pp. 280–316. Speaking of Husserl, Paul Ricoeur tells us at p. 289: 'Il n'y a pas de réflexion directe sur l'histoire comme flux d'*événements*, mais indirecte comme *avènement* d'un sens.' It is in this way that we are speaking of historicity.

[54] More on painting and the body, in particular in relationship to perception, see Chap. 4 below.

[55] S, p. 69/p. 111.

[56] Ibid., p. 68/pp. 109–110: 'If it is characteristic of the human gesture to signify beyond its simple existence in fact, to inaugurate a meaning, it follows that every gesture is *comparable* to every other.' [Italics in the original]

sense of an institutional name, as in impressionism or cubism. What he does mean is better grasped as 'skill', or even 'knack', as in the phrase 'to get the knack of something' which refers to the *bodily* understanding (and fun!) of a certain movement or action, the skill that binds me bodily to the world in the singular way I engage with it in expression, while, at the same time, making it possible to share the world with others. So, in the field of painting, we are dealing with the singular way of expression of an artist. According to Merleau-Ponty, skill is the bodily, and thus pre-reflective, being in the world of a subject. The skill of painting is found in the painter *at work*. It is to be found in the *living* artist. Yet, interestingly, a painter is unaware of his own skill of painting. While painting is making something visible, it rests on an invisible core. With this notion of skill, Merleau-Ponty points to an understanding of expression in which the factual and the ideal are completely intertwined in the singular act of the painter. To understand expressive gestures as intrinsically meaningful makes it possible to draw a line from the very first expressions to the ones of today. In other words, it enables us to think of painting as a unity. This unity has no real beginning, since it is rooted in the expressive gestures of the body. Nor does it have an end, since every expressive act is 'both a beginning and a continuation which, insofar as it is not walled up in its singularity and finished once and for all like an event, points to a continuation or recommencements.'[57] Merleau-Ponty refers us to an important feature of the emergence of meaning. Existing works form a tradition: The order of expression should be understood as an order of advent, of originating meaning, and as such it possesses a fecundity that asks for ever more expressions. That is why Merleau-Ponty can say that '[a]dvent is a promise of events.'[58] As we shall see in the next section, this has important consequences for the field of history and politics.

3.4   Constitution and Being in the World

As I wrote above, the distinction between speaking speech and spoken speech is part of a general philosophy of expression. Later Merleau-Ponty inscribed this dynamic relationship into a ground structure that I call constitution. Let us now take a look at what type of anthropology and ontology may sustain such a view of constitution-making. While we have discussed the structure of expression, and the theme of historicity in the previous two sections, I will start here by connecting the two, and give a definition of constitution: 'Those events in experience which endow it with durable dimensions, in relation to which a series of other experiences will acquire meaning, will form an intelligible series or a history – or again, those events which sediment in me a meaning, not just as survivals or residues, but as the invitation to a

---

[57] Ibid., p. 68/p. 110.

[58] Ibid., p. 70/p. 112.

sequel, the necessity of a future.'[59] The movement of constitution is a chiastic inter-relatedness of past, present and future, and in this knot, meaning is formed. It takes up sedimentations in both their aspects of duration and fertility, and brings them to bear on the present, thus unfolding their potentialities. This view of constitution roots in an anthropology that holds that the ability to take up existing meaning is given with man's embodied-being-in-the-world. Meaning, in other words, is found and formed in this engagement, i.e., in the bodily encounter of man and world. And it is exactly this engagement that is the chiasm: Man's implication in the world. In this respect, it is important to stress that the notion of the chiasm presupposes an interval: There is no question of fusion here. Rather, the chiasm in its ontological form is the structure in which 'every relation with being is *simultaneously* a taking and a being taken, the hold is held, it is *inscribed* and inscribed in the same being it takes hold of.'[60] This shows the chiasm at the heart of constitution: One can only be constituting by embodying the situation as already constituted, and the other way around. Man's ability to take up existing meaning towards an uncertain future while, at the same time, engaging new meaning as if nothing more could be estab-lished, is possible because of his chiastic relation to the world. Accordingly, man always dwells between absolute meaning and complete nonsense.

In this context, Merleau-Ponty's discussion of Max Weber's famous thesis on the relationship between Protestantism and capitalism forms an interesting case to show what this amounts to.[61] As is well known, Max Weber wanted to understand the rational and modern character of Western society. In his research, he was struck by the temporal coincidence of the rise of capitalism and a severe, Calvinistic Protes-tantism from the Sixteenth until the Eighteenth Centuries. He found that what binds these two movements together is a specific ethos of labour. According to Merleau-Ponty, to come to this conclusion, Weber breaks with a representationalist under-standing of history.[62] He understands the relationship between these two move-ments as neither causal, nor simply reciprocal. Furthermore, there is no question of the development of an idea in history.[63] Rather, religion and economy grasp each other and, in their intertwinement, give meaning to history. Between them exists what Merleau-Ponty calls 'a kinship of choice'. In this way, meaning in history is formed in the encounter with contingency, through historical sedimentation. Protes-tantism and capitalism are inserted in one and the same matrix that is the history of Western rationalisation. In other words, in the symbolic system of history, meaning

---

[59] M. Merleau-Ponty, *L'institution. La passivité. Notes de cours au Collège de France (1954–1955)*, Paris: Belin 2003, p. 124. [My translation, LC] Hereafter, this book will be referred to as IP.

[60] VI, p. 266/p. 313. [Italics in the original]

[61] Cf. M. Merleau-Ponty, *Adventures of the Dialectic*, trans. J. Bien, London: Heinemann 1974/M. Merleau-Ponty, *Les aventures de la dialectique*, Paris: Gallimard 2000 [1955], Chap. I. Hereafter, this book will be referred to as AD, with first the English pages, then the French ones. Cf. G. La-belle, 'L'oeuvre de Weber et ses prolongements selon Merleau-Ponty: de l'historicité à la recher-che de l'absolu dans le relatif', in: Christian Nadeau (dir.), *La philosophie de l'histoire. Mélanges oferts à Maurice Lagueux*, Québec: PUL 2007, pp. 395–434.

[62] AD, p. 20/p. 11.

[63] Ibid., p. 27/p. 16.

is formed in the reference of historical acts to each other. Meaning is the absolute in the relative; it is meaning formed in intelligible knots, in symbolic matrices.[64]

These matrices form a world 'in between' subjects and object, which is the place of historical action, and thus of politics. Meaning is formed in the interval *between* the signifiers (and their differences) on the one hand and embodied practice on the other. This is why human action is symbolic. To understand history and politics as symbolic domains means to take seriously their dimension exceeding the merely factual, the dimension that is formed by actions that refer to each other, and where meaning emerges in this fertile encounter. History, in other words, is a system of symbols.[65] A symbol refers to the opening of multiple perspectives, thereby showing the virtual possibilities *of* an actual state of affairs.[66] It points to man's ability to give another meaning to what is given to him, to his ability to go beyond the simple vital meaning of things. He owes this to his bodily being in the world as is already shown in perception.[67] This emphasis on perception is crucial to Merleau-Ponty's understanding of the symbol, for it points to the ties between the sensible and the ideal: While meaning may differ, it always comes in a concrete form that is its sensible vehicle. This is a necessity: Meaning is not available without being given in a sensible form, and as human beings, we can only perceive meaning because of its sensible form. Furthermore, these meanings are inextricably linked with our bodily insertion in a concrete situation. Our body not only allows us to take a different perspective on things, unlocking their symbolic potential. More importantly, our body is what can be called 'the first' symbolic form. Our hands, for example, can wash our face, they can join in prayer, help us to swim and knead the dough for the bread. There is thus no gap between the factual, on the one hand, and the symbolic, on the other hand. There is only a symbolisation *of* the factual. The symbolic appears not

---

[64] Merleau-Ponty bases this understanding of the emergence of meaning on a (rather odd) reading of some aspects of the theory of the Swiss linguist Ferdinand De Saussure. Cf. M. Merleau-Ponty, *In Praise of Philosophy and Other Essays*, trans. by J. O'Neill, Evanston, Ill.: Northwestern University Press 1988, p. 55/M. Merleau-Ponty, *Éloge de la philosophie et autres essays*, Paris: Gallimard 2002 [1953], p. 56: 'The theory of signs, as developed in linguistics, perhaps implies a perception of historical meaning (...) Saussure, the modern linguist, could have sketched a new philosophy of history.'

[65] AD, p. 65/pp. 93–94: 'Torn by all the contingencies, repaired by involuntary actions of men who are caught in it and want to live, the web deserves the name of neither spirit nor matter but, more exactly, that of history. This order of "things" which teaches "relationships between persons," sensitive to all the heavy conditions which bind it to the order of nature, open to all that personal life can invent, is, in modern language, the sphere of symbolism, and Marx's thought was to find its outlet here.'

[66] M. Merleau-Ponty, *The Structure of Behavior*, trans. A.L. Fisher, Boston: Beacon Press 1963, pp. 120–124/M. Merleau-Ponty, *La structure du comportement*, Presses Universitaires de France: Paris 1942, pp. 130–133.

[67] Cf. M. Rainville, *L'expérience et l'expression: essai sur la pensée de Maurice Merleau-Ponty*, Montréal: Éditions Bellarmin 1988, p. 26: 'Il y a, en effet, dans la perception humaine vue comme conduite symbolique, un élément qui fait qu'elle ne se réduit pas à l'ouverture perspective ni a une succession d'événements sans connexion les uns avec les autres. Cet élément, c'est le pouvoir qu'a l'être humain de prendre un donné comme signe.' For more on perception, see Chap. 4 of this inquiry.

as something completely different from, but rather as the other side of, what is given factually. The factual has a 'symbolic pregnancy'.[68]

This openness to multiple perspectives which our body provides us with is characteristic for our relationship with the world as embodied beings. In other words, this openness is given in our chiastic relation to the world. It shows that the world has *depth*: We experience the world as always already loaded with meaning, always already given in an origin that cannot be retrieved.[69] Yet, we cannot cut loose from our seeing this depth, nor from our ability to penetrate it, up to some point. The depth of the world entails that 'there is meaning'.[70] Constitution takes this brute fact seriously, and builds further meaning by starting from this irreducible moment of factuality or positivity.[71] However, it would be mistaken to think that constitution is a matter of simply going further along the lines the world shows. Man's implication in the world, the ties that root him are never neutral.[72] For '*seeing* depth' already implies a moment of ordering, a moment of creation, indeed, that makes constitution always more than 'reading the signs as they are laid out in front of us'. As Merleau-Ponty warns us, 'perception already stylizes'.[73] And style (i.e., skill or knack) as we have seen, is that moment of singularity that is a stain on everything we do, a stain that remains invisible to us but is exactly what makes us able to 'see' in the first place.

And what we see is 'the world'. With all his emphasis on perception, one might almost forget that Merleau-Ponty regards perception as only the privileged *locus* of access to 'the world'. While the concept of perception and its exact relation to constitution will be the topic of the next chapter, it might be worthwhile to unveil at least the basic idea of what perception teaches us of our relationship with the world, all the more so since it has important consequences for the sphere of history and politics. Perceiving 'the world' reveals exactly that 'the world' is not an object at my disposal, nor a construction of my thinking, my relationship with it is much more intimate, much more chiastic, indeed.[74] Merleau-Ponty's interpretation of some thoughts of Marx is of importance in this respect. What Marx has pointed to, argues Merleau-Ponty, is that our relationship with the world cannot be reduced to that of a subject towards an object. In other words, on the most fundamental level, our relationship with the world is not that of a knowing subject. First and foremost,

---

[68] PP, p. 340/337.

[69] B. Waldenfels, *Order in the Twilight*, p. 101: 'An order that on the whole cannot be ascribed to any orderer stems from a *primary production* that has always already happened and escapes from any reach.' [Italics in the original]

[70] PP, pp. xiv–xv and 454/pp. xxii and 454. [Translation slightly altered, LC]

[71] Cf. B. Waldenfels, *Order in the Twilight*, pp. 66–67.

[72] For more on these ties or attachments, see: R. Visker, *Truth and Singularity: Taking Foucault into Phenomenology*, Dordrecht (etc.): Kluwer Academic 1999 and R. Visker, *The Inhuman Condition: Looking for Difference After Levinas and Heidegger*, Dordrecht (etc.): Kluwer Academic 2004.

[73] PW, pp. 59–60/pp. 83–84.

[74] R. Visker, *Truth and Singularity*, p. 104.

we are in the world as bodily beings, our relationship with it is practical but in a *potential* mode. In short, *pace* Descartes, as a human being I am not, first of all, a *Je pense*, but rather a *Je peux*, i.e., in the double sense of 'having an ability' and 'being enabled'.[75] In this alternative reading, Marxism should, therefore, be understood as an anti-dualistic philosophy, an attempt to describe the ambiguous relationships between man and world and between man and history. In order to take these relationships seriously, the total existence of man should be taken into account. One could, therefore, call Marxism a philosophy of expression in the sense described above.

3.5   Chiastic Constitution in Politics and Law

Let us quickly recapitulate what we have discovered about constitution in the previous section. Constitution in its chiastic form should be located in the interval between me and the world my body provides me with. There is no fusion, nor a relationship of subject towards object. The world is where I always already dwell, and what always already confronts me with possibilities of meaningful action without ever giving the reassurance that I will succeed. In other words, meaning can be constituted by following what is already meaningful, by taking it up on a bodily level, by forming meaning in man's implication in the world. And, it is this implication that has been called chiastic. In this section, I will give three examples in the legal-political sphere of what I have called the chiastic account of constitution.[76]

Remember that I argued that the dualism underlying the different theories of constitution-making concerned a clear-cut distinction between two separate domains. These are politics and law, absolute power and limited power, presence and absence, formless forming and form, original and representation. The theory of constituent power reads the dualism from the viewpoint of a sovereign constituent power; constitutionalism turns this view around by taking its vantage point from constituted power. Now, we have argued that the concept of constitution should be understood by thinking the relationship between constituent power and constituted power as a chiasm. What does this entail in the sphere of constitution-making? I will discuss the examples of universal suffrage, and the relationship between rule of law and rule of man. Yet, first of all, I will look at some features of Arendt's discussion of revolution, the paradigm of constituent power in Modernity.

Hannah Arendt's treatment of revolutions is an extensive one, both historically and in terms of philosophical ideas. Giving a full account of all the interesting features she distinguishes would take us too far away from our topic. Instead, I would like to concentrate on one specific aspect of her exposition, one that appears in the last chapter of her book. There, she writes the following: 'To the extent that the

---

[75] PP, pp. 366–367/p. 363. Cf. H. Arendt, *On Revolution*, London: Penguin 1973 [1963], p. 150.
[76] For an account of constitution very close to the one developed here, see also: H. Lindahl, 'The paradox of constituent power. The ambiguous self-constitution of the European Union', *Ratio Juris: An International Journal of Jurisprudence and Philosophy of Law*, vol. 20 (2007), pp. 485–505.

greatest event in every revolution is the act of foundation, the spirit of revolution contains two elements which to us seem irreconcilable and even contradictory. The act of founding the new body politic, of devising the new form of government, involves the great concern with the stability and durability of the new structure; the experience, on the other hand, which those who are engaged in this grave business are bound to have, is the exhilarating awareness of the human capacity of beginning, the high spirits which have always attended the birth of something new on earth. (…) To be sure, these opposites have their origin, and ultimately their justification, in the revolutionary experience as a whole, but the point of the matter is that in the act of foundation they were not mutually exclusive opposites, but two sides of the same event, and it was only after the revolutions had come to their end, in success or defeat, that they parted company, solidified into ideologies, and began to oppose each other.'[77] Arendt thus recognises two aspects in a revolution that part ways after the revolution. These two aspects are the concern for stability and durability, on the one hand, and beginning something new, on the other. While Arendt goes on to assign these moments to the major ideological movements in Western *politics,* and then goes on to search for a new type of politics that holds the two moments together, I would like to point to something else. Her remarks teach us something about the very relationship *between* politics and law as it emerges in revolutions.

The question is, I think, how to understand the durability and something new as 'two sides of the *same* event', as Arendt rightly calls them. The concept of constitution that I have developed above, captures exactly these two moments as part of one movement. Remember that constitution was characterised as the inauguration of *new* meaning that is *durable.*[78] Its structure was analysed as one of creative expression, a 'coherent deformation'. This means the following: Every new claim to power, however revolutionary, should present itself as being coherent with what has already been established as authoritative. This entails that a new claim to power should present itself as *legal* power, power under the law, even if this law is not necessarily the very same positive law that gives power to the *status quo*—this may be the very reason why references to 'higher law' or 'divine authority' are so common in revolutions. And only if it does this successfully, if it is coherent, will its deformative power work and found a new beginning. Yet, this new beginning is again dependent on other acts that take it up in the hopes of making it (always retrospectively) the beginning of a new order. A claim to power should always present itself as part of already established and, thus, legal power in order to be successful and found a new polity. A *re*-volution always involves a moment that connects it with a (forgotten) past. And so, what emerges from Arendt's argument is a chiastic relationship between law and power.

---

[77] H. Arendt, o.c., pp. 222–223.

[78] IP, p. 124: 'those events in experience which endow it with durable dimensions, in relation to which a whole series of other experiences will acquire meaning, will form an intelligible series or a history – or again those events which sediment in me a meaning, not just as survivals or residues, but as the invitation to a sequel, the necessity of a future.' [My translation, LC]

At some points in her book, Arendt seems to point to this chiasm. She reads it first and foremost in the "Roman" tradition of thinking of law and politics. Machiavelli, whom she calls 'the spiritual father of revolution',[79] seemed already aware of it. In this regard, Arendt points to a twofold perplexity that haunted Machiavelli and all revolutionaries that came to follow him: 'The perplexity consisted in the task of foundation, the setting of a new beginning, which, as such, seemed to demand violence and violation, the repetition, as it were, of the old legendary crime (Romulus slew Remus, Cain slew Abel) at the beginning of all history. This task of foundation, moreover, was coupled with the task of lawgiving, of devising and imposing upon men a new authority which, however, had to be designed in such a way that it would fit and step into the shoes of the old absolute that derived from a God-given authority, thus superseding an earthly order whose ultimate sanction had been the commands of an omnipotent God, and whose final source of legitimacy had been the notion of an incarnation of God on earth. Hence, Machiavelli, the sworn enemy of religious considerations in public affairs, was driven to ask for divine assistance and even inspiration in legislators – just like the 'enlightened' men of the eighteenth century, John Adams and Robespierre, for example. This 'recourse to God', to be sure, was necessary only in the case of "extraordinary laws", namely of laws by which a new community is founded.'[80] As I have argued above, this is the necessary structure of a new claim to power: It must inscribe itself in the register of what is already established as authoritative. Or, in the terms Arendt uses to describe the Roman tradition: Every constitution must be cloaked as a re-constitution.[81]

For my second example of chiastic constitution in the legal-political sphere, I draw on the work of Claude Lefort, political philosopher, and former student of Merleau-Ponty. While he is not speaking of constitution-making in the strict sense of the term, he gives a very interesting analysis of what is at stake in elections, surely a constitutive moment in any polity. Lefort points to the paradoxical relationship at the heart of universal suffrage in modern democracy. In Modernity, at least since Rousseau, democracy has been understood as popular sovereignty, as the whole people ruling the whole people. However, bigger and more complex societies have made it impossible for the people to really rule themselves. Instead, representatives have taken their places, and in elections, the people itself emerges on the political scene in order to choose its representatives. Universal suffrage is, then, the most eminent way in which this popular sovereignty is manifested. While in everyday politics the people is represented, this is surely not the case at those moments when representatives are chosen, so it is argued. In other words, in elections, one would

---

[79] H. Arendt, o.c., p. 37.

[80] Ibid., pp. 38–39.

[81] Ibid., pp. 207–208: 'Inherent in the Roman concept of foundation we find, strangely enough, the notion that not only all decisive political changes in the course of Roman history were reconstitutions, namely, reforms of the old institutions and the retrievance of the original act of foundation, but also that even this first act had been already a re-establishment, as it were, a regeneration and restoration.'

expect the people to appear in all its unity, in all its sovereignty. In elections, the people, normally *absent,* becomes *present.*

But is this really the case? Claude Lefort argues that something else happens in elections, something that is telling for the very nature of modern democracy: 'It is at the very moment when popular sovereignty is assumed to manifest itself, when the people is assumed to actualize itself by expressing its will, that social interdependence breaks down and that the citizen is abstracted from all the networks in which his social life develops and becomes a mere statistic. Number replaces substance.'[82] In elections, individual citizens thus take the place of the one sovereign people. It is this 'indeterminacy',[83] argues Lefort, that characterises modern democracy, this *'dissolution of the markers of certainty'*.[84] See here the chiasm: In a modern democracy, the way in which the people can be sovereign as a people (i.e., a unity) is through elections whereby individual citizens (i.e., a disunity) cast their votes. On the other hand, individual citizens in all their (discordant) social relationships can only appear because of the political scene that acts as a stage on which these conflicts can take place.[85] As is well known, Lefort argues that opening the political sphere is an act that consists of pointing to a place transcending society, a reference that makes it possible to speak of *a* society (in the singular, as a unity) in the first place.[86] This is 'a gesture towards something *outside,* and that it [i.e., the society, LC] defines itself in terms of that outside.'[87] In a democracy, this symbolic place of power is empty, argues Lefort. The people as sovereign (constituent power) can only appear by way of those powers that represent them (constitutional powers). The analysis of Lefort shows how, in modern democracy, unity and disunity, presence and absence are chiastically interrelated.

The third example I would like to discuss concerns the establishment of new rights, and the relationship between rule of law and rule of man. I will draw here on the analysis of the American political philosopher Bonnie Honig.[88] She takes her cue from the case of Louis Freeland Post, an Assistant Secretary of Labor during what was later called the First Red Scare. This Red Scare was a series of (attempted) terroristic bombings during the year 1919, by anarchist and communist groups. As a response hereto, people like Attorney General Palmer, and a very young J. Edgar Hoover, started with mass deportations of people who could be linked to anarchist or communist movements. These deportations were made possible under the so-

---

[82] C. Lefort, *Democracy and Political Theory*, trans. D. Macey, Cambridge: Polity Press 1988 [1986], pp. 18–19.

[83] Ibid., pp. 16 and 19.

[84] Ibid., p. 19. [Italics in the original]

[85] Ibid., p. 18.

[86] Ibid., pp. 226–227.

[87] Ibid., p. 225. [Italics in the original] Cf. D. Loose, *Democratie zonder blauwdruk. De politieke filosofie van Claude Lefort*, Best: Damon 1997, especially Chaps. III–V.

[88] B. Honig, *Emergency Politics: Paradox, Law, Democracy*, Princeton and Oxford: Princeton University Press 2009, Chap. 3.

called Sedition Act.[89] Post tries to stop these deportations, and the way in which he does this is very instructive. He first claims the right to make decisions on individual deportation cases.[90] Then, Post continues to restrict the category of deportability in a threefold way. In the words of Honig: 'First, he got Labor Secretary Wilson to rule that membership in the Communist Labor Party was not a deportable offense. (…) Second, Post decided, again contra Hoover, Palmer, and Caminetti, that what he coined "automatic membership" was not grounds for deportation. (…) Third, and most radically, Post applied to administrative cases standards of evidence and due process that normally would have been thought at the time to obtain only in judicial settings, not administrative ones. (…) Finally, Post used all his powers of reasoning and all of the law's resources to find in favor of aliens marked for deportation whenever possible.'[91]

In Honig's view, what Post, an administrator, does can neither be called completely legal nor can it be dismissed as a simple act of discretion. Indeed, discretion is exactly what Palmer and Hoover accuse him of. Yet, Honig argues that it is not so simple: There is no clear-cut distinction between acting according to the rule, on the one hand, and exercising discretion, on the other hand. Her point emerges, if we read what she has to say about Post's defence of his actions in front of the House Committee on Rules: 'Palmer and Hoover cast Post as an arbitrary, untrustworthy administrator whose aim was to undo the law. They claimed, by contrast, to be law's servants, operating in adherence to the requirements of the Sedition Act and the will of the legislators who passed it. Post responded by casting himself as law's strictest adherent and casting his opponents as arbitrarians and securitarians whose own decisionism was poorly cloaked by pseudo-legality. The success of his strategy depended largely upon whether Post's use of technicality would persuade or enrage the public and the members of the House Committee on Rules.'[92] This is how I read these comments of Honig: The case of Post shows the chiastic structure of transgression. Post, while going beyond the meaning of the Sedition Act, claims to do nothing else than act according to this law. In this way, he transgresses the law in a chiastic way: While acting as a constituent power (giving a *new* meaning to the Sedition Act by reading in it rights it did not contain)[93] he claims to do nothing else than act as a constitutional power (reiterating the *established* meaning of the Sedition Act). Technicalities *of* the law are thus used to go *beyond* the law, or even to undo it. This is Post acting as a legal mastermind: 'He understood the power and powerlessness of law. He knew that law cannot be pressed into new directions

---

[89] Ibid., p. 70: 'From late 1919 to early 1920, a series of raids known as the Palmer raids swept up five to ten thousand (estimates differ) aliens and lined them up for deportation under the Sedition Act of 1918.'

[90] Ibid., p. 71.

[91] Ibid., pp. 71–72.

[92] Ibid., p. 76.

[93] Ibid., p. 79: 'As aliens subject to administrative power, the detainees lacked the rights Post attributed to them. Post used his administrative powers to grant them rights they did not have juridically.'

unless claims, even – or especially – illicit ones, are made in its name and using its terms.'[94] And, he will only be successful if he can convincingly stage his use of technicalities as 'always already part of the law'. This is a claim that necessarily comes too early: Whether or not the technicalities are considered to be part of the established meaning of the Sedition Act can only be determined in retrospect, to wit, when Post has to appear in front of the House Committee on Rules, and 'the harm' has already been done.[95] Note, moreover, that the decision whether or not Post's acts are, indeed, within the meaning of the Sedition Act depends on the public and the Committee on Rules. In the vocabulary introduced above: Whether or not the act of creative expression of Post is successful depends on sedimentation, i.e., on whether others follow him in his reading of the Sedition Act. In this sense, and *from the perspective of Post,* there is only an anticipation of a *possible* reading of the Sedition Act.[96] Whether or not this reading is feasible is only decided afterwards.

Making the law turn in a new direction by making a claim in its name, us-ing its very terms—this was the structure through which Post could do his inge-nious work. In the words of Honig, we might say that Post engaged in a 'politics of technicality'.[97] And in this felicitous turn of phrase, Honig catches exactly the broader issue lurking in the back of the Post episode: The paradoxical relationship between rule of law and rule of man. What is most of all interesting about the posi-tion taken by Honig is that she rejects the 'Exceptionalism of the State of Exception' as defended by Schmitt and Agamben, on the one hand, and an a-political concep-tion of rule of law, on the other. Honig rejects the simple dichotomy between the decision of the sovereign and the agency of the law. Against Schmitt and Agamben, she puts forward that decisionism is a much more mundane phenomenon than they claim it is. As the story of Post has made clear, in an American context it is as-sociated with the discretion of the administrative branch.[98] Against a procedural con-ception of law, she holds that juridical procedures do not guarantee the just use of the law and that, therefore, a decision needs to be taken time and again. Her com-ments on the phrase 'he got off on a technicality' are illuminating in this respect and worth quoting in full: 'The phrase's force relies on the assumption that the law's

---

[94] Ibid.

[95] Ibid.: 'And then Post (before the Committee, in his practice at the Labor Department, in rela-tion to the Justice Department) acted as if these rights, which had no juridical existence apart from his own contestable administrative rulings, bound him. That is, Post acted as if he had not granted those rights, as if they existed ex ante, as if they bound him, and as if he merely deferred to the force of those rights or channeled them, acknowledging their power to limit the range of his discretion – the very discretion whereby he granted or acknowledged the rights in the first place.'

[96] I thus use the term 'anticipation' in a different context from the one criticised by Honig. Cf. ibid., p. 82 etc.

[97] Ibid., p. 76. See also p. 24: 'Technicalities tend to be discovered or invented post hoc, they are not normally broadcast in advance, as the rule of law requires. Often they apply only to an individual case, and not to a general class of cases and so they violate the rule of law's generality requirement. In short, technicality, a necessary postulate of the rule of law (an outgrowth of inter-pretation and implementation), also threatens to corrupt or undo the rule of law.'

[98] Ibid., p. 67.

proceduralism is perfect, that the rule of law, if only unhampered by crooked de-vices such as technicality, will imprison only the guilty and free only the innocent. When we say "he got off on a technicality," we imply he is guilty but has been found not to be so under law not because the law errs, but rather because the law erred in this instance only because it was exceptionally corrupted by a lawyerly device.'[99] Yet, procedures can be used for both just and unjust means. Moreover, as the dis-cussion of the actions of Post has made clear, this use of the law entails a moment in the rule of law that cannot be caught in strictly legal terms. Political, moral and other practical reasons play a role. Yet, as we have seen above, these can only make the law turn in a certain direction when they are convincingly made as claims in the name of the law. What Honig's discussion of the actions of Post shows is not only that 'the binary distinction between rule of law and rule of man is overdrawn and misleading', as she says herself.[100] But also, it shows the chiastic interrelatedness of rule of law and rule of man.

These three examples all considered, in one way or another, the relationship be-tween law and politics. In the previous chapter, we have seen that existing theories of constitution-making (implicitly) start from a dualism of law and politics. I reject-ed that view, and am now able to state my alternative. As the specific legal-political version of the relationship between speaking speech and spoken speech, the relation between constituent and constitutional power should also be conceptualised as a chiasm. This entails that law and politics are chiastically related. In constitutional thinking, there can be no clear-cut distinction between law, on the one hand, and politics on the other, since in constitutional practice the domains are always inter-mingled. Accordingly, legal powers always operate in between politics and law. Note that this is only the beginning of a viable alternative for the theories described in Chap. 2. In the next chapter, I will continue exploring the relationship between constituent and constitutional power, now focusing on rule-following. How will a chiastic approach understand this phenomenon?

3.6   Conclusion

In this chapter, I have laid the conceptual foundations for a new and non-dualistic theory of constituent power. For this purpose, I have related the legal notion of con-stitution as the creation of a legal order with the more general philosophical issue of the constitution or creation of meaning. Then, taking my cue from Merleau-Ponty's concepts of speaking speech and spoken speech, I have developed a philosophy of expression that understands creation (of meaning) as metamorphosis: Something new is formed in acts that take up the old to transgress it, and then sediment. The structure is thus one of 'coherent deformation'. I went on to show what view on historicity this entailed. Expression has its own historicity of life that takes its cue

---

[99] Ibid., p. 78.
[100] Ibid., p. 84.

from the act of expression, itself. In the next section, I showed the anthropological and ontological views underlying this concept of expression. It leads to a concept of man as an embodied actor (*Je peux*) and a notion of constitution that captures expression in the legal-political sphere as a chiastic action. In the last section, drawing on the work of Arendt, Lefort and Honig, I have shown that a chiastic understanding of the relationship between constituent and constituted power can shine light on phenomena like revolution, universal suffrage and the relationship of rule of law and rule of man.

Chapter 4
Embodying the Rule: The Passivity of Constitution

In this chapter, I will further develop my theory of the relationship between constituent and constituted power in order to shed new light on the discussion on competences in the European Union, especially on the way in which the Court of Justice deals with them. I will show why the concept of constitution developed in the previous chapter is important for the legal sphere, by taking up the problem of rule-following. Rule-following will be the lens that allows me to focus on the dynamics of constitution, and thus, on the notion of competence as the specific legal form of this phenomenon. In the first section, I will critically follow Vincent Descombes, in his journey to understand the subject in modern and contemporary philosophy. He takes up the famous question of Wittgenstein, of what it means to follow a rule. I will argue that Descombes' notion of the grammatical subject fails to make sense of Wittgenstein's theory of rule-following. That is why, in the second section, I will develop my own reading of this theory, drawing on Merleau-Ponty's work once more.[1] The leading hypothesis will be that rule-following is, first and foremost, a *bodily* activity. Then, in Sect. 4.3, I will elaborate this point by looking into the domain of art to show the central significance of the body for any form of constitution. Special attention will be paid to how constitution always brings with it what Merleau-Ponty calls 'passivity'. Continuing on this theme, in the fourth section, I will further elaborate the concept of *praxis,* taking this dimension of passivity into account. Surprisingly perhaps, the paradigm of *theoria,* namely perception or 'seeing', will serve as a model to demonstrate what is at issue in *praxis.* The body, as perceiving-perceived, will provide us with a non-dualistic account of how sense comes about. In other words, a theory of perception is already a theory of how sense-giving occurs on a bodily level. In the final section, I will come back to Descombes to discuss his interpretation of Wittgenstein's emphasis on 'customs' in rule-following. Instead of a conventionalist reading of this concept, I will argue that with the notion of 'customs', Wittgenstein is pointing to the importance of our embodied being in the world for rule-following.

---

[1] Yet, I would like to stress that it is not my purpose to make a full-fledged comparison between the thought of Merleau-Ponty, and Wittgenstein.

4.1   Auto-Institution and Rule-Following

In a thought-provoking book, the French philosopher, Vincent Descombes, engages in an inquiry into the notion of the subject in modern and contemporary philosophy. The first results of his inquiry were that the only tenable interpretations of the subject in practical philosophy were the logical *subjectum,* and the grammatical subject, the agent of the action. Now, the question central to the last part of his journey is whether a third notion, the subject as a self, should be added to this couple, as so many philosophers in Modernity demand. Descombes turns to the field of law in order to find an answer to this question. He does this in two stages. First, he investigates whether the grammatical subject is similar to the legal person, insofar as the latter may be seen as a final, but purely formal, point of attribution. In other words, his question is whether the autonomous subject, and the bearer of individual rights and duties, are one and the same. After analysing the different positions taken in the French debate on individual rights, he concludes that this is not the case. The reason is that no solid notion of the legal subject exists.[2] As a consequence, the legal subject cannot function as the philosophical 'self'.

Proceeding to the second stage of his inquiry in the field of law, Descombes states that 'a last argument remains to be investigated. It concerns the domain of positive law, taken as an example of a normative system instituted by man. The power to institute would be, according to that argument, a subjective power, in the sense that this adjective has in this exposition. This means the power that a subject confers to himself in an auto-institution of himself as author of the institutions on which he models himself in order to act.'[3] In other words, what still needs to be investigated is autonomy, in the sense of acting by rules man himself has instituted. The legal order is thus not seen as an order given by nature or by gods. Instead, what interests Descombes is exactly the legal order as an order of *positive* law, i.e., *nomos* in the sense of convention.[4] What we encounter here is auto-nomy, which is self-reflexivity under its normative guise.[5] In other words, Descombes wants to know what it means to act in a normative context. That is why he can take his cue from the later works of Ludwig Wittgenstein. There, Wittgenstein is interested exactly in that topic. In his own words: 'How can one follow a rule? That is the question I want to pose.'[6]

To answer this question, Wittgenstein asks us to imagine what it takes to direct ourselves in perhaps the most elementary sense of the word: How can someone steer himself in a straight line? Descombes immediately sees what is at stake in this

---

[2] V. Descombes, *Le complément de sujet. Enquête sur le fait d'agir de soi-même*, Paris: Gallimard 2004, p. 430: 'Toutefois, il s'agit moins de supprimer une notion solide de «sujet de droit» que de signaler que cette notion solide n'existe pas.'

[3] Ibid., p. 433. [My translation throughout, LC]

[4] Ibid.

[5] Ibid., p. 434.

[6] L. Wittgenstein, *Remarks on the Foundations of Mathematics*, Oxford: Blackwell 1978, VI § 38. Hereafter, this work will be referred to as RFM.

question. This seemingly innocent example of Wittgenstein is crucial for practical philosophy since it can be linked to the core problem of sovereignty. Descombes argues that the question entails the return 'to the very foundations of the notion of sovereignty, that originally meant the power of the *rex* to *regere fines* (literally, to trace the right line of the frontier between the interior of the kingdom or temple and its outside).'[7] Indeed, we are at the very 'root of sovereignty because what is at stake is the *instituent power* itself.'[8] Needless to say that what Descombes calls here *pouvoir instituant* is what, since Sieyès, goes by the name of *pouvoir constituant,* and what I have analysed in the previous chapter with the notion of constitution. In the work of Wittgenstein, one may thus find (the nucleus of) a theory of constituent power.

Now then, how do rules guide our behaviour? Wittgenstein answers that a rule guides us like signs on a road do. We read them, for instance, as saying 'this way'. However, it is important not to regard this as the intellectual process often called interpretation. It suffices that one acts in accordance with the sign. As Descombes remarks about 'following a rule': 'To describe this small episode, we just need to mention the rule or the directive plus the reaction. It is not necessary to insert between the two a work of interpretation or appropriation by which the subject had conferred a meaning upon the indication that he had obtained from outside.'[9] The rule thus offers me a model to follow *in this way.* It asks for a 'technical' capacity, a practical understanding in a more immediate sense than is usually assumed. This practical understanding is more fundamental than any intellectual comprehension.

Now, this practical understanding makes me follow the rule as I am used to do. However, Descombes asks, does this not lead to the statement that we never follow rules for the first time? This would be problematic, since it seems to be completely contrary to our experience. Is it not possible that I invent a totally new rule and then follow it for the first time? Wittgenstein has foreseen this objection, and remarks: 'Certainly I can give myself a rule and then follow it. But is it not a rule only for this reason, that it is analogous to what is called "rule" in human dealings.'[10] So, what makes a rule, a rule? According to Descombes, for Wittgenstein, this is the 'commerce' between people. Now, Descombes' interpretation of 'commerce' is important for his argument. He understands 'commerce' as 'a background of practice, of established uses and institutions (in the large sense of the words "pre-established models of behaviour").'[11] That is to say, in the end Descombes understands this as conventions.[12]

Wittgenstein's remark has an important consequence. I can only say that I invented a 'rule' to follow, if I am able to impose this 'rule' upon others. This is exactly where things go wrong, and why the example of me inventing a 'rule' does not hold: 'I can give a rule to others but I cannot, properly speaking, give them a *usage,* an *institution,* a *custom.* To determine the content of a rule is one thing, to

---

[7] Descombes, o.c., p. 443.

[8] Ibid., p. 444.

[9] Ibid., p. 445.

[10] RFM, VI § 41.

[11] Descombes, o.c., p. 452.

[12] Cf. ibid., p. 450. Especially the beginning of the page is telling.

make it into an established practice is another. If we would call "to establish a rule" the operation of laying down what would henceforth be the use, it seems impossible for an individual, however powerful he may be, to establish use by himself. In this sense, the instituent power does not have an individual nature.'[13] Ultimately, *others* determine the use of the rule because the establishment of an accepted custom is dependent on others who are going to follow the rule 'in this way'. In other words, before one may speak of a 'rule', one has to take into account that more people must be able to follow it. Inventing a rule for myself, I have to act as if it were invented already, and I were one of those following it.

Yet, another problem arises: What will I do with someone who does not understand the concept of a rule? Normally, when I give a rule to others, I can just tell them what to do in order to comply with it. However, this presupposes that one knows the meaning of the word 'rule'. So, for someone who does not understand the concept of a rule at all, this does not work: It is impossible simply to *tell* him what acting according to a rule means. Again, Descombes claims to join Wittgenstein in the answer to this question. Ultimately, the problem is 'to educate (*former*) him to follow a rule *that he does not yet understand. To oblige to the rule without yet knowing what the fact to be in line with (en règle) consists of.*'[14] Now, what is so interesting in the work of Wittgenstein is that he shows that the paradox encountered here is inherent in language itself. On the one hand, one cannot teach someone her first language through language, yet, on the other hand, one cannot teach her to speak a language without speaking to her.[15] What this boils down to, argues Descombes, is that Wittgenstein approaches the circle of autonomy by the circle of learning, as paradigmatic for the concept of rule itself. In other words, to understand autonomy, one should first of all understand the learning process. Therefore, what becomes essential is the role of the instructor.

What Descombes ultimately wants to show is that there is a purely practical way to understand the meaning of normative concepts. In order to make this point, he discusses some propositions of Elizabeth Anscombe, a philosopher of language and former student of Wittgenstein's. Anscombe makes a distinction between two kinds of reasons why someone must do something. There are, first of all, natural reasons. These are independent of language. They are teleological, and appeal to practical rationality. Descombes gives the following statement as an example: 'You cannot pass by that road because it is flooded.' The second group of reasons Anscombe discerns are called non-physical. These statements have a deontic meaning. As an example, could serve: 'You cannot pass by that road because only X has the right to do so.' This distinction is important for the purpose of understanding rule-following or, more generally, participating in an institutional practice. In the case of natural reasons, an agent will not get to where he wants to be by 'the facts on the ground', so to speak. A teacher can point to these and warn the pupil, but if the agent ignores them, she will be put to the test, sooner or later. But what would 'pointing' amount

---

[13] Ibid., p. 454. [Italics in the original]

[14] Ibid. [Italics in the original]

[15] Ibid., p. 455.

to in the case of institutional reasons? The example is that of a chess game: How to teach someone to play chess? Descombes distinguishes two phases in this process. In the first phase, the teacher should *bodily* stop the pupil when she wants to make a move that is not allowed, and tell her the reason for stopping her (e.g., it was not her turn). In the second phase, it is enough to *say* that a certain move is not allowed, and to give the reason for this. According to Descombes, from the moment when we do not have to tell the student anymore what the rules prescribe, we may say that she knows the rules of the game, that she is autonomous.

It is important to observe, stresses Descombes, that the learning process consists of giving examples, and not definitions. Since the student moves from a prohibition that she accepts without understanding why (phase one) to a prohibition that she accepts while acknowledging that she should have known it (phase two), there is a circle involved. This is the moral circle: '(…) The exercise aims at developing capacities of agency in the pupil, dispositions to act, aptitudes, habits, so, *morals* (*moeurs*).'[16] Descombes points to conventions once again, and again he does so without formulating a theory that may explain where they might come from. This time, however, he acknowledges that this cannot be the final answer to the problem: '(…) One cannot let the whole of norms repose on a fundamental norm (which would, by force, be empty because it would in fact say: There is a rule that wants that there are rules).'[17] One should, therefore, found human conventions on a practical necessity, i.e., the natural reasons of Anscombe.

Notwithstanding its value as far as it goes, one can wonder whether Descombes' solution is ultimately convincing. His example of the game of chess rests on a specific interpretation of Wittgenstein's work. In this interpretation, the 'technical capacity' required to follow rules is finally embedded in what Wittgenstein called 'human dealings'. As we have seen, Descombes understands this as 'commerce', in the sense of conventions. Now, it is exactly this interpretation that I find unconvincing. My main problem is that, if rule-following is at issue, conventions are part of what is to be explained, rather than part of the explanation. Unless conventions are regarded as purely uniform patterns of behaviour in a certain population, i.e., if one wishes to address conventions as regulating behaviour, they are just instances of rule-following. Of course, Descombes makes clear that he speaks of human conventions, in the sense of agreements. Yet, what are the conditions under which people would be willing to come to agreements, to comply with them, to stop some who don't, and to not stop still others who don't? Who may be part of these agreements? Who is to decide on this? These questions show that conventions are not the ultimate answer. Contrary to what Descombes argues, it is my claim that Wittgenstein's theory of rule-following does not, first and foremost, point to the need and importance of conventions. The pivotal point seems to me as what to make of that element in the theory of Wittgenstein that Descombes called 'technical capacity'. In the next section, I will develop an alternative interpretation of Wittgenstein's theory by rethinking what this 'technical capacity' might entail.

---

[16] Ibid., p. 463. [Italics in the original]

[17] Ibid., p. 464.

4.2 "How to Take the Next Step": Rereading Wittgenstein

Descombes' interpretation of Wittgenstein's ultimate explanation of how to follow a rule—the teacher example—is unconvincing. Yet, the relevance of this case seems central to any theory of rule-following: 'Once you have described the procedure of this teaching and learning, you have said everything that can be said about acting correctly according to a rule.'[18] In order to understand what Wittgenstein tries to show us, we must, therefore, return to this example. The first thing we should bear in mind is that many rules we know have a field of application that is (at least virtually) infinite. A rule is made for all kinds of applications in the unknown future. For example, the rule 'You cannot eat bread on Sundays' does not apply only to the coming Sunday, and white bread. The rule applies to all the next Sundays, and all kinds of bread. Now, in contradistinction to the infinite range of application of rules, '[t]he number of illustrations and examples a teacher can offer a pupil must always be *finite*. (…) The point cannot be emphasized too strongly. In learning such rules, there is always going to be the problem of taking the next step, of moving from previously known cases to new ones.'[19] The number of examples is always finite, simply because no one can foresee all the different situations to which a rule may apply. Secondly, and by implication, the teacher's understanding of the rule is limited: 'If you use a rule to give a description, you yourself do not know more than you say. I.e., you yourself do not foresee the application that you will make of the rule in a particular case. If you say "and so on", you yourself do not know more than "and so on".'[20]

How, then, does Wittgenstein resolve this problem? How are we to understand rule-following? As we have already seen in the previous section, for Wittgenstein, interpretation does not play a decisive role in rule-following. Let us go back to the example of road signs. Signs are immediately meaningful by virtue of our 'engaging' with them. This immediacy is critical towards any approach to rules which claims that one should first 'interpret' (by an intellectual act) the rule, before one is able to follow it. Such a theory of interpretation regards rules as containers with a number of pre-existing meanings from which we may retrieve the most appropriate one to meet the case at hand, i.e., the situation 'outside' the rule. The problem with this is that one is always able to argue that a new case does or does not fall under the rule, simply because the rule is silent about new cases. It would be entirely our semantic decision to say whether we were following the rule or not, and thus we would lose the idea of receiving guidance from the rule. This difficulty cannot be bypassed through an appeal to intuition, so Wittgenstein tells us. It would still entail a dualistic scheme, as if the application of a rule is just a copy, a re-presentation, of a pre-given meaning to a reality 'outside'. But the meaning retrieved from the rule

---

[18] RFM, VII § 26.

[19] D. Bloor, *Wittgenstein, Rules and Institutions*, London and New York: Routledge 1997, p. 11. [Italics in the original] Bloor calls this characteristic of the theory of Wittgenstein, 'meaning finitism'.

[20] RFM, IV § 8.

does not leave the rule behind. It is as much in need of interpretation as the original one. So, why would one not be able to follow the original one straight away? The problem of interpretation is thus that symbols are simply replaced with other symbols. In other words, 'interpretation is not a process that generates meaning: It is a transformation that takes the notion of meaning for granted. (...) After the interpretation we will still be left with a set of symbols to which we must respond, i.e., upon which we must act.'[21]

In contradistinction to this representationalist, thus dualistic, scheme, Wittgenstein provides us with a non-dualistic theory of what it means to follow a rule: 'What this shows is that there is a way of grasping a rule which is *not* an *interpretation*, but which is exhibited in what we call "obeying the rule" and "going against it" in actual cases.'[22] In other words, 'we create meaning as we move from case to case.'[23] Wittgenstein's proposition seems weird at first sight: 'I want to regard man here as an animal.'[24] Learning a rule happens automatically, without justification. It involves 'something that lies beyond being justified or unjustified (...) something animal.'[25] Rule-following is thus ultimately something pre-reflective, i.e., we take the next step in the way we were taught to do. We act like machines; Wittgenstein even calls it explicitly 'an ungrounded way of acting.'[26] Rejecting the concept of interpretation, and opting for a piecemeal approach to the constitution of meaning, he shows us that rule-following is not a matter of choosing one of a given set of possible interpretations. Rather, we follow rules blindly.[27] We take step after step, and 'it *looks* as if a ground for the decision were already there; and it has yet to be invented.'[28] Even though Wittgenstein's own examples are mostly taken from the field of mathematics (number sequences in particular), he surely does not confine his theory of rule-following to this domain. His theory is a general one, applying to all kinds of rule-following: 'And what is in question here is, of course, not merely the case of the expansion of a real number; or in general, the production of mathematical signs, but every analogous process, whether it is a game, a dance, etc., etc.'[29] Wittgenstein's theory of going '*von Fall zu Fall*' applies to all cases of rule-following.

Until now, my explanation of Wittgenstein has not differed in any significant way from the reading of Descombes. Indeed, Descombes also appeals to Wittgenstein in order to find an alternative for an approach to rule-following that would re-

---

[21] Bloor, o.c., p. 18.

[22] L. Wittgenstein, *Philosophical Investigations*, Oxford: Blackwell 1967, § 201. Hereafter, this work will be referred to as PhI. Notice that the German original reads 'von Fall zu Fall'.

[23] Bloor, o.c., p. 19.

[24] L. Wittgenstein, *On Certainty*, Oxford: Blackwell 1979, § 475. Hereafter, this work will be referred to as OC.

[25] OC, § 358–359.

[26] OC, § 110.

[27] Cf. PhI, § 219.

[28] RFM, V § 9. [Italics in the original]

[29] Ibid.

duce it to an intellectual process.[30] Yet, what needs further elaboration is what this going '*von Fall zu Fall*' means. We have seen how Descombes argues that this asks for a 'technical capacity' that can ultimately be reduced to learning conventions. Yet, I think that 'taking the next step' should be taken literally, to wit, in a bodily way. In other words, when Wittgenstein says that a rule provides us with a model to follow, 'in this way' he is saying that it asks for a technical capacity that should be interpreted as the ability *to go with the rule in a way that is bodily entrenched.* How are we to understand this bodily nature of rule-following?

Saying that a rule gives me a model to follow 'in this way' means to say that it guides me as signposts do.[31] Take the example of a traffic sign that tells us what to do by showing us an arrow. We can only do what the sign tells us if we project ourselves at the beginning of the arrow, i.e., if we project ourselves at some point we call the beginning of the arrow and follow its movement. To even find this beginning, we should already know what 'to point' means, and we know this because when we point (to) ourselves we use our arms and hands, or our noses. To follow the sign post, we follow it as we would follow pointing hands. In other words, following a sign post indeed asks for a technical capacity, but this is not only a matter of conventions.[32] Rather, following a sign post is, first and foremost, grasping it on a bodily level as a direction indicator. What we do when we follow a sign post is that we direct ourselves in the direction the sign shows by *bodily* inserting ourselves into the picture and moving along with the movement of the arrow. Therefore, we also understand that an arrow that points upwards does not ask us to ascend, but to go straight ahead. It is this ability that is needed to understand mathematical sequences and city maps, but also instructions by IKEA on how to construct a new commode.

Now, the same goes for the example of someone learning to play chess as a paradigmatic example of rule-following. Also in playing chess, rule-following asks for being bodily immersed in the world. One can only make sense of the situation and grasp the next move on this level. It means getting there on the board and experiencing the pieces fighting.[33] It involves, ultimately, not thinking and finding a new move, but seeing it immediately, knowing it on a much more intimate level: 'It is no mistake of language for the chess master to say that he "sees" the right move.'[34] Even following a mathematical sequence implies a bodily engagement: One literally *feels* the steps, and steps along until one can take the next step by oneself. Generalising over these paradigmatic cases of traffic signs, games, and sequences, we may say that rule-following can only be understood as a bodily projection of oneself into the rule, attaching oneself to it in a bodily way. This is also how I under-

---

[30] See for example: Descombes, o.c., pp. 440–442 and 448.

[31] Cf. Bloor, o.c., pp. 27–28.

[32] However, I am not claiming that there are no conventions involved, at all. Signs always involve conventional elements.

[33] Cf. W. G. Chase and H. Simon, 'Perception in Chess', *Cognitive Psychology*, vol. 4 (1973), pp. 55–81, at p. 55: 'By analyzing an expert player's eye movement, it has been shown that, among other things, he is looking at how pieces attack and defend each other.'

[34] Ibid., p. 56.

stand Wittgenstein when he says: 'One follows the rule *mechanically*. Hence, one compares it with a mechanism. (…) "Mechanical" – that means: without thinking. But *entirely* without thinking? Without *reflecting*.'[35] In this way, rule-following is, indeed, a pre-reflective action, something that I do with my body. In Wittgenstein's words: 'Also obeying a rule is a practice.'[36]

4.3   Following the Trail: Perception in Art

As is commonly recognised, Wittgenstein's theory of rule-following pivots on the concept of *praxis*. Usually, this is interpreted as conventions. I argue, however, that this notion points, first and foremost, to our bodily commitment to a pattern that we recognise as 'moving', rather than to conventions. It is this bodily entanglement of joining a movement that has already set in which binds us to others as it binds us to the world. In other words, *praxis* implies an embodied being, indeed a *Je peux*.[37] It involves an immediate grasping of the world we are "in" by the world we are "of", since my body is always in, part of, and open towards the world, and vice versa. This basic ability precedes the usual distinctions between theory and practice, thinking and doing, perceiving and making things happen. Or rather, there is a basic sense in which the notion of *praxis* pervades both of these terms. In particular, it throws some light on perception as the apex of experience. My goal in this section and the next one is, therefore, to show how perception as *praxis* should be understood as the paradigmatic way in which we are bodily in the world.

In the previous chapter, I have shown how the relationship between constituent and constituted power should be understood as a chiasm. The dynamics of this chiasm was caught with the notion of 'constitution'. Thus, my argument in this section will be that perception is the privileged *locus* to understand constitution. Strange as this may sound at first, perception offers us insight into the active and passive intertwinements of body and world that are characteristic of 'rule-following', provided that we refrain from reducing perception to observation in the specific praxis of science. To avoid such reduction, I will focus on the way in which sense-constitution occurs in perception in art. My reason to focus on art perception is, as Merleau-Ponty argues, that here, the constitution of sense is not mediated beforehand by the models of an established scholarly community, and the corresponding instruments that are geared to measure certain values according to pre-set parameters. In art, perception occurs, first of all, on an immediate bodily, i.e., pre-reflective, level: Hence, it is exactly the realm where it is shown that perceiving my body-being-

---

[35] RFM, VII § 60. [Italics in the original]

[36] PhI, § 202.

[37] M. Merleau-Ponty, *Phenomenology of Perception*, trans. C. Smith, London and New York: Routledge 2003, pp. 159 and 366/M. Merleau-Ponty, *Phénoménologie de la perception*, Paris: Gallimard 1945, pp. 160 and 363. Hereafter, this book will be referred to as PP, with first the English pages, then the French ones.

in-the-world constitutes sense. So, an understanding of perception is, by itself, an understanding of our embodied being in the world, which is, in turn, crucial to understanding rule-following. I will discuss perception in art by looking, first of all, at the way *artists* perceive in their creative activity. Then, I will discuss perception in art by focusing on the perception of *art viewers*. As I will shortly show, these perspectives only differ relatively. Following Merleau-Ponty, the discussion will concentrate on the art of painting.

In their creative activity, artists have often experienced a very peculiar relationship with the world, a relationship that combines the activity of creative expression with the experience of being caught in the world, or participating in it in the double sense of co-establishing it while being part of it. Merleau-Ponty calls this second dimension of the artist's experience, 'passivity'. With this concept he, first of all, draws our attention to the relationship between the visible world and the artist's body. Looking at the world, the artist does not experience it as a spectacle. Rather, she feels intimately related to the world, as if there is a secret bond that binds her body and the world together. Indeed, the light that allows her to see something makes her become visible together with what she sees. This body, seeing and visible at the same time, is on a par with the visible world, as if it is made of the same matter. The world, in turn, is not only visible, but also seeing, indeed looking at her, addressing her seeing, and attracting her attention.[38] Therefore, nature, through its light, colour and depth, is able to move the painter, and to awaken echoes in her body. Her paintings are the answers to what she sees; the bodily echoes of what moved her eye.

> The pressure of my hand on the canvas, its evolutions over the surface of the emerging picture, the exhaustion of my back after hours of work, the rhythm of my breathing, my eyes' perception of colour, my hesitation and my inspiration converge as the invisible depths of the painting, the brushstrokes of which stand as the visible traces of my body's "*quasi* presence". The painting *echoes* my body.[39]

It is important to grasp more precisely what happens when a painter starts to paint: What does the bond between body and world tell us about the artistic process? First of all, this bond shows how the process of creating art is a *physical* process.[40] Of

---

[38] Cf. Marchand speaking, after Klee, quoted in: M. Merleau-Ponty, 'Eye and Mind', in: T. Baldwin (ed.), *Merleau-Ponty. Basic Writings*, London and New York: Routledge 2004, pp. 290–324, at p. 299./M. Merleau-Ponty, *L'Oeil et l'Esprit*, Paris: Gallimard 2003 [1964], p. 31. Hereafter, this book will be referred to as EM, with first the English pages, then the French ones.

[39] M. Nijhuis, *Echoes of Brushstrokes*, Paper presented at '100 Years of Merleau-Ponty, A Centenary Conference', March, 14–16 2008, Sofia University, Bulgaria, p. 6. Thanks to Marta for giving me permission to quote from her paper. Marta Nijhuis is both an artist and a philosopher; for more information on her work, see: http://www.martwork.net/.

[40] This is also true for the art of writing novels, cf. H. Murakami, *What I Talk About When I Talk About Running*, New York: Knopf 2008, pp. 79–80: 'Writing novels, to me, is basically a kind of manual labor. (…) You might not move your body around, but there's gruelling, dynamic labor going on inside you. Everybody uses their mind when they think. But a writer puts on an outfit called narrative and thinks with his entire being; and for the novelist, that process requires putting into play all your physical reserve, often to the point of overexertion.'

course, this can be read as an obvious remark, in the sense that the creative process often requires artists to get their hands dirty. However, there may be a deeper meaning hidden in this phrase. It goes to the materiality of the work of art, and the artist's relationship with this material. The notion of passivity stresses that in the act of creation the artist participates in, takes part in, by becoming part of, the visible world, even if only for a moment. Artistic creation is thus only possible because the artist is bodily immersed in the world: She takes up this situation and takes it further along a movement suggested by the material. Indeed, artistry does not simply consist of creating something new, but rather, of resonating with something that is already there. This is the specific bodily understanding of *praxis*. Consequently, the artist is someone who can see something, someone who understands what the material (the paint, the marble, the music) is saying, and is able to express this in her work. The artist can listen to the material and tell what it asks for. She gets close to it and, in touching it, she is being touched, herself.

> I am in front of a canvas, my brush in my hand. The canvas is in front of me. As soon as I approach its immaculate surface following the invisible sketch that my vision of the world traces upon it, something unexpected happens. Depending on the quality of my first touch – strong or delicate, shy or dashing, circumspect or confident – the canvas suggests to me, in a play of activity and passivity, where to move my next step. Painting is expressing, yes, but it is also listening. To the smooth *voices of silence*.[41]

The question is how to understand this process: How do artists take the next step? The relationship between artist and material is crucial in this respect. Artists are those people who can listen to the material and, ultimately, this is something that is determined physically. What I called 'listening to the material' should, therefore, also be understood in a bodily way: An artist is able 'to bodily get into the material'. A painter is someone who is able to get inside the paint, someone who has the ability 'to become paint'. These moments are rare, and even artists who have been successful in the past can never be certain that they will really paint again. On some days it just does not work; she can look and look and look at something, and still… there is nothing she feels, nothing she hears. However, what really makes her a painter is her ability to become paint on some days, at some rare moments, to catch a glimpse of what the visible world is saying, and make the world into a painting. As mentioned before, these moments do not occur often, and when they do, they are gone in a blink of an eye. If the artist cannot get hold of them precisely at the moment that the fusion would occur, everything escapes and she has to start all over again.

Thus, art requires a kind of sensitivity. Though it may be characterised as a certain 'intelligence', this sensitivity is not something intellectual, something that has to do with reflective thinking. Rather, it is pre-reflective because it is the sensitivity of the body. Artistry requires, first of all, a bodily aptitude for, a physical disposition towards, contact with the matter at hand. This sensitivity clearly comes under different forms (for colours, shapes, lines, sounds, bodies, images or words) and it is not given to all of us in equal amounts; therefore, not all of us are destined to

---

[41] Nijhuis, o.c., pp. 5–6. [Italics in the original]

become artists, or artists in the same field. Yet, bodily aptitude is not a zero-sum game either; there are differences in degree, and also, one might develop one's skills. Nevertheless, someone with little talent may practice and practice, and perhaps advance little by little, but she will never know what it is to be a painter. On the other hand, one should take care not to make more of this aptitude than it is. It may be the first, but it is certainly not the only, condition for becoming an artist. For example, someone with sensitivity for language may become a literary critic; it takes more to become a poet. In the same vein, there is more to being a violinist than just being able to play the violin. As the Dutch conductor, Jaap van Zweden, once said about Janine Jansen: 'The instrument is an extension of her being. You only see that with very few. So natural. She does not play the violin, she is a violinist. That is an enormous difference.'[42]

In the process of artistic creation, there seems to exist, however, another experience, that of the material becoming human. This experience is not so strange as it may seem at first glance.

> I was looking at a rock formation, when suddenly I saw a host of massive warriors from another time and place, solemnly marching over the sea. The rocky warriors turned to me and their eyes of stone crossed the eyes of my body. I was amazed. The people round me probably thought I was miles away then. Yet, I wasn't. In fact, there I was, next to them, my feet on the same ground, but more deeply, as I felt the eyes of the world staring at me for the first time in my life.[43]

Probably, this experience is nowhere better described than in the tale of Pygmalion.[44] A sculptor, Pygmalion, makes a statue of a girl of ivory. He finds the statue so beautiful that he falls in love with it.[45] Apparently, the ivory is able to trick the artist, even to the extent that he forgets about it and treats the girl of ivory as if she is truly human.[46] Ultimately, Venus herself fulfils his wish and blows life into it: The ivory girl becomes human.[47] This experience of the material becoming human

---

[42] 'Het instrument is een verlenging van haar wezen. Dat zie je maar bij een enkeling. Zo natuurlijk. Ze speelt geen viool, ze is violiste. Dat is een enorm verschil.', quoted in: R. Gollin, 'De viool als verlengstuk van haar wezen. Dinsdagprofiel Janine Jansen', de Volkskrant, 16 October 2007. [My translation, LC]

[43] Nijhuis, o.c., pp. 7–8.

[44] Ovid, Metmorphoses, trans. M. Innes, London (etc.): Penguin 1955, Book X, 243–297, at pp. 231–232.

[45] Ibid., p. 231: 'But meanwhile, with marvellous artistry, he skillfully carved a snowy ivory statue. He made it lovelier than any woman born, and fell in love with his own creation. The statue had all the appearance of a real girl, so that it seemed to be alive, to want to move, did not modesty forbid. So cleverly did his art conceal his art.'

[46] Ibid.: 'Often he ran his hands over the work, feeling it to see whether it was flesh or ivory, and would not yet admit that ivory was all it was. He kissed the statue, and imagined that it kissed him back, spoke to it and embraced it, and thought he felt his fingers sink into the limbs he touched, so that he was afraid lest a bruise appear where he had pressed the flesh.'

[47] Ibid., p. 232: 'She seemed warm: he laid his lips on hers again, and touched her breast with his hand – at his touch the ivory lost its hardness, and grew soft: his fingers made an imprint on the yielding surface, just as wax of Hymettus melts in the sun and, worked by men's fingers, is fashioned into many different shapes, and made fit for use by being used. The lover stood, amazed,

seems to be the opposite of the one described above. However, this is merely appearance. Both experiences are intimately bound to one another. In both, the artist has the feeling of becoming one with the material, one with the ivory, one with the music, one with the movement, entangled in a texture between the world and her body. In both, nevertheless, this coincidence cannot be kept. At the moment the unity is felt, it immediately escapes. Both experiences are that of passivity: In her creative activity, the artist experiences how her body and the body of the world are related to each other. It shows that in order to create, she has to let herself be moved by the movement of the world, follow the traces in the material in order to take them further and make them her own. This does not mean that she appropriates what is given, but rather, that she respects the direction pointed at, lets herself be guided and takes the next step on her own account.

We have thus seen that the relationship between artist and material is a very specific one. The material limits the artist: For example, a specific piece of marble is, by itself, cold, and has a certain colour, roughness, weight and size. All these qualities may limit the artist in her creative wishes. Nevertheless, this remains half of the story. These qualities guide her eyes, her hands, her touch, and she cannot but follow them if something is to be created. It is the particular piece of marble, there on the floor of her atelier, with its specific qualities, that makes a specific work of art possible. A statue made of a different piece of marble would not be the same, let alone one made of a completely different material, such as wood. Following the rules, the next step is possible: Only by going along with the lines of the marble, as if these are the signs for the artist to follow, can she create something. Here, we can see why passivity is not equal to receptivity. The material both limits and enables creation. It is not simply 'ready to be received', but also has a certain roughness, robustness or stubbornness that forces the artist into a certain position towards it. The concept of passivity stresses that creation is something that is made possible not so much by the artist, but rather, *via* her.[48] The experience of creation is that of something coming to life through her. The artist experiences that she is a medium, that her work is something that does not come entirely, perhaps not even primarily, from her. It is the experience that I described earlier: The painter becoming paint. The artist can only experience this because she is *bodily* engaged in the world. Passivity and creation go hand in hand, and hence can only be experienced together. It follows that passivity is not opposite to but, rather, is the other side of creation.

The experience of passivity in activity, the entanglement of passivity and activity, should be distinguished from both a radical form of activity and a radical form of passivity. Until now, I have especially criticized the former by showing how a philosophy that departs from the constituting powers of a sovereign consciousness cannot make sense of the experience of creation. The latter, however, is not able to escape these flaws, either. Understanding passivity in an absolute sense, i.e., the ex-

---

afraid of being mistaken, his joy tempered with doubt, and again and again stroked the object of his prayers. It was indeed a human body!'

[48] S. Ménasé, *Passivité et création. Merleau-Ponty et l'art moderne*, Paris: Presses Universitaires de France 2003, p. 11.

perience of being totally possessed by the surrounding world, makes creation equally mysterious. Both radicalisations remain trapped in the subject–object dualism. What is forgotten in these readings is that creation requires a bodily interaction with the world, and that interaction means, ultimately, that the world and I do not coincide. In other words, *praxis* always presupposes passivity, as the interaction has to sense the fissures that open up to something new from, and therefore, together with, the thickness of what one is perceiving. This passivity is not opposed to the creative part of the painter's work. Therefore, it is not a radical passivity that can be experienced by itself. Rather, this passivity is always *the other side* of constitution. It reminds one that constitution is never done *ex nihilo* but, rather, that it always involves a moment of inspiration. Far from being some kind of whispering in your ear that comes from above, inspiration comes from beneath, from the visible world. Inspiration does not come after the long silence of reflection; it is not an intellectual achievement. Rather, inspiration comes to her who has her feet in the dirt instead of her head in the clouds. Inspiration is the moment when the artist manages to become one with her material.[49]

Concluding this part of the section, we can say that the concept of passivity refers to a specific dimension of the perception of the artist. Several points are important for our inquiry. First of all, passivity focuses on the relationship between artistic creation and the artist's body. Artistic creation can only come about when the artist is situated, to wit, bodily immersed in the field. Secondly, this brings with it a special relationship between the artist and the material. We have illustrated this with the twin experiences of the artist 'materialising', and the material 'becoming human'. Thirdly, it is exactly this bodily sensitivity that enables the artist to take the next step. She is being guided by the trail the material offers, and this makes that she can bodily follow in the direction in which she is pointed. The fourth important point is that we are dealing here with a passivity *of* creation. This dimension is only opened up in the process of artistic activity. Finally, this entails that the artist and the world are bodily intertwined in a chiastic way, without ever coinciding. In other words, there is a chiasm between constitution and passivity.

Let us now turn to the *art viewer* and the way he perceives. Again, my argument focuses on the way the body constitutes sense while perceiving. There is something like a sensuous attraction between me, as an art viewer, and the work. This is, first of all, felt in the way works of art situate me in a bodily way. That is to say that a work asks me to take up a specific position in relation to it: 'For each object, as for each picture in an art gallery, there is an optimum distance from which it requires to be seen, a direction viewed from which it vouchsafes most of itself: At a shorter or greater distance we have merely a perception blurred through excess or

---

[49] EM, p. 299/pp. 31–32: 'We speak of "inspiration" and the word should be taken literally. There really is inspiration and expiration of Being, respiration in Being, action and passion so slightly discernible that it becomes impossible to distinguish between who sees and who is seen, who paints and what is painted. We say that a human being is born the moment when something that was only virtually visible within the mother's body becomes at once visible for us and for itself. The painter's vision is an ongoing birth.'

deficiency.'[50] In other words, the work positions me and puts me in a certain situation, i.e., the one that allows me to perceive it at its best. In this situation, I am able to experience the work of art as it is supposed to be experienced.

It would be a mistake to think that I can catch the sense of an artwork outside of, or separate from, its material. Only through my body can I grasp its sense, which is intertwined with the material way in which the work presents itself to me. In the case of painting, I am referring to the colours, lines, shadows, figures, depth of the work. What we touch upon here is what Merleau-Ponty has called '*idée sensible*'. With this notion, he refers to works of art (paintings, music) treating them as paradigmatic for perceivable or visible, and thus sensuous, phenomena. His point is that in sensuous phenomena, materiality and sensibility, sensation and meaning, are intertwined. Meaning is not available without or separate from, but only in or through, the sensation of material, however abstract this meaning may grow to become. Marcel Proust gives the pre-eminent example of this phenomenon in his *À la recherche du temps perdu*, when he writes on the '*petite phrase*'. As Merleau-Ponty comments: 'No one has gone further than Proust in fixing the relations between the visible and the invisible, in describing an idea that is not contrary to the sensible, that is its lining and its depth.'[51] The piece of music described by Proust that hides in it the essence of love for Swann, is paradigmatic for 'all cultural beings', 'the passions, but also the experience of the world.'[52] These are all examples of an '*idée sensible*': 'The ideas we are speaking of would not be better known to us if we had no body and no sensibility; it is, then, that they would be inaccessible to us. (…) [T]hey could not be given to us *as ideas* except in a carnal experience. (…) Each time we want to get at it [i.e., the idea, LC] immediately, or lay hands on it, or circumscribe it, or see it unveiled, we do in fact feel that the attempt is misconceived, that it retreats in the measure we approach.'[53] The interaction here is on an immediate, pre-reflective level.[54] Merleau-Ponty calls it 'a cohesion without concept, which is of the same kind as the cohesion of the parts of my body, or the cohesion of my body with the world.'[55] This 'cohesion without concepts' is my body grasping the world while being grasped by it.[56] That is why these ideas are not at my disposal as if I had them. No, I am, rather, caught in them by a kind of magnetic force that makes me dive into them.

---

[50] PP, p. 352/p. 348.

[51] M. Merleau-Ponty, *The Visible and the Invisible*, trans. A. Lingis, Evanston, Ill.: Northwestern University Press 1968, p. 149/M. Merleau-Ponty, *Le visible et l'invisible*, Paris: Gallimard 2003 [1964], p. 193. Hereafter, this book will be referred to as VI, with first the English pages, then the French ones.

[52] Ibid.

[53] VI, p. 150/p. 194. [Italics in the original]

[54] This implies a new understanding of aesthetics as aesthêsis. For more on this subject, see: M. Carbone, *La visibilité de l'invisible. Merleau-Ponty entre Cézanne et Proust*, Hildesheim [etc.]: Georg Olms Verlag 2001 especially Chapter 6 and J. Slatman, *L'expression au-delà de la representation. Sur l'aisthêsis et l'esthétique chez Merleau-Ponty*, s.n., Wageningen, 2001.

[55] VI, p. 152/pp. 196–197.

[56] Cf. VI, p. 266/p. 313.

Now, how does this 'cohesion without concepts' work? My ability to make sense of the situation is inextricably linked to the sensuous signs or clues that the work offers. I can only be moved by art if I am able to 'read' these signs and move along the movement of the work. Only then can I obtain its 'sense'. This means that by moving me on a bodily level, the work makes me go along with the movement it suggests. What can be called the 'depth' of something sensuous is its ability to situate me and suck me into it. Depth is exactly the dimension that cannot be seen by taking a bird's eye view. Consequently, in order to be able to see the depth of a certain work, one should, first of all, be situated bodily. Then, one should follow the 'depth clues' in order to be able to constitute sense in following the sense the work offers. Take the example of Bernini's sculpture of Apollo and Daphne. It is the vibrant form of the marble that moves me in such an intense way that it (literally) demands that I circle around it. And, step-by-step, it makes me not simply witness the metamorphosis. No, as I follow the events taking place before my eyes, I am caught in the work. For, only if I take the next step does Daphne change from a beautiful nymph into a laurel tree. I am really *executing* the metamorphosis to the extent that I am drawn into it. I cannot remain the object unless I become the subject of metamorphosis myself. It is this ability of art, its ability to suck me into its movement and get me moving, that Merleau-Ponty has analysed in his latest writings. Yet, it is not something that is restricted to art. Rather, it is part and parcel of all *bodily,* and thus *sensuous,* phenomena. Art, as an intensified mode of perception, is the paradigm of 'sense-constitution'.

Notice that the passivity described here is the passivity *of* experiencing art. One cannot simply evoke this passivity at one's own demand. One only experiences this passivity in the process of perceiving art. Only then, situated bodily vis-à-vis the work, confronted with its materiality, can one be guided by its signs and follow these, taking one step at the time, towards its depth. One should really experience the work with one's whole body in order to feel oneself being guided. This entails that one should really look at a painting carefully and with attention before one can experience passivity. Passivity is not a preparatory stage: Rather, it is the upshot of concentrated activity. A quick glance, or a look at a reproduction will probably not suffice. For movies this means that one should probably watch them in a cinema, where the quality of sound and image is at its best. To be able to get sucked in by a play, one should be able to see the facial expressions of the actors. Yet, the best seats in the theatre are not necessarily those closest to the stage. The best seats are those where one can see the play at its best. Depending on such things as the nature of the particular play, lighting, sound and set, the best seats might well be far more to the back. What is important, however, is that all these examples show that depth clues do their work best in the particular situation of the art viewer who is really able to experience the work.

There is, finally, one last thing to say about this experience of passivity of the art viewer. A work of art can have different meanings for different people, in different places and at different times. Its meanings are never fixed; if they were, one could simply repeat them infinitely. The sense of a work of art would be an infinite repetition of the same. One should, rather, think of a work of art as pregnant with sense; it is open because it can be taken up endlessly, and is able to say different things again and again, without ever being determined completely.[57] However, it does not give *carte blanche*. In its materiality, it offers us a trail to follow. Any sense to be given to it must take its cue from this materially given sense: 'A successful work has the strange power to teach its own lesson. The reader or spectator who follows the clues of the book or the painting, by setting up stepping stones and rebounding from side to side guided by the obscure clarity of a particular style, will end by discovering what the artist wanted to communicate.'[58] Only by following the signs can the art viewer step with the movement, and take the next step on his own account. Experiencing the passivity of being guided, he will be able to constitute new sense starting from the sense offered. Since it is the passivity *of* constitution, there is a chiastic relationship between passivity and constitution.

Concluding this section, one may say that the art viewer also experiences passivity while perceiving. Five points are important in this respect. First of all, in the process of perceiving art, the work situates the viewer. Secondly, there is a bodily interaction between the art viewer and the work. Thirdly, the work will guide the viewer with the help of 'depth clues'. Fourthly, this experience is only available in the process of perceiving the work of art. It requires a bodily confrontation with the work. Lastly, there is a chiasm of passivity and sense-constitution in the experience of the art viewer. So, following Merleau-Ponty, I argue that also the perception of art viewers is ultimately understandable by the very same points as that of the artist himself. Of course, this experience is strongest with the artist himself: The experience of the art viewers is derived from it. Yet, the difference is one of degrees. Notwithstanding differences in emphasis, in the end we are dealing with one and the same experience of passivity-in-activity. This can be explained when we realise that the artist is himself also, first of all, viewing, i.e., perceiving, the work by following the 'depth clues', such as colours, lines, etc. Guided by these clues he picks up his brush and starts to paint. On the other hand, if the art viewer does not, in a minimal sense, grasp what the artist was perceiving, he will certainly not grasp the work at all. In order to follow the 'depth clues' of a work, the viewer should, in a minimal sense, perceive what the artist perceived. In perception in art, there is, therefore, a chiastic intertwinement of sense-constitution and passivity. In the next section, I will further elaborate on perception as the privileged place where the constitution of sense comes about. A theory of perception is a theory of an embodied subject, and, as I will show, this is exactly the subject implied in Wittgenstein's theory of rule-following.

---

[57] For this notion of openness (*offen endlos*), see: M. Merleau-Ponty, *Husserl at the Limits of Phenomenology*. Including texts by Edmund Husserl, trans. and eds. L. Lawlor with B. Bergo, Evanston, Ill.: Northwestern University Press 2002, pp. 22 and 39/M. Merleau-Ponty, *Notes de cours sur* L'origine de la géométrie *de Husserl*, Suivi de Recherches sur la phénoménologie de Merleau-Ponty, dir. R. Barbaras, Paris: Presses Universitaires de France 1998, pp. 25 and 46. Hereafter, this book will be referred to as HL, with first the English pages, then the French ones.

[58] M. Merleau-Ponty, *Sense and Non-sense*, trans. P.A. Dreyfus, Evanston, Ill.: Northwestern University Press, pp. 19–20/M. Merleau-Ponty, *Sens et non-sens*, Gallimard: Paris 1996 [1948], pp. 25–26.

4.4   Perception and Rule-Following: The Embodied Subject of Constitution

Usually, perception is understood as one-way traffic. Such an understanding may be exemplified by theories of so-called sense-data in which what is perceived is something completely external to us (perceivers). These theories entail a view of perception as representation: 'A sense-datum theory might be called a *representative realism* because it conceives perception as a relation in which sense-data represent perceived external (hence real) objects to us.'[59] Thus, perception is predicated on there being a distance between perceiver and perceived. Contrary to this, in this section I will show that perception is predicated on the intertwinement of perceiver and perceived; and that, therefore, it can function as the ground model for rule-following and the wider concept of constitution. That is to say, all constitution (of sense) begins on a bodily level, and thus in the process of my body perceiving. The five important points that could be derived from an analysis of perception in art are paradigmatic for perception, in general. In this section, I will first show how perception always bodily situates us in a field. Then, I will concentrate on the bodily sensitivity towards the world which this entails. Thirdly, I will show how perception is guided by signs that show the direction in which to take the next step. After this, I will argue that there is a passivity *of* our perceptive activity, and show what this entails for the subject of perception. Finally, I will focus on the chiasm between the embodied subject and the world.

First of all, let us see how the notions of situation and field help us to break with dualistic thinking. Already in his early work, Merleau-Ponty showed that perception cannot be grasped by the dualistic model of a spectator watching a spectacle. This is so because my body—i.e., me-perceiving—is not something opposite to what it perceives. Since my body is also perceivable, it is already a part of the perceived world. It not only enables me to perceive, but also my body makes me perceivable. So, perceiving, I also always belong to the perceived world: Because of my body, I am *situated* in the same world as the one I am perceiving. Therefore, perception has a special nature. Perceiving, I am not locked up in myself, but I nestle myself there where I am looking.[60] This is why seeing, hearing, smelling, etc., can be understood according to the model of touching, and vice versa.[61] In perception, I cling to the perceived world and the world is clung to me. There is a constant interplay of touching and being touched between me and the world. Activity and passivity cannot be distinguished in the relationship between me as a perceiving body, and the perceived world. My body is, first and foremost, the agent of my perception.[62] Thanks

---

[59] R. Audi, *Epistemology. A Contemporary Introduction to the Theory of Knowledge*, London [etc.]: Routledge 1998, p. 33. [Italics in the original]

[60] EM, p. 317/p. 81.

[61] Cf. J. Slatman, 'The Sense of Life: Husserl and Merleau-Ponty on Touching and Being Touched', *Chiasmi International*, no. 7 (2005), pp. 305–325.

[62] PP, p. 94/p. 97.

to my body, I am not a purely internal subject, a spiritual entity totally different from the objects in their strange world, but rather, I am an embodied perceiver amidst the objects in a world that is the place of my bodily being. In other words, perceiving is not predicated on the subject–object relationship; quite the contrary, the latter is an abstraction scheme operating in a more original mode of perception.

As the agent of perception, my body is always directed towards, and open to, the world.[63] Yet, I do not simply perceive 'everything' without any form of differentiation. When something shows itself to me, I see it because it attracts my attention. More precisely, I see it because it appeals to my body. Take the example of a row of chairs, one after another. My attention will be drawn by the one chair that does not stand in line. Yet, this chair, stubbornly resisting the row, can only attract my attention because it stands out against the background of other chairs. This simple example shows the way in which I perceive things: I always perceive a certain structure or *Gestalt* of things, i.e., something that appears in a context.[64]

This structure points to a fundamental characteristic of perception. Perception is never a full grasp of things, never a total control of a sovereign subject. The opposite is true: Perception is never complete, because it always implies a *field*.[65] Each of our senses has its own field of perception, and while perceiving, I do not catch every object within the field, but only those that correlate with the sense I am activating. As the example of the chairs shows, in our everyday practice we are fully familiar with this phenomenon. What we do perceive depends on what we give our attention to.[66] Perceiving always involves attention; I cannot see without looking, and looking always involves attention in the sense of directing my body towards the world.[67] It would be a mistake, however, to conceive of attention as a neutral, purely passive phenomenon. Though it is rooted in picking up the resonance of movement in the intertwinement between body and world, it gradually evolves into the ability to continue the movement in 'a next step', which entails moving to and from this intertwinement. This is where attention becomes directive of perception, or, in other words, where perception becomes the paradigm of creation. Here, perception ushers in the creation of sense or, what amounts to the same thing for Merleau-Ponty, the constitution of sense.[68]

We are now able to see the scope of the initial thesis, that perception helps us refine what happens in constitution. The above-mentioned field of perception is important in this respect. Constitution of sense should be understood as the opening of a field. A perceptive field always involves a horizon, to wit a figure-background struc-

---

[63] Merleau-Ponty calls this 'l'être au monde', cf. PP, p. 90/p. 93 and following.

[64] B. Waldenfels, *Das Leibliche Selbst. Vorlesungen zur Phänomenologie des Leibes*, Frankfurt am Mein: Suhrkamp 2000, p. 45.

[65] PP, p. 4/p. 10.

[66] PP, pp. 33–34/pp. 37–38.

[67] Cf. EM, p. 294/pp. 16–17: 'My mobile body makes a difference in the visible world, being a part of it; that is why I can steer it through the visible. Conversely, it is just as true that vision is attached to movement. We see only what we look at.'

[68] PP, p. 34/p. 38.

ture.[69] In other words, perception is always perception *in perspective*. It is a power to order, to restructure certain elements so that they become a window giving out onto a new world, just as expression.[70] To take another example, when I look at a specific apple tree (the figure of my perception) the surroundings (the meadow, other trees, the mill and the farm that form the background) seem to disappear.[71] However, the background has a very important function. The structure of object and horizon is the way in which objects appear. Indeed, the background (the surroundings that seem to disappear) makes it possible for a specific object (the apple tree) to appear in the first place. This illustrates the very first meaning of order as a *spatial* structure. Far from being a disadvantage, perspective is thus constitutive of the appearance of objects.

What the analysis of perception reveals, and this will be my second point, is that there is a specifically bodily way to deal with the situation with which I am confronted. Since it is my body that makes that I am situated, it is the nexus where being situated gradually develops into being able to situate, i.e., being able to put myself in a situation.[72] This entails a concrete liberty.[73] This locomotion should be understood in the sense of me being bodily orientated towards objects in the world, as my body orients itself towards the tasks at hand. My body makes me an inhabitant of the world. Being is, therefore, *being orientated*.[74] This not only means that I am able to orient myself with respect to actual objects, or an actual state of affairs. It entails the possibility to situate myself towards everything that has meaning for me, even when it is not (yet) actually there.[75] This is crucial in playing.[76] For example, in tennis, the player awaiting the service of her opponent already assumes a certain bodily position, projecting herself in the situation of returning the ball. She adjusts and refines that position as the moment to hit draws nearer, both reading and anticipating her opponent's movements in relation to her own. Note (in passing) that this is actually the *fun* of tennis, i.e., what makes it playful. That we can turn this play into a game, and then into a contest with constitutive and regulative rules, is entirely secondary. The primary rules of tennis do not derive from an authoritative body setting rules, but from how two or more people can extract fun from a drive with a ball, a net and some rackets. The fun is to surprise each other by anticipating projection of oneself in the world of each other's movements and corresponding action.

---

[69] PP, pp. 78–79/pp. 82–83.

[70] Cf. R. Visker, *Truth and Singularity. Taking Foucault into Phenomenology*, Dordrecht (etc.): Kluwer Academic 1999, pp. 97–98.

[71] See for a radical example of this the painting by Piet Mondriaan, *Flowering apple tree*, 1912.

[72] PP, p. 157/p. 158.

[73] PP, p. 156/p. 158: '(…) that concrete liberty which comprises the general power of putting oneself into a situation.' See also PP, p. 190/p. 191.

[74] PP, pp. 293–295/pp. 291–293.

[75] PP, p. 163/p. 165: 'This is because the normal subject has his body not only as a system of presence positions, but besides, and thereby, as an open system of an infinite number of equivalent positions directed to other ends.'

[76] PP, p. 156/p. 157.

This notion of projection is very important for our inquiry into rule-following. It is the body's ability to launch itself into new space-vectors, i.e., to bodily evoke this new situation in order to live it.[77] As it is the perceiving body that allows one to do this, it shows in how wide a sense Merleau-Ponty interprets the notion of perception. For him, perception is the primordial openness of my body towards the world: In perception, my body is directed towards, and receptive to, the world. One should also keep in mind that 'world' has a specific phenomenological meaning in this context. What is perceived by me is not simply what is directly in front of me. No, the broad reading of perception has an impact on the perceived, as well: 'It [i.e., the perceived, LC] may be a "unity of value" which is present to me only practically. (…) I perceive everything that is part of my environment, and my environment includes "everything of which the existence or non-existence, the nature or modification, counts in practice for me" (…).'[78] In other words, my field of perception also comprises everything that has a practical meaning for my situation, everything that moves me. The world I perceive is the world in which I move, therefore every movement has a background which 'is immanent in the movement, inspiring and sustaining it at every moment. The plunge into action (*l'initiation cinétique*) is, from the subject's point of view, an original way of relating himself to the object, and is on the same footing as perception.'[79] Perception and action (in its basic, bodily sense of moving) are thus intimately related.

Furthermore, perception brings with it a specific skill or knack (*style*). As we have seen in the previous chapter, skill refers to my singular bodily interaction with the world, which, at the same time, makes it possible to share the world with others.[80] It is the specific way of dealing with the perceptive field of *praxis,* my specific pre-reflective bodily contact with the world. Take the example of swimming. My swimming skills are linked to the way my body moves naturally through the water. If I want to swim a longer distance, I will have to learn to swim more efficiently so that I will last longer. This means that I have to learn to control my breathing, and to adjust the way my arms and legs move in the water. For example, it might be wise to make my strokes just a little longer. It is thus my body that learns in the situation by adapting itself to the task it has to perform. My skill is pre-reflective and thus never completely known to myself. What is most intimate to me, remains hidden from my sight.

The third important point in my analysis of perception concerns the way in which the constitution of sense precisely occurs. To understand this, it is crucial to look into the relationship between perception and space, as spatial existence is 'the primordial condition of all living perception.'[81] This relationship is of particular interest if we conceive of perception as a form of rule-following, since this always

---

[77] Merleau-Ponty points to the fact that projection can be understood as evocation in the sense that a medium evokes an absent, see PP, p. 129/p. 130.

[78] PP, p. 371/p. 374. Merleau-Ponty quotes Scheler.

[79] PP, p. 127/p. 128.

[80] Cf. Chap. 3, Sects. 3 and 4.

[81] PP, p. 126/p. 127.

involves the problem of taking the next step in a certain direction. An important distinction should be made between spatiality of position and spatiality of situation.[82] Objects have a place in the world, they are positioned somewhere. In contradistinction with this spatiality of position, my body has the *spatiality of situation:* Bodily space is the ground on which an object can appear. In this regard, the notion of the body-scheme means that my body is the zero point of space. As a bodily being, I am situated in the world, and from 'here' I determine the place of objects, or state of affairs. My bodily space is thus constitutive for space at large. This also changes the notion of object. Objects in the world are no longer completely manageable things. As was made clear above by the analysis of perception, objects emerge (or fade away) in a field, i.e., in perspective. They never completely show themselves to us. Never appearing to us fully, they retain their mystery. They are never completely known to us. Moreover, what appears to us is what we give attention to. The spatiality of situation opens up to a field of action in which an object can appear as the goal of our action.[83] In other words, the space of our situation is linked with the tasks in which we are engaged: Our bodily situation opens up a specific space that differs from case to case, depending on what we are doing.[84]

Back to rule-following: Following meaning while creating meaning is the problem of the next step. How does this occur? Wittgenstein gives us a clue when he writes that someone following a rule 'does just let himself go on when he follows the rule or the examples; however, he does not regard what he does as a peculiarity of *his* course; he says, not: "so *that's* how I went", but: "so *that's* how it goes".'[85] This should also be understood in a phenomenological way.[86] Indeed, how is one to follow it, how to follow the direction the rule points to? The analysis of perception enables us to give a more detailed account of what this entails. From Merleau-Ponty, we have learned that it is ultimately my perceiving (immersed/immersing) body that gives sense to all things, to the extent that it picks up the sense of its surrounding world. As a translation of the French *sens,* we should understand sense as both direction and meaning.[87] Furthermore, as we appreciate its bodily meaning, the term reminds us that perception has all the connotations of sensation, feeling and experience.

The analysis of perception as a form of moving along certain lines following their directions, i.e., of perception as an achievement in space, thus leads to a new understanding of sense, one that breaks with the analysis of a constituting consciousness.[88] My body moving, directing itself through the world, directs the objects

---

[82] PP, pp. 114–115/p. 116.

[83] Cf. PP, p. 117/p. 119.

[84] Cf. B. Waldenfels, *Das Leibliche Selbst. Vorlesungen zur Phänomenologie des Leibes*, p. 115.

[85] RFM, VII § 4. [Italics in the original]

[86] Interestingly enough, David Bloor explicitly mentions this possibility. Cf. Bloor, o.c., p. 52.

[87] Cf. C. Lefort, 'Le sens de l'orientation', in: M. Merleau-Ponty, *Notes de cours sur* L'origine de la géométrie *de Husserl*, Suivi de Recherches sur la phénoménologie de Merleau-Ponty, dir. R. Barbaras, Paris: Presses Universitaires de France 1998, pp. 221–238.

[88] PP, p. 170/pp. 171–172.

and state of affairs, gives them meaning. At the same time, however, the body is also situated by the objects in the world, first and foremost, in the sense that it is guided by these objects. Movement and perception are intertwined in the living body and it is thus through my body that I can extend myself towards the world: 'Everything I see is, in principle, within my reach, at least within reach of my sight, and is marked upon the map of the "I can".'[89] My body is a *Je peux;* the opening of the world, presupposed in perception. In other words, by virtue of my body I have a world, and by virtue of the world I have my body, which is to say—indeed, to repeat—that my first grasp of the world is always a bodily grasp.[90]

Closely connected to this are my last two points. First of all, as we have seen, perception always involves passivity. Remember the previous section on the relationship between artist and material. The same idea explains how, in perception generally, the next step can be taken. It is because of my body that I am a *sensuous* being, and this allows me to connect to other people or things or states of affairs. Following the sense given in the world, I learn to take the next step on my own account. An analysis of perception shows how intimately body and world are related: Perception as the paradigm of sense-constitution presupposes a very specific subject, what Merleau-Ponty has called the *Je peux.* However, in his last writings, we do not find this notion anymore. There, trying to rethink perception once again, he radicalises his early thought without rejecting it completely. Instead of stressing the bodily nature of our being in the world, and intentionality, he goes one step further. Against dualistic thinking, he now stresses the intimate bond between body and world. The notion he uses to describe this phenomenon is '*j'en suis*', 'I'm part and parcel of it'.[91] There is not a subject, on the one hand, and a world, on the other. Because of my body, I am a visible being in a visible world.

Of course, my body is not simply a part of the visible world. It is a special part because it is a subject. First of all, my body is both directed and open towards the world it lives in. It is that part of the visible world that can perceive. Secondly, the body is animated, it possesses a spirit or mind. Yet, this does not mean that Merleau-Ponty silently reintroduces the dualism of Descartes. The spirit should be thought of as the other side of the body, and vice versa: '*Define* the mind (*l'esprit*) as the *other side* of the body – We have no idea of a mind that would not be *doubled* with a body, that would not be established on this *ground* – (…) There is a body of the mind, and a mind of the body, and a chiasm between them.'[92]

Finally, my last point: I cannot see *something* if I cannot feel a certain change, a movement in the relationship between me and the world. Now, I experience something coming to me from the twilight of the world, something I cannot distinguish at first but is like a certain pressure I feel, as the world rubbing me. Yet, I can only feel this rubbing as an embodied being. This rubbing is a moment of being touched by the world while touching it. In other words, my ability to sense this rubbing and

---

[89] EM, p. 294/p. 17.

[90] PP, p. 169/p. 171: 'The body is our general medium for having a world.'

[91] Cf. VI, pp. 134–135/pp. 175–176.

[92] VI, p. 259/ p. 307.

to make sense of it, presupposes my being wrapped up in the world and the world being wrapped up in me. It is this moving-movable texture, this dynamic element that makes perception (and thus all sense-constitution) possible, that Merleau-Ponty calls 'flesh'. We have seen that I cannot perceive without a texture that encompasses both me and the world, and that lies on the other side of us and sustains us. This texture is the 'flesh'. It is like the light that illuminates both me and the world, but that belongs neither to the one nor to the other.[93] In this texture I am linked to the world in a chiastic way: '[T]he idea of *chiasm,* that is: Every relation with being is *simultaneously* a taking and a being taken, the hold is held, it is *inscribed* in the same being that it takes hold of.'[94]

It is in this chiastic relationship of body and world that sense-constitution occurs. This means that sense is something that comes about not before or independent of, but only *in* action (*en acte*). Whoever can see the signs, the sense of the situation, will be able to read in them the direction to follow.[95] Man is not a dweller in truth, but given the contingency of life, and the fragility of sense, he can initiate meaning (sense) by following the direction (sense) of the world.[96] And, stepping in the footprints of sense the world gives, he will learn to step by himself, to make his own footprints and give sense to the world. Sense-constitution is, therefore, a radical type of creation: '[A] creation that is, at the same time, an adequation, the only way to obtain an adequation.'[97] The paradox is obvious here: While sense is always constituted starting from the clues the world gives, the only way to experience these clues and to follow them is to constitute (create) a world for oneself.[98]

In this section, I have further elaborated on perception as the privileged place where the constitution of sense occurs. As I have shown, a theory of perception is a theory of an embodied subject. In this respect, I pointed to five important aspects. First of all, perceiving always means being bodily situated in a field. Secondly, there is a specifically bodily way of dealing with the situation at hand, and the tasks that need to be performed. Thirdly, it is my perceiving body that constitutes sense by following the sense of the world. Fourthly, the intimate bond between subject and world is caught in the new notion of the subject as '*j'en suis*'. Lastly, there is a chiasm of passivity and sense-constitution in perception, and this chiasm is made possible by the ontological element that Merleau-Ponty calls 'flesh'.

---

[93] Cf. VI, p. 130/p. 170.

[94] VI, p. 266/p. 313. [Italics in the original]

[95] HL, p. 29/p. 34: '[I]n remaking the path which has led from the natural world to this superstructure, the path which is not only in the past which has unfolded but also in us.'

[96] PP, pp. 152–153/p. 154.

[97] PP, pp. 152–153/p. 154.

[98] VI, p. 197/p. 248.

4.5   Rules and Customs: The Furrows of the World

We can now return to Descombes, and his reading of Wittgenstein. As we have seen in the previous section, the chiasm helps us to refine *praxis* as our relationship towards the world. We have seen that the subject of *praxis* is what Merleau-Ponty called a *Je peux,* or also the *'j'en suis'*: A bodily-being-in-the-world, a subject intimately related with the world it inhabits. This is very different, both from the authoritative subject Descombes criticises, and from the empty grammatical subject he proposes. In the remainder of this chapter, I want to argue that his own solution to what he called the moral circle of autonomy—Wittgenstein's theory of rule-following—is untenable without a conception of *praxis*. Indeed. Descombes' failure to understand the subject of rule-following has as its consequence that he cannot make sense of rule-following at all. In this section, I will come back to Wittgenstein's example of teaching someone to play chess in order to point out where Descombes' mistake lies, and how it can be solved. Then, I will argue that this has everything to do with what to make of Wittgenstein's concept of 'customs'.

Taking into account our argument of the previous sections means that we should reject a view saying that learning to play chess as the example of following a rule should, first of all, be understood as learning a set of conventions, the rules of the game. Rather, what should be learned, first of all, is the *situation* of the chess player. A teacher should make his pupil familiar with the field as a battle field, and the different pieces as forming an army, indeed *his or her* army, attacking and defending. Without this first-person agential viewpoint, the rules do not tell anybody anything, though there is no rule telling that one should take that viewpoint. Indeed, beyond that first-person singular viewpoint of the chess player, the agent should take the viewpoint of a first person plural agent, as it takes two to get involved in playing *the game* of waging a battle, as distinct from getting involved in waging a battle. The pupil should then get to know every particular piece and its characteristics. The way in which the pieces can move says something about their value in the game. What should be learned by the pupil is how to *perceive* the game. But, this is only possible by situating oneself as a player touching and moving the pieces, even if one does not actually play. Only by (would-be) playing will one learn to see what makes a 'good' move, when to attack or to defend, etc. Indeed, it is not a spirit that plays chess, but an embodied, and thus situated, subject. Understanding this situation, and the fun it may bring, one is caught by the game and already learning the rules.[99] Game after game, one will become more experienced, better at 'seeing' the

---

[99] In this respect, I tend to disagree with Waldenfels, who sometimes seems to think that the bodily situation is something preceding (and thus separate from) rule-following in the strict sense. Cf. B. Waldenfels, *Das Leibliche Selbst. Vorlesungen zur Phänomenologie des Leibes,* p. 195: 'Die erste Vorbedingung für die Anwendung einer Regel und eines Gesetzes besteht deshalb darin, daß überhaupt *eine Situation entsteht,* in der diese Regeln oder Gesetze anwenbar sind.' [Italics in the original] Yet, it is my point that rule-following is also a form of sense constitution that is done on a bodily level. In other words, being situated by the rule is already following it. There is no hard distinction between 'being-bodily-situated', on the one hand, and applying a rule, on the other.

right move.[100] One will learn to know directly what a specific situation in the game asks for, and one will learn to respond with the right move. Like this, little by little, one will learn to play the game, learn to follow the rules by becoming not simply 'someone who happens to play chess', but a real chess player.

Now, this alternative reading of the chess example is connected with a specific interpretation of Wittgenstein's concept of 'customs'. This was the question: Should we accept Descombes' emphasis on conventions as the basis of *praxis*? At a certain moment, Wittgenstein tells us that '[a] game, a language, a rule is an institution.'[101] The problem is, however, that he has never explained what he means by this.[102] Let us delve deeper into the issue by returning once again to the example of teacher and pupil. When can we say that a pupil has understood the rule? Wittgenstein answers: 'Let us suppose that after some efforts on the teacher's part, he [the pupil, LC] continues the series correctly, that is, *as we do it*.'[103] In other words, the yardstick by which to judge whether the pupil follows the rule is if his acts are the same as those of (the vast majority of) the other rule-followers.[104] Wittgenstein points to a consensus, the importance of which should not be underestimated: 'This consensus belongs to the essence of *calculation*, so much is certain. I.e.: This consensus is part of the phenomenon of our calculating.'[105] As a consequence, whether or not someone is following a rule depends on 'us', the community of rule-followers. In this way, we may predict their behaviour. However, in this context, it is important to keep in mind that '[t]he prophecy does *not* run that a man will get *this* result when he follows this rule, (...) – but that he will get this result when we *say* that he is following the rule.'[106]

The interesting point that Wittgenstein makes is that rule-following entails an approach to the meaning of a rule that is bound up with what a community of rule-followers says about it. Rule-following ultimately amounts to acting 'as we do it', which Wittgenstein explains with the notion of customs. That is the reason why Descombes points to a conventional element in Wittgenstein's theory of rule-following. Indeed, several other philosophers later developed the concept of institution Wittgenstein hints at in similar ways.[107] His concept of customs is, accordingly, understood as an agreement between the rule-followers on how the rule should be

---

[100] PhI, § 231: '"But surely you can see...?" That is just the characteristic expression of someone who is under the compulsion of a rule.'

[101] RFM, VI § 32.

[102] Cf. Bloor, o.c., p. 27: 'Wittgenstein at no point explained or defined the words "custom", "convention" or "institution".'

[103] PhI, § 145. [My italics, LC]

[104] RFM, VI § 39: 'Here, it is of the greatest importance that all, or the enormous majority of us, agree in certain things. I can, e.g., be quite sure that the colour of this object will be called "green" by far the most of the human beings who see it.'

[105] RFM, III § 67. [Italics in the original]

[106] RFM, III § 66. [Italics in the original]

[107] Most famously, this interpretation was defended by Saul Kripke. It has also been popular among legal philosophers such as H. L .A. Hart.

followed. Consequently, an institution is commonly defined as 'a collective pattern of self-referring activity.'[108]

But perhaps… there is more. How should we picture this self-referential character of rules? David Bloor gives the following explanation.

> Thus the rule "exists" in and through the *practice* of citing it and invoking it in the course of training, in the course of enjoying others to follow it, and in the course of telling them they have not followed it, or not followed it correctly. All of these things are said to others and to oneself, and are heard being said by others. In standard sociological parlance, the rule is an "*actor's category*".[109]

What are we to make of this 'practice'? What does it ultimately mean to say that rules are 'an actor's category'? Is the 'practice' involved in following a rule 'as we do it' really a sort of agreement? Interpreting conventions as agreements would mean that the practice of rule-following is ultimately bound up with an engagement on a linguistic and, thus, intellectual level. There are at least two problems with this interpretation. First of all, this would not correspond to Wittgenstein's emphasis on the 'animal' character of rule-following and the immediacy involved in such an approach. Above, I have developed an interpretation that does try to do justice to these elements.[110] Secondly, and more importantly, understanding conventions as linguistic agreements would entail a relapse into a dualistic theory of rule-following. After all, rule-following would again be dependent on an intellectual act of interpretation; in this case, a joint interpretation by the community of rule-followers.

The question remains then: How does one make sense of Wittgenstein's reference to 'customs' in his explanations of rule-following? Remember that Wittgenstein does not point to rule-following as a practice 'as we *say* we do it'. His reference to action is immediate, i.e., without the detour via language: Rule-following as a practice 'as we *do* it'. Contrary to what Descombes and Bloor seem to suggest, there is a fundamental difference between conventions and customs, when it comes to their social function. What Wittgenstein seems to tell us is that the action involved in rule-following is not of a clearly defined, linguistic character, obtained by intellectual agreement between the members of a community of rule-followers. Rather, 'we' rule-followers act according to a pre-reflective uniformity. Still otherwise, in following a rule we do not act *together*, but *one by one*. This is the only way in which following a rule 'as we do it' does not refer to an intellectual comprehension of the way in which we act.

Indeed, 'as we do it' points to the same immediate practice that we encountered earlier in this chapter.[111] In following the rule 'as we do it', I argue that Wittgenstein

---

[108] Bloor, o.c., p. 33.

[109] Ibid. [My italics, LC]

[110] See Sect. 4.2.

[111] Interestingly, Gustav Radbruch also points to the role customs play in education, cf. G. Radbruch, 'Legal Philosophy', in: K. Wilk (ed. and trans.), *The Legal Philosophies of Lask, Radbruch and Dabin*, Cambridge (Mass.): Harvard University Press 1950, pp. 47–226, at p. 90: 'No education in its beginnings can do without the categorical norm: "That is not done" – which after all is a reference to custom.'

is not pointing to agreements on an intellectual level; once again, he is asking attention for the 'animal' character of rule-following. Following a rule 'as we do it' means that we do not know *how* we do it, but only *that* we do it. This has serious consequences for the 'self' involved in rule-following. This is not a 'we' made by agreements, not a 'we' acting together according to rules agreed upon in advance. Rather, the plural self of rule-following is indiscernible from this very practice.

In one of his texts, Wittgenstein, indeed, refers to 'customs' in order to understand the ability to follow a rule.[112] Yet, the original German term, '*Gepflogenheiten*', helps us to see better what is at stake here. This concept refers to 'the things we do just so', but it does so in a rather specific way. The word is connected to the verb '*pflügen*' which means 'to plough'. If '*Gepflogenheiten*' translates as 'customs', we should hear the association with furrows rather than (tacit) agreements. In ploughing a furrow one follows a line, projecting oneself to a reference point far ahead, and approaching it step by step by mediating reference points or 'depth clues'. But, in the context of action and *praxis,* one should also read this in reverse order: One can only follow a line (a rule) by ploughing, i.e., by taking a direction step by step, one 'depth clue' after another, until one is sure that one is going straight ahead. So, what Wittgenstein is alluding to, in my view, is a much more direct and pre-reflective interaction with the world and others than the term 'conventions' suggests. He refers to our bodily being inserted into the world. The 'technical capacity' demanded for rule-following amounts to this: The *praxis* of following a rule always presupposes a subject that is already embedded in the world, and a world that is something so familiar at those moments, that I feel myself guided, bound by the rule.

There is, then, an obvious agreement between the thoughts of Merleau-Ponty and Wittgenstein. The bodily insertion into the rule, the moment of *attaching* myself to it, being guided by it, is the 'cinematic plunge' described by Merleau-Ponty. It is exactly this ability of *bodily* taking up the situation that we described above, that is always presupposed in Wittgenstein's theory of rule-following. The practical capacity necessary to follow a rule that Wittgenstein alludes to is the bodily being-in-the-world of Merleau-Ponty. Put differently, when it comes to an understanding of constituent power, the analytic philosopher, Wittgenstein, and the phenomenologist, Merleau-Ponty, are much closer to each other than Descombes wants us to believe. The specific subject that is able to follow rules as Wittgenstein alluded to is the one Merleau-Ponty described, the *J'en suis* or *Je peux.* What I have tried to show is how this specific notion is necessary in order to make sense of the practical capacity involved in political and legal philosophy.[113]

This also entails a new understanding of the meaning of rules.[114] Following a rule 'as we do it' means that, going from case to case, the meaning of the rule itself

---

[112] PhI, § 199: 'To obey a rule, to make a report, to give an order, to play a game of chess, are *customs* (uses, institutions).' [Italics in the original]

[113] Cf. P. Ricoeur, o.c., p. 181: 'To understand the term "capacity" correctly, we must return to Merleau-Ponty's "I can" and extend it from the physical to the ethical level.'

[114] For this understanding of meaning, see: PP, pp. 170 and 192/pp. 172 and 193.

is at stake, time and again. In other words, meaning is formed in the practice of following, i.e., meaning is 'originating'.[115] The meaning of a rule does not exist independently from its application as if it were some kind of ideal reality. Applying a rule to a new case means giving it a new life. Paradoxically, if and only if the "original meaning" of the rule is forgotten, can it be truly alive.[116] Following a rule would no longer be an infinite repetition of the same meaning applied to the case at hand, not even by way of an infinite extension of a core meaning. Rather, following a rule is an endless work of taking up what is given. The reason for this is, as Merleau-Ponty says: 'The only way to renew, to remember a production, is by producing.'[117] As we have seen, such a new act, a speaking speech, can only work and become part of the established meanings if one claims that it was always already there. It can only sediment if, retrospectively, one finds the new meaning in what was already given.[118] What we can witness here is what Merleau-Ponty calls 'the "originary" sense, the emerging or arising sense.'[119] As a consequence, a rule is open, as a work of art is. Like works of art, rules, first of all, situate us towards them in a bodily way. Through this bodily being situated, we are able to see the depth of the rule and the direction in which it points. Therefore, legal certainty means, first and foremost, that in the case where I am to follow the rule, it will situate me towards a sense that is perceivable in the specific meaning analysed above. When I am involved in a case (and I always am when I have to follow the rule) the rule will involve me in its movement, will point in a direction that concerns me. Rules open up an endlessly fertile field of meaningful action for those who are able to carry on in the direction in which they are pointed. Only actions that respect this given sense by taking it up may take root and remain as a "meaningful interpretation" of the rule.

4.6   Conclusion

In this chapter, I first followed Descombes' inquiry into the notion of the self that culminated in a specific interpretation of Wittgenstein's theory of rule-following. After rejecting this interpretation, I developed my own by showing how Wittgenstein points to the bodily character of rule-following. In the third section, I scrutinised the bodily nature of sense-constitution by looking into perception in the domain of art. It became clear that constitution always involves passivity, and that it should, therefore, be understood as the creative-passive activity of an embodied

---

[115] VI, p. 124/p. 163.

[116] I am paraphrasing what Merleau-Ponty says about traditions, cf. HL, especially pp. 28–29/pp. 32–34.

[117] HL, p. 42/p. 51.

[118] HL, p. 19/p. 21: 'In the geometry which results from it, this sense is read as a necessity. It belongs to its essence.'

[119] HL, p. 18/p. 19.

subject. In Sect. 4.4, this was connected with Merleau-Ponty's notion of perception as the model of *praxis*, our bodily being in the world. This analysis of perception has helped us to understand the nature of the subject of sense-constitution and rule-following. With Merleau-Ponty, this subject was characterised as *Je peux*, a notion that was later replaced by its ontological counterpart *J'en suis*. Finally, in Sect. 4.5, I returned to Descombes' reading of Wittgenstein, one last time. Instead of a conventionalist reading of the latter's notion of 'customs', I argued that an interpretation that emphasizes the meaning of our embodied being in the world is crucial to understand how to follow a rule.

Chapter 5
Constituting Competence: The Court of Justice and the European Legal Order

Let me recapture the trajectory until this point. I started out with the thesis that the problem of creeping competences, and the doctrine of implied powers in EU law, questions the traditional way in which the relationship between constituent (constituting) power and constituted (constitutional) power is understood. After rejecting the current theories on constitution-making in Chap. 2, an alternative model was developed in Chaps. 3 and 4. This alternative was inspired, above all, by the work of Maurice Merleau-Ponty. I held that constitution of a polity is a species of a more encompassing genus: constitution of sense. With Merleau-Ponty, I argued that constitution of sense always occurs on a bodily level, as it is intimately bound up with the specific structure of perception. Five points were important in this respect. First of all, perceiving always means being bodily situated in a field. Secondly, there is a specific bodily way of dealing with the situation at hand, and the tasks that need to be performed. Thirdly, it is my perceiving body that constitutes sense by taking its cue from (in both the active and the passive sense of the word) the sense of the world. Fourthly, the intimate bond between subject and world is caught in the new notion of the subject as '*j'en suis*'. Lastly, this notion involves a chiasm of passivity and activity in sense-constitution, bearing out the ontological element that Merleau-Ponty calls 'flesh'.

It is now time to return to the legal problems discussed in the first chapter of this inquiry. There, I have outlined the phenomenon of 'creeping competences' of the European Union. In this regard, special attention was paid to the role of the European Court of Justice (ECJ) and its doctrine of implied powers, as an emblematic case of creeping competences. It was my thesis that the doctrine of implied powers questions the traditional way in which the relationship between constituent (constituting) power and constituted (constitutional) power is understood. The alternative I developed pivots around a chiastic understanding of the relationship between the two poles, which amounts to taking seriously a dimension of passivity in constitution. In this chapter, I will show what the philosophical investigation has brought us in terms of a better understanding of competence and constitution in the context of European Union law. There can be little doubt that these issues arise mainly in the politico-legal relationships between the Union (or the Community) and the

Member States.[1] Moreover, the major part of these issues passes through the sieve of the European judiciary under the guise of (often vigorously debated) procedures. Granting that in an important sense, all courts in the Member States participate in the 'European judiciary', I will focus on the specific situation of the European Court of Justice in the European legal order to see if my theory is able to throw new light on the authoritative decisions that purport to end these conflicts. But, even if it turns out to have some explanatory potential, my theory will certainly not usher in a full-blooded account of the ECJ's decision-making in matters of legal competence. In Sect. 5.1, I will explore two features that are characteristic of the ECJ's position in its relation to the national courts: The preliminary question procedure, and the *acte clair* doctrine. I will argue that this specific institutional constellation situates the ECJ in such a way that its activity can only be understood as the other side of passivity. Then, I will turn to more substantive competence issues by submitting three case studies, firstly (Sect. 5.2), with regard to the rise of 'a federal common law' in Europe; secondly (Sect. 5.3), with regard to the 'Europeanisation of public (here: administrative) law'; thirdly (Sect. 5.4), with regard to fundamental rights in European law. Central to the analysis of these three case studies will be how the chiastic relationship between constituent and constitutional power appears in the reasoning of the ECJ. Finally, in Sect. 5.5, I will come back to the issue of passivity once more. This will be done in a discussion of the constitutionalisation of European Union law, claiming that a better understanding of competence developments does not always imply approval, but sometimes lends support to a critical attitude.

5.1   Situating the European Court of Justice: Preliminary Ruling and *Acte Clair*

The position of the ECJ, in the wider context of politico-legal relationships between the Union and its Member States, may be characterised by at least two peculiar features: The preliminary question procedure, and the *acte clair* concept. The former follows from the Treaty, the latter has developed as part of the ECJ's ruling in *CILFIT*. What will interest us most in these features is the way in which competence oscillates between the poles of constituent and constitutional power, in view of re-enforcing the common market.

---

[1] As this chapter will discuss some case law from before the coming into force of the Treaty of Lisbon, both the terms 'European Union' and 'European Community' will have to be used. Between 1993 and 2009, the European Union encompassed three pillars. The first pillar consisted of the three (now two) European Communities: The European Atomic Energy Community (EAEC or EURATOM), the European Community (EC) and the now-expired European Coal and Steel Community (ECSC). The second pillar was formed by the Common Foreign and Security Policy (CFSP) and the third pillar was made up of the Police and Judicial Cooperation in Criminal Matters (PJCC). With the coming into force of the Treaty of Lisbon (1 December 2009) the pillar structure has been abolished.

The preliminary question procedure is enshrined in Article 267 TFEU (ex Article 234 EC): 'The Court of Justice of the European Union shall have jurisdiction to give preliminary rulings concerning: (a) the interpretation of the Treaties; (b) the validity and interpretation of acts of the institutions, bodies, offices or agencies of the Union; Where such a question is raised before any court or tribunal of a Member State, that court or tribunal may, if it considers that a decision on the question is necessary to enable it to give judgment, request the Court to give a ruling thereon. Where any such question is raised in a case pending before a court or tribunal of a Member State against whose decisions there is no judicial remedy under national law, that court or tribunal shall bring the matter before the Court. If such a question is raised in a case pending before a court or tribunal of a Member State with regard to a person in custody, the Court of Justice of the European Union shall act with the minimum of delay.' This procedure was especially made in order to enable the ECJ to guard the unity of EU law. In other words, with the help of this procedure, the ECJ, prompted by the Member State courts, establishes what is to be regarded as *law* in the EU legal order.[2] As such, it constitutes 'the "jewel in the crown" of the ECJ's jurisdiction.'[3] The relevance of this procedure, for our inquiry, is beyond dispute since '[i]t is through preliminary ruling that the ECJ has developed concepts such as direct effect and supremacy,'[4] in other words, the fault-lines of competence issues.

The ECJ itself has always characterised the nature of the preliminary question procedure as cooperative, implying some sort of horizontality. Yet, recent case law has led some commentators to speak of a changed picture. Craig and De Bùrca, for instance, argue that the ECJ has introduced what is, 'in effect', a system of precedent.[5] In this respect, the first important case was the ECJ's decision in *Da Costa*. Since the factual and legal situation of this case was equal to that which gave rise to the ECJ's decision in *Van Gend en Loos,* the Court held that the national judge could be referred to that decision.[6] This line has been developed further in the case of *CILFIT,* where the Court formulated its thoughts on the preliminary question procedure in more detail. In this case, the ECJ established the doctrines of *acte clair* and *acte éclairé,* and en passant, gave a lesson in how to interpret Community law.[7] First, the

---

[2] Important in this respect is also the Court's mandate in Article 19, paragraph 1 TEU. See my comments on this Article later in Sect. 5.5, below.

[3] P. Craig & G. de Bùrca, *EU Law. Text, Cases, and Materials* (4th edition), Oxford (etc.): Oxford University Press 2008, p. 460. On the importance of this procedure, see also: P. Craig, 'The Jurisdiction of the Community Courts Reconsidered', in: G. de Bùrca and J.H.H. Weiler (eds.), *The European Court of Justice,* Oxford (etc.): Oxford University Press 2001, pp. 177–214, at pp. 181–182 and A. Arnull, *The European Union and its Court of Justice* (2nd edition), Oxford (etc.): Oxford University Press 2006 pp. 97–104.

[4] P. Craig & G. de Bùrca, o.c., p. 461.

[5] P. Craig & G. de Bùrca, o.c., p. 468. See also A. Arnull, o.c., pp. 625–633.

[6] Cases 28–30/62, *Da Costa en Schaake NV, Jacob Meijer NV and Hoechst-Holland NV v. Nederlandse Belastingadministratie* [1963] ECR 31.

[7] On the importance of this lesson, given that the Treaties do not contain a specific provision regarding the interpretation of EC law: G. Itzcovich, 'The Interpretation of Community Law by the European Court of Justice', *German Law Journal*, vol. 10 (2009), pp. 537–560, at pp. 546–549.

ECJ argued that a national judge has to take into account the different languages in which Community law is drafted, and the fact that a particular concept in EC law that also exists in a Member State may still have another meaning than the one in the national legal order. Then, the ECJ concluded as follows:

> Finally, every provision of Community law must be placed in its context and interpreted in the light of the provisions of Community law as a whole, regard being had to the objectives thereof and to its state of evolution at the date on which the provision in question is to be applied.
>
> (...) [A] court or tribunal against whose decisions there is no judicial remedy under national law is required, where a question of Community law is raised before it, to comply with its obligation to bring the matter before the Court of Justice, unless it has established that the question raised is irrelevant or that the Community provision in question has already been interpreted by the Court or that the correct application of Community law is so obvious as to leave no scope for any reasonable doubt. The existence of such a possibility must be assessed in the light of the specific characteristics of Community law, the particular difficulties to which its interpretation gives rise and the risk of divergences in judicial decisions within the Community.[8]

Thanks to the cases of *Da Costa* and *CILIFIT,* so it is argued, the very nature of the preliminary question procedure has changed: a judgment of the ECJ is now valid, not only for the referring national court, but for all national courts in all Member States.[9]

However, it is questionable whether the term 'precedent' covers the crucial part preliminary rulings have played and continue to play in the development of EC law. As is well-known, the concept of precedent comes from the system of common law. There, it refers, first of all, to the *past,* to wit, to an existing and, therefore, authoritative way of following the rule. It finds a home in the policy of *stare decisis,* which is, in the words of the Ninth Circuit Court of Appeals, '(...) but an abbreviation of *stare decisis et quieta non movere* – "to stand by and adhere to decisions and not disturb what is settled."'[10] In the vocabulary of the third chapter of this study: the doctrine of precedent means the primacy of spoken speech, i.e., the primacy of established or settled legal sense. Note that this philosophical vocabulary neither implies that courts are bound by the wordings of a previous decision by a superior court, nor that courts are obliged to replicate the reasoning behind the decision in a relevant case. It solely points to how a *given* line of mapping certain facts to certain legal consequences should be continued and extended. Since all sorts of teleological ramifications can enter the court's re-construction of this line, the doctrine of precedent involves not only the past, but also the future.

Now, is this the way in which the preliminary question procedure functions? I think it is not. First of all, in an important sense, Member State courts refer is-

---

[8] Case 283/81, *Srl CILFIT and Lanificio de Gavardo SpA v. Ministry of Health,* [1982] ECR 3415, par. 20–21.

[9] Craig and De Bùrca mark this change as one from a bilateral to a multilateral system. Cf. P. Craig & G. de Bùrca, o.c., p. 477.

[10] Cf. United States Internal Revenue Serv. v. Osborne (In re Osborne), 76 F.3d 306, 96-1 U.S. Tax Cas. (CCH) par. 50, 185 (9th Cir. 1996), available at: http://laws.findlaw.com/9th/9455890.html [visited on 30 October 2009].

sues to the ECJ, precisely if and when they see *no* precedent to guide them with regard to the interpretation or the validity of a certain provision. Indeed, as the above quote from *CILFIT* illustrates, the ECJ encourages them not to request a preliminary ruling if '(…) the Community provision in question has already been interpreted by the Court, or (…) the correct application of Community law is so obvious as to leave no scope for any reasonable doubt.' This twofold condition reflects what *acte éclairé* (the first part) resp. *acte clair* (the second part) amount to. So if there is a *doctrine* of precedent in EU law, it appears under the guise of the twin doctrines of *acte clair* and *acte éclairé,* not under the practice of preliminary procedure itself. This procedure is the institutional framework in which legal certainty is provided in the European legal order and, as we will examine more closely below, the relationship between national court and ECJ is characterised by both hierarchy and cooperation. Telling for the difference with the doctrine of precedent is that, under *acte clair,* national courts are supposed to do exactly what the doctrine of precedent expects them to do: To (re-)construe from the past a line of decision-making that is 'obvious' (*clair*), while taking their cue, not from a specific case (as with precedent and *acte éclairé*) but from an authoritative action (*acte*) of the European legislator.

Secondly, together with what I called the ECJ's encouragement to apply precedent, comes a warning that courts should not assume too easily that the rule in the matter is obvious. In order to avert abuse by means of self-proclaimed obviousness, the ECJ, in fact, conveys the message that, in general, there will not easily be precedent in cases where courts struggle with the interpretation or validity of provisions of EU law. To this effect, it provides its acceptance of *acte clair* with a number of qualifications which, according to some lawyers,[11] tend to willingly suffocate the whole point of the doctrine. The general qualification is that the meaning some national court believes to be obvious, should be equally obvious to the courts in other Member States and to the ECJ. The ECJ is quick to detail along which cumbersome paths such a conviction may be reached. The path of comparative linguistics is only the first one: To compare the different versions of the provision in (presumably all) languages of the Community. This may have been a feasible exercise in 1982, when *CILFIT* was decided, but it is virtually impossible with the present 23 official languages in the EU. The second methodological exercise is in comparative law: Legal concepts and terminology do not necessarily have the same meaning in EU law as in national law.[12] Last but not least, the ECJ emphasises that 'every provision of Community law must be placed in its context, and interpreted in the light of the provisions of Community law as a whole, regard being had to the objectives thereof, and to its state of evolution at the date on which the provision in question

---

[11] Cf. H. Rasmussen, 'The European's Court *Acte Clair* Strategy in *CILFIT*', *European Law Journal,* vol. 9 (1984), pp. 242–259.

[12] For a recent study on conceptual divergence in EU law, cf. S. Prechal and B. van Roermund (eds.), *The Coherence of EU Law: The Search for Unity in Divergent Concepts,* Oxford (etc.): Oxford University Press 2008.

is to be applied.'[13] In this respect, most lawyers will acknowledge, for instance in the wording by T. C. Hartley, that '(...) in the case of Community law (...), the policy-oriented approach of the European Court can produce very different results from the more traditional methods of an English judge.'[14] That is to say, the main parameter in these decisions is not the past and the precedent, but rather, the future and the new meaning that a provision may get in circumstances that are, by default, unprecedented. In sum, by virtue of these qualifications, the ECJ suggests that a national court's appeal to *acte clair* will rarely be justified, unless pursued along the lines the ECJ itself habitually decides cases.

A third reason why the preliminary ruling procedure does not amount to the introduction of precedent in EU law, is offered by the fact that the ECJ ruling received by the national court(s)—though 'in effect' binding (as Craig and De Bùrca correctly observe)—is binding in ways different from the doctrine of precedent. For one thing, it is imposed by *another* judge, rather than self-imposed by (re-)construction. In this respect, it resembles appeal, rather than precedent. To the extent that this ruling decides the case in point of fact as far as European law is concerned, it is not 'pre-liminary' at all, but simply 'liminary', or final. Of course, it is still the national judge who should ultimately decide the case before him. Nevertheless, the ECJ's answer to the national judge's question is often so detailed that it leaves little room for manoeuvre.[15] The case thus decided by the ECJ is an 'in-cident', rather than a 'pre-cedent'. For another thing, and more importantly, the preliminary ruling is imposed as an answer in response to a question, rather than as a justification of a decision. In this respect, reference is something quite different from appeal. It is also a procedure that is at odds, in principle, with the idea of a legal order as a 'ratio scripta'. In many a civil law system, the judge who decides not to decide on a case 'under the pretext of silence, obscurity, or incompleteness of the law, may be prosecuted on grounds of refusal of the court to exercise its powers.'[16] This basic provision finds its roots in the problems around separation of powers in late Eighteenth Century France. After the Revolution, statutory law became so sacrosanct that the judges were obliged to refer to the maker of statutory law, i.e., the legislator, if they believed the rules to be silent, unclear or incomplete.[17] Thus the legislator was explicitly invited to take over from the judiciary, and to interfere in specific cases—with undesirable consequences. Hence the move to the opposite principle: A judge has to decide, under the pretext that the law harbours an answer—indeed

---

[13] Case 283/81, *Srl CILFIT and Lanificio de Gavardo SpA v. Ministry of Health,* [1982] ECR 3415, par. 20.

[14] T.C. Hartley, *The Foundations of European Community Law* (3rd ed.), Oxford: Clarendon 1994, p. 292.

[15] Cf. P. Craig & G. de Bùrca, o.c., pp. 493–494.

[16] According to Dutch law, Art 13 Wet Algemene Bepalingen. This provision is a literal translation of Article 4 of the Code Napoléon, see: Ch. Perelman, *Logique juridique: Nouvelle rhétorique,* Toulouse Dalloz 1976, n°14.

[17] The loi de 16–24 août 1790 on the organisation of the judiciary. See also Ch. Perelman, o.c., n°14.

'one right answer'—to all cases that the judiciary is competent to hear. If the answer is wrong, this will be decided in appeal, but not by referring. Now the preliminary procedure—as for instance Perelman already noted[18]—does not refer to the legislator, but to a higher judge. So, separation of powers is not at issue. But, at least to some extent, legal certainty *is*: Here is a national court, granting by its preliminary question, that it is quite sure that European law is a necessary source in the case at hand, but unsure what this source says. If the judge does not know prior to ruling by the ECJ, how are legal subjects supposed to know?

On closer inspection, however, the responsive structure of the preliminary ruling procedure appears to be the specific mode in which legal certainty is provided, and by which it reveals its true meaning. Firstly, the preliminary procedure drops the presupposition of the doctrine of precedent that, by legal definition, the future is an extension of the past, thus upholding a practice of rule-following that stays closer to the perception of the politico-legal environment in which the decision is to be made. This may be counted as a loss by those who define legal certainty as the certainty that a legal order will always reduce new cases to old ones, and blindly replicate the decisions made in the latter to apply to the former. But, this is not how law is envisaged, and this is not what legal certainty means, from an agential point of view. For an agent, certainty in law means access to justice in the justified expectation that one's case will be heard in all its singular details, rather than as a token of some well-known type. And, even if one favours an observational angle on a legal order, i.e., even those who defend the view that legal certainty amounts to predictability, one will admit that predicting legal decisions may be much harder than giving a five days weather forecast for Iceland, precisely because all sorts of parameters have to be calculated, without there being much of a model defining how their values are to be measured.

Secondly, the responsive structure of the preliminary procedure rests on the various intertwinements of question and answer, revealing how the discursive structure of judicial decision-making, in the European context, is built. Only the most superficial of these would be that there is no preliminary ruling (by the ECJ) without reference (by the Member State courts) and no reference without preliminary ruling. There are more subtle intertwinements between question and answer.[19] One of them is the chiasm of time. Though trivially, the question precedes the answer, it cannot be denied that it precedes the answer *in anticipating it*. By asking a question, the speaker opens up a question-realm in which the answer is expected to appear. This clearly applies to the preliminary question procedure: Article 267 TFEU says, in so many words, that the request by the Member State courts to give a ruling should be raised upon the consideration 'that a decision on the question [i.e., on an EU law issue; LC] is necessary to enable it to give judgment.' Thus, the national courts are supposed to anticipate the relevance of EU law in the matter, in a rather specific way. Indeed, it is not just 'relevance' in general which they anticipate, but (a) relevance in the case at hand, and (b) relevance in the sense of a necessary

---

[18] Ch. Perelman, o.c., n° 14, footnote 35.

[19] Cf. B. Waldenfels, *Antwortregister*, Frankfurt am Main: Suhrkamp 1994.

condition for deciding the case. From a European law perspective, theirs is a pre-judgment in the matter, while the ECJ's judgment is final; but from a Member State perspective, the reverse is true: The ECJ's judgment is preliminary, the national court gives final judgment.[20] Another intertwinement between question and answer regards the distinction between the *contents* of question and answer, on the one hand, and the *act* of addressing someone in questioning and answering, on the other. Following Husserl, Waldenfels points to 'the bi-polarity between *Sachfrage* and *Anfrage*;'[21] and with Karl Bühler, he explains how the multifarious functions of the latter condition the former, and vice versa. For instance, not all questioning is intended to have a gap in one's knowledge filled out by the respondent, not even if the question pertains to a state of affairs. Some questions are meant to show that the addressee's gap of knowledge is even bigger than the adressant's (e.g., 'Which other operas did Beethoven write, apart from Fidelio?'). Others are meant to elicit an explanation, sometimes as a step towards accusation or excuse. If one does wish to have one's knowledge gap filled out, this requires a specific way of addressing one's interlocutor. This brings us to the next feature of the preliminary procedure, pertaining to the mutual relationships that are established by references and rulings.

So thirdly, the preliminary question procedure ensures the *unity* of EU law by a give-and-take between the Union and the Member States, with regard to the monopoly on the interpretation of EU law.[22] Lawyers have observed that introducing binding preliminary ruling, and the *acte clair*-doctrine, has led to 'a more effective regime of Community law.'[23] The national courts have become more involved in the process of interpreting and applying EU law.[24] Collaboration is thus the key term, at first sight. At the same time, however, the ECJ has made it clear that it regards itself, and itself only, as the final instance that is to give an authoritative decision on European law. In the second case of *Foglia*, the ECJ took an active stance towards its own jurisdiction:

> Whilst the spirit of cooperation which must govern the performance of the duties assigned by Article 177 [now Article 267 TFEU] to the national courts, on the one hand, and the Court of Justice, on the other, requires the latter to have regard to the national court's proper responsibilities, it implies, at the same time that the national court, in the use which it makes of the facilities provided by Article 177, should have regard to the proper function of the Court of Justice in this field.[25]

---

[20] Ibid., p. 23: 'Fragen werden gestellt, wie Urteile gefällt werden'.

[21] Ibid., p. 31.

[22] Cf. Itzcovich, o.c., p. 545 and footnote 17 for references to relevant case law.

[23] Cf. P. Craig & G. de Bùrca, o.c., p. 477. Of course, now we would say 'EU law'.

[24] Cf. P. Craig & G. de Bùrca, o.c., p. 478: 'The national courts are, in this sense, "enrolled" as part of a network of courts adjudicating on Community law, with the ECJ at the apex of that network. They become "delegates" in the enforcement of EC law, and part of a broader Community judicial hierarchy.' For more on the (sometimes) difficult relationship between the ECJ and national judges, see: D. R. Phelan, *Revolt or Revolution: The Constitutional Boundaries of the European Community,* Dublin: Round Hall Sweet & Maxwell 1997 and M.L.H.K. Claes, *The National Courts' Mandate in the European Constitution,* Oxford: Hart Publishing 2006.

[25] Case 244/80, *Pasquale Foglia v. Mariella Novello (No. 2)* [1981] ECR 3045, par. 18–20.

In this case, the ECJ emphasized its task as a Court, i.e., a body giving *binding* decisions, and not just legal advice. Craig and De Bùrca argue, therefore, that there has been a shift from horizontality to verticality in the preliminary ruling procedure.[26] Even though this might seem an innocent conclusion, the underlying legal-philosophical problem is that of the final legal authority in the European legal order. In other words, the problem of judicial *Kompetenz-Kompetenz* arises here. By interpreting the second case of *Foglia* as the final stage of a shift from horizontality to verticality, some lawyers seem to argue that the question which court holds the ultimate legal authority in the European legal order, is solved in favour of the ECJ.[27]

But is this really the case? A close reading of the excerpt of the second case of *Foglia* reveals that the ECJ sticks with the language of cooperation. This 'spirit of cooperation' makes that 'the duties' assigned to the national courts and the ECJ, should be seen against the background of 'the proper function of the Court of Justice in this field', and 'the national court's proper responsibilities.' This shows, in essence, what I would call the chiastic structure of the preliminary question procedure. As agents in the gradual unfolding of European law, the ECJ and the national courts are dependent on each other. To return once more to *Foglia*:

> (...) it should be pointed out that, whilst the Court of Justice must be able to place as much reliance as possible upon the assessment by the national court of the extent to which the questions submitted are essential, it must be in a position to make any assessment inherent in the performance of its own duties in particular in order to check, as all courts must, whether it has jurisdiction. Thus the Court, taking into account the repercussions of its decisions in this matter, must have regard, in exercising the jurisdiction conferred upon it by Article 177 [now Article 267 TFEU], not only to the interests of the parties to the proceedings, but also to those of the Community and of the Member States. Accordingly it cannot, without disregarding the duties assigned to it, remain indifferent to the assessments made by the courts of the Member States in the exceptional cases in which such assessments may affect the proper working of the procedure laid down by Article 177.[28]

This language neither trades means for ends, nor collaboration for hierarchy, nor verticality for horizontality. It re-arranges them, so that the poles become interdependent and mutually productive. On the one hand, from the perspective of the ECJ, it is directly linked up with its own function, or as I will call it, 'end', that is to safeguard the unity of EU law. On the other hand, from the perspective of a national court, the preliminary question procedure seems to be a means ('the facilities') to come to a decision in the conflict at hand. But, even the language of 'on the one hand' and 'on the other hand' falls short of what is really argued here. The issue of collaboration and hierarchy may perhaps clarify what is at issue. The point is that there can be no collaboration without hierarchy, nor hierarchy without collaboration. The common error is to think that hierarchy is

---

[26] Cf. P. Craig & G. de Bùrca, o.c., p. 500.

[27] Cf. P. Craig & G. de Bùrca, o.c., pp. 493–494, where the authors argue that also the fact that the ECJ has been willing to make more and more specific decisions under the preliminary ruling procedure shows how the co-operative nature of the procedure goes hand in hand with the role of the ECJ, as ultimate decision-maker.

[28] *Foglia*, par. 19.

necessarily linked with the metaphor of a pyramid. But it is not; the metaphor of the web or the network, though more fashionable in our day, is equally expressive of hierarchy. Draw a realistic picture of a network of interactions, and you will immediately see where the main crossing points are. Hence, you will realise which points you have to occupy in order to play the game, whatever its name. As soon as you start playing the game, you will detect the need for hierarchy from the inside: No collaboration without coordination, and no coordination without authority. Similarly, if you hold on to the pyramid metaphor of a hierarchy, and picture yourself at the top as final authority, you will soon detect how dependent you are on people at 'lower' places to keep exercising this authority successfully. So, what the preliminary procedure does, in point of fact, is to defuse the language of monopoly, to neutralise sterile oppositions, and to propose that the unity of the European legal order lies as much in the common enterprise of referring and ruling, as in a grand idea of Europe that has to be deployed.

In this light, the problem of judicial *Kompetenz-Kompetenz* in Europe merits rethinking.[29] Usually, this issue, i.e., the question who holds ultimate judicial authority in the EU legal order, is answered by pointing either to the ECJ, or to the national judiciary. What is taken for granted in these answers is a view of legal competences as a hierarchy, i.e., a chain of legal powers that leads right to a highest authority. However, my analysis makes clear that grasping competences in a hierarchy does not solve the problem because posing a 'highest authority' will always lead to the call for a new highest authority, etc. What should be recognised is that, in legal constitution, there remains a moment that cannot be legally captured. Some would call this a moment of violence. I have argued, however, that this is a moment of passivity *in* constitution.[30] This moment bears witness of the chiastic interrelatedness of constituent and constituted power, of how constitution roots in passivity. EU law is oriented to the ends that take root in that dimension. Thus, in answering a preliminary question, the ECJ will try to find the solution that is best for the future development of EU law. Its decisions often create new legal meaning, however, without cutting its rulings loose from the legal traditions of the Member States in which they are to be applied.

A fourth, and last, point to characterise the position of the ECJ, via the features of the preliminary procedure and its responsive structure, may be added. It goes to the role of 'passivity' in this procedure. To avoid misunderstandings, let me say that I introduce this notion here, neither in order to play down the active role of the ECJ in the development of EU law, nor to promote or criticise what some call the 'judicial

---

[29] There is also, of course, that other European court, the European Court of Human Rights (ECtHR). For the relationship between the ECtHR and the ECJ, the latter's case law on fundamental rights is important, see Sect. 5.4, below.

[30] In an article to which I am much indebted Hans Lindahl already points to the passivity *of* constitution, see: H. Lindahl, 'The paradox of constituent power. The ambiguous self-constitution of the European Union', *Ratio Juris: An International Journal of Jurisprudence and Philosophy of Law*, vol. 20 (2007), pp. 485–505. He does not, however, connect this to the bodily character of constitution.

activism' of this Court.[31] Quite different issues are at stake. These issues are immediately linked with what understanding constitution as constitution *in passivity* entails for the ECJ's role as 'a decision-making authority', as Everling has once characterised it.[32] The first is that the ECJ is 'passive', not only in that it awaits requests for rulings from the Member State courts, but also, and more importantly, in the sense that it will only give a ruling if it is really in the position of 'being placed before a decision'. The ECJ denies that it has jurisdiction on advisory opinions, in general, or hypothetical questions.

> It must in fact be emphasized that the duty assigned to the Court by Article 177 [now Article 267 TFEU] is not that of delivering advisory opinions on general or hypothetical questions but of assisting in the administration of justice in the Member States. It accordingly does not have jurisdiction to reply to questions of interpretation which are submitted to it within the framework of procedural devices arranged by the parties in order to induce the Court to give its views on certain problems of Community law which do not correspond to an objective requirement inherent in the resolution of a dispute. A declaration by the Court that it has no jurisdiction in such circumstances does not in any way trespass upon the prerogatives of the national court but makes it possible to prevent the application of the procedure under Article 177 for purposes other than those appropriate for it.[33]

It has to sense the full weight of the conflict that it will have to decide,[34] in order to take the right decision in the light of what the European legal order requires.

This 'light'—a claire-obscure surely, rather than a ready-made truth—is a second sense in which the ECJ is 'passive', and here again, two aspects may be distinguished. On the one hand, in seeking arguments, the Court follows the line of its previous decisions, also where it decides to take a turn. It either distinguishes where a turn seems appropriate, or it argues that there is a basis in the Treaty, 'after all'. On the other hand, it is passive, in that it is open and sensitive to the ever-changing environment in which European law has to prove its politico-legal value. The policy rationales that are characteristic of its way of argumentation, and that keep an all too formal *stare decisis* at bay, testify to the self-conception of the ECJ as part of the European 'body politic'. That is to say, there is a certain passivity of the Court in what is normally called its 'activism'.

In concluding this section, let me sum up this characterisation of the preliminary procedure on a more general level, and announce how I am going to substantiate this more general view again in the remainder of the present chapter. In this section,

---

[31] Cf. H. de Waele, *Rechterlijk activisme en het Europees Hof van Justitie,* Den Haag: Boom Juridische Uitgevers 2009 and S. Weatherill, 'Activism and Restraint in the European Court of Justice', in P. Capps, M. Evans and S. Konstadinidis (eds), *Asserting Jurisdiction: International and European Legal Perspectives,* Portland (Oregon): Hart 2003, pp. 255–282.

[32] Cf. U. Everling, 'The Court of Justice As an Decisionmaking Authority', *Michigan Law Review,* vol. 82 (1983–1984), pp. 1294–1310.

[33] *Foglia,* par. 18.

[34] Cf. B. van Roermund, *Het verdwijnpunt van de wet. Een opstel over symboolwerking van wetgeving,* Deventer: Tjeenk Willink 1997. See also: B. van Roermund, 'The Origin of Legal Rules', paper presented on the Conference 'The Species of Origin', Glasgow, 13–14 December 2007. Available at: www.speciesoforigin.org/FCKeditor/File/BVR_Origin.pdf [Visited on 25 October 2009].

I have characterised the preliminary question procedure as one that is distinctively different from a system led by the rule of precedent, especially because of its orientation towards the future. Taking my cue from the *acte clair* doctrine, I have argued that the preliminary procedure constitutes the specific way in which legal certainty is provided in the EU legal order. This specific constellation shows, first, an emphasis on the specific situation (in all its details) of the case to be decided; second, the intertwinement of answer and response on different levels; third, the chiastic interdependence between national courts and ECJ that blurs a strict distinction between hierarchy and cooperation; and fourth, the passivity of adjudication in Europe in the twofold sense of the ECJ being placed 'before the decision', and open to the changing conditions in which European law should function, while proceeding from the line of decisions already taken. Thus, the general form in which legal certainty is provided is the ECJ following the rule in a chiastic way: In its judging, constitution and passivity are intertwined. Or, with the closing words of the Israeli Supreme Court Judge, Aharon Barak: 'Whenever I enter the courtroom, I do so with the deep sense that, as I sit at a trial, I stand on trial.'[35]

Now, how does this relate to a better understanding of the 'competence creep'? This will be the question central to the remainder of this chapter. In the next three sections, I will first look into several case studies that articulate the chiasm of constitution in the sphere of competence issues. In other words, I will argue that in different domains, the ECJ's reasoning on legal powers reveals the chiastic interrelatedness between constituent power and constituted power. Together, these case studies provide us with a good overview of the ECJ's case law in fields as far removed from each other as private law and administrative law and in the important field of human rights. Accordingly, I will, first of all, critically examine the cases on implied powers by connecting these with a broader development in the Court's case law known as 'federal common law.' Then, I will pay attention to the so-called 'Europeanisation of Public law', and especially to the much debated Pupino-judgment. Thirdly, I will turn to the case law concerning human rights, where the ECJ takes up the 'common traditions of the Member States.' At the end of this third case study, I will also explain what the passive dimension of this constituting activity amounts to. In the last section of this chapter, I will try to understand how the ECJ's so-called activism relates to its mandate that calls upon it 'to ensure that the law is observed.'

5.2   'Federal Common Law' and the Conundrum of Implication Solved

As I showed in the first chapter, implied powers are an emblematic case of a phenomenon that continues to cast doubts on the authority of European law, in general, and the position of the European Court of Justice, in particular. This phenomenon

---

[35] A. Barak, *The Judge in a Democracy,* Princeton, NJ: Princeton University Press 2008 [2006], p. 315.

was referred to as 'creeping competences,' a process in which competences are taken from the Member States, and given to the European Union. The case law of the ECJ has played a major role in this development, and the doctrine of implied powers is a case in point. Now, in order to show that the doctrine of implied powers is not unique, that it is indeed what I claim it is, a paradigmatic case of a larger phenomenon, I would like to discuss the case of 'federal common law' in Europe.

At first glance, it might seem rather strange to use the concept of 'federal common law' in the context of the European Union. With the term 'common law', one usually refers to the Anglo-Saxon legal system, in which the role of case law as a legal source is much bigger than in the continental system of 'civil law'. The concept of 'federation' says something about the way in which power is distributed between the local and the central level of a state. So, why would one speak of 'federal common law' in the context of the EU? One cannot simply say that the European legal order constitutes a system of common law, nor that the EU, in its present state, is a federation like the United States of America. There are, however, good reasons to speak of 'federal common law' in Europe, as Koen Lenaerts and Kathleen Gutman argue. Following their definition, this notion captures 'Union and Community concepts, principles and rules of decision formulated by the Court of Justice, that are not clearly suggested from the face of a provision of primary or secondary Community law.'[36] In other words, we are dealing here with judge-made law. Given the crucial role of the ECJ, it is thus justified to use this concept in the EU legal order. Furthermore, one can now understand why this phenomenon is of particular interest to this study: Like the implied powers doctrine, 'federal common law' is an outstanding example of the ECJ, in its constituting activity. The full meaning of this activity can only be grasped if one takes into account the specific role of the judge: Whatever the judiciary does, it is always bound by the law. So, even in the creative work of *making rules,* the judge is, at the very same time, *following the rule.* Lenaerts and Gutman analyse exactly this phenomenon, and their conclusions regarding the reasoning of the ECJ provide us with new insights that improve our understanding of the implied powers doctrine. The other way around, a renewed understanding of implied powers may prove valuable to acknowledge what is philosophically at stake in 'federal common law'.

It is, first of all, important to realise what the making of 'federal common law' entails. Every time the ECJ is confronted with a case revolving around a concept for whose elaboration the EU has not been given competence, but that is needed to reach goals in areas in which the Union does possess competence, the Court finds itself in a situation where it could make federal common law. Interestingly enough, most of the cases of European 'federal common law' arise in the field of private law. For example, in a number of cases, the ECJ was called upon to enlighten the Community concept of '(the leasing and letting of) immovable property'. Now, what is of interest for this inquiry is not so much what this definition of the Court is. Rather,

---

[36] K. Lenaerts and K. Gutman, '"Federal Common Law" in the European Union: A Comparative Perspective from the United States', *The American Journal of Comparative Law,* vol. 54 (2006), pp. 1–121, at p. 7.

we will focus on the steps the ECJ takes to reach the conclusion that it was mandated to formulate such a uniform concept, in the first place. What the Court does in these cases is that it 'is fashioning key concepts within the field of real property law for which the Community legislator has not been given explicit competence, yet doing so within the context of interpreting measures for which the Community legislator has been given competence.'[37] As one might remember, this manner of reasoning is akin to the one the ECJ uses in its case law on implied powers. However, before turning to this similarity, let us now first take a closer look at the scope of "federal common law". As a preliminary, it is important to understand the rise of "federal common law" against the background of the EC Treaty as a *traité cadre*.[38] Instead of a full-fledged blueprint of the European integration project, the Treaty only offered the basic lines. It is deliberately left open for the institutions to fill out. As a consequence, there remains some room for the Court of Justice for lawmaking activity; however, certain limits must be taken into account. These limits are dealt with by a framework, and they can be broken down into questions concerning power, and questions concerning content.[39]

With regard to the power to make "federal common law", a distinction between substantive and adjudicatory power may be drawn. In order to fashion "federal common law", the ECJ should possess a sufficient degree of both. This is a direct consequence of the principle of attributed powers. Regarding the *substantive* power, two bases may be distinguished, and it is exactly at this point that we encounter interesting material for our inquiry. 'Federal common law' may be derived from either "the system of the Treaty", or from other provisions of the Treaty, or secondary community law. The first base is especially important, since it was used when the autonomy of the European legal order was at stake.[40] In other words, while making "federal common law", the ECJ often refers to "the system of the Treaty". In this way, the Court links its own actions directly with the autonomous nature of the European legal order. That is to say, making "federal common law" is connected with what makes the EU order distinct, with what defines its very identity. "Federal common law" is not an anomaly, rather, it follows directly from what it means to say that the European legal order is autonomous.

This is confirmed when we look at the second basis: Provisions of primary or secondary Community law. In this regard, Article 19 TEU is of crucial importance. As one may remember, this provision contains the mandate of the ECJ, and it is

---

[37] Ibid., pp. 65–66.

[38] Cf. L. Senden, *Soft law in European Community law. Its Relationship to Legislation*, Nijmegen: Wolf Legal Publishers 2003, pp. 36–37.

[39] K. Lenaerts and K. Gutman, o.c., p. 12: 'The framework governing the scope of the European "federal common law" serves to allay both confusion as to the basis of the Court of Justice's lawmaking power and tensions regarding the limits of such power.'

[40] Ibid., p. 13: 'The Court's power to fashion "common law rules" from "the system of the Treaty" is reserved for those rules that are inherent to the very nature and establishment of the European Community as a distinct and autonomous legal order.'

formulated very broadly.[41] Accordingly, it leaves the Court plenty of discretion. What is clear, however, is that the ECJ is appointed the task of guarding the EU legal order. So, a quick analysis of the grounds of the case law concerning "federal common law" shows that what is at stake is nothing less than the autonomy of the European legal order, and the ultimate unity of European law. This is also apparent when one realises that the *adjudicatory* power of the Court to make European "federal common law", has mostly been derived from Article 234 EC (now Article 267 TFEU), the provision on the preliminary ruling procedure. As we have seen above, this procedure has been devised especially in order to ensure the unity of the European legal order.

A second interesting point can be found when we turn to the content of European "federal common law". In the EU, "federal common law" was made, above all, in the fields of torts (the case law on state liability offers an excellent example) and contracts.[42] Let us take a closer look at the judgment that introduced the principle of state liability for breaches of EU law, and still forms the starting point of such a claim: The case of *Francovich and Bonifaci*. In this case, applicants held Italy responsible for their damages, which were a direct result of the state's failure to implement a directive. After considering that the question was to be decided 'in the light of the general system of the Treaty and its fundamental principles,'[43] the ECJ continued to answer the principle question of the existence of State liability, as follows:

> It should be borne in mind at the outset that the EEC Treaty has created its own legal system, which is integrated into the legal systems of the Member States and which their courts are bound to apply. The subjects of that legal system are not only the Member States but also their nationals. Just as it imposes burdens on individuals, Community law is also intended to give rise to rights which become part of their legal patrimony. (…)
>
> Furthermore, it has been consistently held that the national courts whose task it is to apply the provisions of Community law in areas within their jurisdiction must ensure that those rules take full effect and must protect the rights which they confer on individuals. (…)
>
> The full effectiveness of Community rules would be impaired and the protection of the rights which they grant would be weakened if individuals were unable to obtain redress when their rights are infringed by a breach of Community law for which a Member State can be held responsible.
>
> The possibility of obtaining redress from the Member State is particularly indispensable where, as in this case, the full effectiveness of Community rules is subject to prior action on the part of the State and where, consequently, in the absence of such action, individuals cannot enforce before the national courts the rights conferred upon them by Community law.
>
> It follows that the principle whereby a State must be liable for loss and damage caused to individuals as a result of breaches of Community law for which the State can be held responsible is inherent in the system of the Treaty.
>
> A further basis for the obligation of Member States to make good such loss and damage is to be found in Article 5 of the Treaty [now Article 4, paragraph 3 TEU], under which the Member States are required to take all appropriate measures, whether general or particular, to ensure fulfilment of their obligations under Community law. (…)

---

[41] See my comments on this article in Chap. 1, Sect. 1.3, and below in this chapter, Sect. 5.5.

[42] K. Lenaerts and K. Gutman, o.c., par. V.

[43] Joined cases C-6/90 and C-9/90, *Francovich and Bonifaci v Italian Republic,* [1991] ECR I-5357, par. 30.

It follows from all the foregoing that it is a principle of Community law that the Member States are obliged to make good loss and damage caused to individuals by breaches of Community law for which they can be held responsible.[44]

The importance of this case for the subject under discussion cannot be overemphasized.[45] What is of special interest for our analysis is that this case reiterates a figure we are already familiar with: The structure of implication. Basically, the ECJ holds that the principle of state liability is implied in the European legal order, being an 'own legal system,' the effectiveness of which should be ensured by the Member States, following the principle of loyal cooperation. Indeed, it is justified to speak of 'implied remedies' in the field of state liability.[46] And this is not the only time the figure of implication comes up. In the same vein, the right of compensation in contract law is said to be 'implied'.[47] In other words, as in the case law on 'implied powers', the ECJ falls back on what can be called an implication of European law. The question, however, is why? Why does the ECJ refer to these concepts as 'implied'? And, perhaps even more importantly, what are they the implication of?

To start with the last question, European "federal common law" seems to be made 'when the objectives of Community law and Community programs are at stake.'[48] It is exactly at this point that our analysis of chiastic constitution becomes relevant. In different cases, the ECJ refers to the autonomous nature of the Treaty, the full effectiveness of Community law, the principle of loyal cooperation, the importance of the uniform application of Community law, the *acquis communautaire*. All these formulas are used by the ECJ to 'derive' from the Treaty a principle that is said to be 'inherent' to it. Yet, let us not be deluded by this. The reason the national judge posed a preliminary question in the first place, was that there is no principle of State liability written in the Treaty. In other words, while following the rule, the ECJ makes the rule. In the process of 'telling what the law says', the ECJ 'creates the law'. This a chiastic act of constitution: While constituting a new meaning of the Treaty, the ECJ cannot but claim to follow the Treaty. This act thus has the structure of a 'coherent deformation' of the Treaty. Yet, this requires a specific way of *perceiving* the European legal order and, subsequently, the Treaty. The principle of State liability can only appear as fundamental to a Court that already presupposes that the issue whether this principle exists should be answered in the light of fundamental principles. State liability is only necessary in the situation of a Court, starting from the 'system of the Treaty', and interpreting it as containing an

[44] Ibid., par. 31–37.

[45] Lenaerts and Gutman call the principle of State liability 'the "fourteen carat gold" example of European "federal common law."' Cf. K. Lenaerts and K. Gutman, o.c., p. 81.

[46] Ibid., p. 81: 'In fact, with American "federal common law" in mind, it may be considered a premier example of European-type "*implied* remedies."' [My italics, LC]

[47] Speaking of the case of Leitner (C-168/00, *Leitner v. TUI Deutschland GmbH & Co. KG,* [2002] ECR I-2631), Lenaerts and Gutman point out that '[t]he Court's judgment signified a Community concept of "damage" that effectively "*implied*" the right of compensation for non-material damages in Ms. Leitner's favour.' Cf. K. Lenaerts and K. Gutman, o.c., p. 107. [My italics, LC]

[48] Ibid., p. 108.

unwritten principle of effectiveness that imposes demands on national authorities. However, the effectiveness of the Treaty can only require the principle of State liability to exist… if one first presupposes that effectiveness requires the principle of State liability.

However, this does not necessarily mean that the structure of implication is used as a silent usurpation of power by the ECJ. In defining new concepts of European law, the Court of Justice is bound to respect the constitutional traditions of the Member States. Moreover, there is yet another reason why the ECJ would try to let its own definitions connect with the ones originating in general principles common to the Member States: Since the national courts are the ones ultimately responsible for the application of EU law in the national legal orders, it would be extremely unwise of the ECJ to come up with a concept completely alien to what most Member States share.[49] What the Court of Justice does in the cases concerning European "federal common law" is trying to start from what is common to the Member States, and connect this with the objectives of European integration. The goal of the ECJ is thus 'to create judge-made rules that embody "the best solutions", or "the most progressive", for the needs of the Community legal order.'[50] One could, therefore, argue that the principle guiding all law-making of the Court is the principle of effectiveness, or *effet utile*.[51] In other words, the ECJ will always look for the concepts and definitions most suitable to reach the objectives of the Union. This teleological type of reasoning is, then, based upon the principle of loyal cooperation, on the reciprocal commitments between Union institutions and Member States.[52] Yet, as we will also see below, this neither entails that the ECJ has a purely instrumental vision of European law, nor that it would impose European objectives on the Member States, without taking into consideration the national legal orders. Indeed, the *effet utile* of European law requires a more complex understanding of the relationship between Union and Member States than the term 'instrumentalism' suggests.

With this in mind, we can return to the doctrine of implied powers, more precisely, to the ECJ's judgment in the case of *AETR*. First of all, confronted with the absence of any specific competence to negotiate and conclude a Treaty such as the

---

[49] Lenaerts and Gutman call this a '"backcheck": Because it is through the implementation of Community law in the national legal orders that Community law maintains its full effectiveness, it would be self-effacing if "federal common law" was not acceptable to the Member States.' Cf. Lenaerts and Gutman, o.c., p. 19.

[50] Ibid., p. 18. Of course, we can also read here 'EU law'.

[51] Cf. L. Senden, 'Twintig jaar Europese rechtsontwikkeling: Versterking van het effet utile van het Europese recht', in A.M.J. van den Biggelaar et al. (eds.), *Twintig jaar rechtsontwikkeling*. Bundel ter gelegenheid van het vierde lustrum van JUVAT, Nijmegen: Wolf Legal Publishers 2008, pp. 107–132. Cf. Former ECJ judge Pescatore, who calls effectiveness 'the very soul of legal rules', quoted in: A. Arnull, o.c., p. 169.

[52] Cf. Lenaerts and Gutman, o.c., pp. 18–19: 'The principle of effectiveness stems from the principle of sincere (or loyal) cooperation enshrined in Article 10 EC, which the Court has made clear is applicable beyond the confines of Community law to areas of Union law in the third pillar, and that it flows both ways as between Member States and the Community institutions.'

one in question,[53] the Court finds itself in the *situation* that it should consider 'the general system of Community law in the sphere of relations with third countries.'[54] The Court starts by referring to Article 281 EC, giving the Community legal personality, and its place in the Treaty as one of the 'General and Final Provisions'.[55] The ECJ concludes from this, that the Community has the capacity to sign Treaties with third countries concerning the whole field of its objectives. Then, confronted with the question whether the Community holds the authority to enter into an agreement such as the AETR, the ECJ can only take the next step if it takes into account the wider context of the problem at stake, i.e., by taking into account 'the whole scheme of the Treaty, no less than to its substantive provisions.'[56] This context, this specific constellation, entails that—and notice that this is the Court taking the next step—competence can be conferred expressly 'but may equally flow from other provisions of the Treaty, and from measures adopted within the framework of those provisions, by the Community institutions.'[57] It then refers to the inseparability of internal and external competences, "Transport" as one of the objectives of the Treaty, and the principle of loyalty, to conclude that in this field, the Community has an exclusive competence. This exclusive character of the competence is to protect the unity of the market, the uniformity and autonomy of the European legal order.[58] Now that all this is said and done, the ECJ concludes that '[t]his is the legal position, in the light of which, the question of admissibility has to be resolved.'[59]

The Court thus followed an elaborated reasoning to come to the conclusion of the existence of implied powers. It did so, and this is crucial, without ever revoking the central importance of the principle of conferred powers, for the division of competences, between the Community and its Member States. What are we to make of this? The recognition of the implied powers of the Community was a creative act, an act of constitution. As such, it had the structure of creative expression which I described above. The accepted meaning of the principle of conferred powers is taken up (the competences of the Community are those explicitly given by the Treaty) and reinvented (the competences of the Community may also be given implicitly by the Treaty, or even by measures adopted by Community institutions) in one single movement. We might say that the Court of Justice *metamorphosed* the meaning of the principle of attributed powers, and its reasoning followed the structure of 'coherent deformation'. This is especially clear when one notes how the

---

[53] In this case: the European Agreement concerning the work of crews of vehicles engaged in international road transport, hereafter referred to as ERTA.

[54] Case 22/70, *Commission v Council (ERTA)* [1971] ECR 263, par. 12.

[55] Article 47 TEU now says that the EU has legal personality.

[56] *ERTA* par. 15.

[57] Ibid., par. 16.

[58] Cf. par. 31: 'These Community powers exclude the possibility of concurrent powers on the part of Member States, since any steps taken outside the framework of the Community institutions would be incompatible with the unity of the common market and the uniform application of Community law.'

[59] Ibid., par. 32.

Court basically holds that implied powers have been part of the Treaty system *all the time*. Going beyond the established meaning of the Treaty, the Court says it only states what has been a part of the Treaty from the very start.

Our theory of chiastic constitution also makes clear that the Court *must* make its argument in this way. Just as an act of creative expression must pose itself as already part of the established order to sediment and remain available for future use, the new reading of the principle of conferred powers must be presented as already existing, in order to be accepted. The Court, in claiming that implied powers have always been a part of the Treaty, refers to 'a past which has never been a present.'[60] Note, furthermore, how the existence of implied powers can only be defended if one presupposes that one should take the specific perspective of the general system of Community law. In other words, the general system of EC law can only require the existence of implied powers... if one first presupposes that the general system requires the existence of implied powers. What rises to the surface in this circularity is the chiasm of constitution, to wit, the chiastic interrelatedness of constituent and constituted power.

Concluding this section, one question still needs to be answered. Why do both Francovich and *AETR* show similar lines of reasoning? In other words, why is the basic structure of creeping competences that of an implication? Here, the market, as the ultimate goal of the integration process, and the emphasis on effectiveness, are connected in such a way that the argument necessarily appears in the form of an implication.[61] The argument of a *telos* (the establishment of a single market) as an ultimate goal that is projected towards the *future*, only works by pointing to commitments taken up in the *past* (the system of the Treaty, the principle of loyal cooperation). These, then, from the perspective of the *present*, appear as *implied*. The implication shows what is finally philosophically at stake in creeping competences, to wit, how legal power moves between power *in* and power *over* the law. What both 'federal common law', and the doctrine of implied powers show is that powers are said to be implied, in the sense that they should appear as 'always already given.' Whether this is really the case can, however, only be judged *retrospectively*, i.e., after a process of sedimentation has taken place. At the moment of this claim, the ECJ is *anticipating* a 'Union-to-be-made', by pointing back to a 'Union-made'.[62] Therefore, legal powers also appear as 'never completely given'.

---

[60] M. Merleau-Ponty, *Phenomenology of Perception*, trans. C. Smith, London and New York: Routledge 2003, p. 282/M. Merleau-Ponty, *Phénoménologie de la perception*, Paris: Gallimard 1945, p. 280. Hereafter, this book will be referred to as PP, with first the English pages, then the French ones.

[61] Without mentioning the cases on implied powers, Hans Lindahl already showed the importance of the structure of implication for the reasoning of the ECJ and the specific philosophy of history this entails, see: H. Lindahl, 'The paradox of constituent power. The ambiguous self-constitution of the European Union', *Ratio Juris: An International Journal of Jurisprudence and Philosophy of Law*, vol. 20 (2007), pp. 485–505.

[62] Cf. see also H. Lindahl, 'Acquiring a Community: The Acquis and the Institution of European Legal Order', *European Law Journal*, vol. 9 (2003), pp. 433–450. For anticipation, see also: A.

In the next section, I will further explore this chiasm by looking into the Europeanisation of public law.

5.3   Making European Public Law: A Story of Effectiveness and Loyalty

Together with the emergence of European substantive law, the EU legal order influences the public law of its Member States. Following the felicitous turn of phrase of a group of Dutch scholars, I will refer to this process as the 'Europeanisation of public law'.[63] Its appearance can be linked directly to the demand for effectiveness of European substantive law.[64] Since EU law is usually enforced by means of administrative law, the influence of European law on the national legal order is very strong in this area. European public (or administrative) law is concerned with the implementation of European law in the national legal order.[65] The broader issue at stake is thus the relationship between national and EU law. This relationship is guided by three principles: The primacy of European law, the principle of loyal cooperation (or simply, loyalty) and the principle of subsidiarity.[66] Since the focus of European administrative law lies on implementation, this brings to light that the final effectiveness of European law in the national legal order is dependent on national administrative bodies, and national judges working within the framework of national law.[67] That is why certain requirements were developed for national administrative and procedural law.

The ECJ has played an essential role in this process. As in the case of "federal common law", the Court let itself be inspired by the common principles of the Member States. Furthermore, the principles of national institutional autonomy, and national procedural autonomy, are relevant in this context. The latter says that national rules of procedure should be used. However, this does not mean that this is possible without posing certain conditions. In the case of *Rewe,* the ECJ formulated two prerequisites.[68] First of all, cases concerning EU law should not be guided by

---

Schaap, The Time of Reconciliation and the Space of Politics, in: S. Veitch (ed.), *Law and the Politics of Reconciliation,* Aldershot (etc.): Ashgate 2007, pp. 9–33.

[63] Cf. J.H. Jans, R. de Lange, S. Prechal and R.J.G.M. Widdershoven, *Europeanisation of Public Law,* Groningen: Europa Law Publishing 2007.

[64] Cf. Ch. Timmermans, 'Foreword', in Jans et al., *Europeanisation of Public Law,* pp. v–vi, at p. vi: 'The development of European public law is more particularly to be regarded as instrumental for that purpose. It is an instrument to ensure the *effet utile* of substantive European public law.'

[65] Jans et al., o.c., p. 13: 'Complying with obligations arising under Community law and, in particular, under regulations and directives, is often referred to as "implementation".' See also: A. Arnull, o.c., pp. 267–334, caught under the well-chosen title 'European rights, national remedies'.

[66] See for a discussion of these guiding principles: Chap. 1, above.

[67] Jans et al., o.c., p. 40: 'Community law is implemented, applied and enforced within the framework of national law.'

[68] Case 33/76 *Rewe* [1976] ECR 1989.

rules less favourable than those concerning national law. This is the principle of non-discrimination, or equivalence. Secondly, there is the principle of (procedural) effectiveness, requiring that procedural rules may neither render virtually impossible, nor excessively difficult, the exercise of rights conferred by European law.

The broader principle of national institutional autonomy is especially interesting for this inquiry. It says that 'unless (secondary) Community law provides otherwise, it is for the Member States themselves to determine how they fulfil their Community obligations, which organs will be made responsible for the implementation and application of Community law (directly or otherwise) and what procedures will be followed.'[69] This principle has interesting consequences in the field of competences: It shows 'how Community law, even though it can create a power, cannot normally designate national bodies to act as competent authorities. These national bodies form part of the national legal order and, it must be assumed, it is the national legal order that confers their powers on them.'[70] In other words, EU law cannot *create* a competence for national administrative bodies.

This is problematic, in relation to the demands of the principle of legality. As is well known, this principle requires a prior legal basis for governmental action. A distinction can be made between a negative and a positive principle.[71] The negative principle holds that 'every act that can be attributed to the Union must be consistent with higher ranking law.'[72] The positive principle demands a legal basis for any act of a Union institution.[73] However, following the principle of national institutional autonomy, these two related aspects do not suffice. There remains a danger of situations that one could call "semi-legal": 'Though it is true that the substantive requirement, or authority, flows from Community law, no institutional basis has been created, and there has been no actual conferral of authority necessary because the national organs are not Community organs.'[74]

While it is true that EU law, in its present state, cannot directly give competences to national authorities, this remains only a part of the story. In case it has direct effect, it can, nevertheless, demand of national authorities not to apply conflicting rules of national law, or even to apply EU rules immediately. The problem, then, is that 'Community law imposes an obligation on the national authorities which they are required to fulfil without necessarily having the power to do so under national

---

[69] Jans et al., o.c., p. 18. Instead of Community, one could now read 'the EU'.

[70] Ibid., p. 24.

[71] Cf. A. von Bogdandy and J. Bast, 'The European Union's Order of Competences: The Current Law and Proposals for its Reform', *Common Market Law Review*, vol. 39 (2002), pp. 227–268, at pp. 229–231.

[72] Ibid., p. 229. In this respect, the distinction between the EC and the EU is not relevant.

[73] Ibid, p. 231: 'Any act at the level of secondary Union law must possess a legal basis which can be traced back to the Treaties. The legal basis can either be contained in the Treaties themselves or in an act of secondary law, which in turn is based on the Treaties.'

[74] Jans et al., o.c., p. 27. On the same page, the authors call this problem 'essentially a constitutional issue'.

law.'[75] The ECJ uses a balanced approach in this respect. So, in the case of *Van Schijndel,* concerning the question whether or not a national judge had the obligation to apply provisions of European law, even when parties had not invoked them, the ECJ first held that, following the principle of loyalty, 'it is for national courts to ensure the legal protection which persons derive from the direct effect of provisions of Community law.'[76] Then, after reiterating the conditions of *Rewe,* it reached the following conclusion:

> For the purposes of applying those principles, each case which raises the question whether a national procedural provision renders application of Community law impossible or excessively difficult must be analysed by reference to the role of that provision in the procedure, its progress and its special features, viewed as a whole, before the various national instances. In the light of that analysis the basic principles of the domestic judicial system, such as protection of the rights of the defence, the principle of legal certainty and the proper conduct of procedure, must, where appropriate, be taken into consideration.
>
> In the present case, the domestic law principle that in civil proceedings a court must or may raise points of its own motion is limited by its obligation to keep to the subject-matter of the dispute and to base its decision on the facts put before it.
>
> That limitation is justified by the principle that, in a civil suit, it is for the parties to take the initiative, the court being able to act of its own motion only in exceptional cases where the public interest requires its intervention. That principle reflects conceptions prevailing in most of the Member States as to the relations between the State and the individual; it safeguards the rights of the defence; and it ensures proper conduct of proceedings by, in particular, protecting them from the delays inherent in examination of new pleas.[77]

For this inquiry, there are two important points in this judgment. First of all, the ECJ holds that a basic principle of national procedural law ought to be respected. This means that the effectiveness of EU law is not a principle, opening the gates to an unrestricted flood of demands on the national institutions. In other words, there are limits to the effectiveness of EU law.

Then, the second important point that can be concluded from this case is that the ECJ makes use of a piece-meal approach.[78] This means that the ECJ, confronted with such a case, will be *situated* in the specific field the case opens. What effectiveness requires is thus something that can only be decided by someone situated in the field. Confronted with the specific case at hand, the ECJ is able to strike the right balance between the purpose of effectiveness, on the one hand, and the national procedural rules, on the other. Effectiveness and national autonomy do not appear as contradicting demands to the ECJ. On the contrary, confronted with a specific case, the European judge is situated in such a way that it can perceive effectiveness and national autonomy as part of one and the same constellation, that is, the intertwinement of the national and the European legal order. What is at stake in this

---

[75] Ibid.

[76] Joined cases C-430/93 and C-431/93 *Van Schijndel and Van Veen* [1995] ECR I4705, par. 14.

[77] Ibid., par. 19–21.

[78] Cf. P. Craig & G. de Bùrca, o.c., p. 321: 'The case states that each national provision governing enforcement of an EC right before national courts must be examined and weighed, not in the abstract, but in the specific circumstances of each case, to see whether, taking its purpose into account, it renders the exercise of that right excessively difficult.'

constellation is the ultimate goal of integration: The market as a project of establishing 'an ever closer union'. Only from this specific perspective can one even begin to make sense of a balance between the two demands. Balancing presupposes a certain similarity, a similarity that can only appear from the specific perspective of the ECJ. *Striking* a balance is always done from a balance *struck*.

Another important case in the field of European administrative law may serve as an example of the ECJ's manner of balancing. The question before the Court was whether or not a national administrative body, 'in particular under the principle of Community solidarity contained in Article 10 EC,' was under the obligation 'to reopen a decision which has become final, in order to ensure the full operation of Community law, as it is to be interpreted in the light of a subsequent preliminary ruling?'[79] After considering that the principle of legal certainty constituted a fundamental principle of EC law, the Court reached the following conclusion:

> However, the national court stated that, under Netherlands law, administrative bodies always have the power to reopen a final administrative decision, provided that the interests of third parties are not adversely affected, and that, in certain circumstances, the existence of such a power may imply an obligation to withdraw such a decision even if Netherlands law does not require that the competent body reopen final decisions as a matter of course in order to comply with judicial decisions given subsequent to those final decisions. The aim of the national court's question is to ascertain whether, in circumstances such as those of the main case, there is an obligation to reopen a final administrative decision under Community law.
>
> As is clear from the case-file, the circumstances of the main case are the following. First, national law confers on the administrative body competence to reopen the decision in question in the main proceedings, which has become final. Second, that decision became final only as a result of a judgment of a national court against whose decisions there is no judicial remedy. Third, that judgment was based on an interpretation of Community law which, in the light of a subsequent judgment of the Court, was incorrect and which was adopted without a question being referred to the Court for a preliminary ruling in accordance with the conditions provided for in the third paragraph of Article 234 EC [now Article 267 TFEU]. Fourth, the person concerned complained to the administrative body immediately after becoming aware of that judgment of the Court.
>
> In such circumstances, the administrative body concerned is, in accordance with the principle of cooperation arising from Article 10 EC [now Article 4. paragraph 3 TEU], under an obligation to review that decision in order to take account of the interpretation of the relevant provision of Community law given in the meantime by the Court. The administrative body will have to determine on the basis of the outcome of that review to what extent it is under an obligation to reopen, without adversely affecting the interests of third parties, the decision in question.[80]

So, in order to retain the effectiveness of European law, while at the same time trying to respect the (national) principle of legality and institutional balance, the Court of Justice again makes use of what has been called the 'structure of implication'. This time, however, the Court refers to an already existing *national* competence. The following conclusion is justified: 'Finally, the case law seems to be developing in the direction of implying what can perhaps best be referred to as a "semi-posi-

---

[79] Case C-453/00 *Kühne & Heitz* [2004] ECR I-4705, par. 19.

[80] Ibid., par. 25–27.

tive" obligation, in the sense that where the national court or national authority has a certain *power*, Community law may imply that it is, in fact, *required* to exercise this power. This requirement follows from Article 10 EC, in some cases in combination with the necessity of effective judicial protection. In other words, a national power implies a Community duty'.[81]

In this way, the ECJ makes use of the 'structure of implication' to help build a European *ius commune* in the field of administrative law.[82] Perhaps even better than the case of *AETR* or 'federal common law', the example of European public law shows that this manner of reasoning is not used as a purely instrumental way of reaching European goals, or—even worse—as a silent usurpation of the powers of the Member States. Again and again, the Court has tried to find a subtle balance between the effectiveness of EU law, on the one hand, and the institutional autonomy of the Member States, on the other. The reference to the principle of sincere cooperation is especially important, since it shows that ultimately European law cannot be effective on a specific level if Member States are not loyal to the obligations they have agreed upon themselves. The goal of an internal market as a concrete reality for the European citizens remains a mirage without the cooperation of the national institutions. This promise to cooperate and implement, apply and enforce European law, so the Court argues, *implies* the duty of national institutions to actually make use of the competences they possess.

The importance of the principle of sincere or loyal cooperation can also be acknowledged if we turn to a recent judgment that concerned the question whether or not national authorities were under the obligation to interpret national law in conformity with a framework decision. In the case against a kindergarten teacher, Maria Pupino, the ECJ was asked whether the Italian judge should interpret Italian law in conformity with a framework decision regarding the protection of vulnerable witnesses. Article 34 of the EU Treaty (now repealed) expressly precluded this possibility, as it mentioned explicitly that framework decisions do not have direct effect. However, the ECJ still held that Italian law had to be explained in conformity with the framework decision under discussion. Now, let us look at the Court's reasoning more closely to find on which basis it could reach this conclusion. The Court started with stating that it had jurisdiction. Furthermore, it observed that the formulation of a 'framework decision' in the EU Treaty was identical to that of a directive, the definition of which one can find in Article 249 EC (now Article 288 TFEU). From this, the Court inferred that national authorities were under the obligation to interpret national law in conformity with the framework decision.[83] It based this conclusion on the following considerations:

> Irrespective of the degree of integration envisaged by the Treaty of Amsterdam in the process of creating an ever closer union among the peoples of Europe within the meaning of the second paragraph of Article 1 EU [now Article 1 TEU], it is perfectly comprehensible that the authors of the Treaty on European Union should have considered it useful to make

---

[81] Jans et al., o.c., p. 53. [Italics in the original]

[82] Ibid., p. 5 and p. 369.

[83] Case C-105/03, *Criminal proceedings against Maria Pupino* [2005] ECR I-5285, par. 34.

provision, in the context of Title VI of that treaty, for recourse to legal instruments with effects similar to those provided for by the EC Treaty, in order to contribute effectively to the pursuit of the Union's objectives.

The importance of the Court's jurisdiction to give preliminary rulings under Article 35 EU [now repealed] is confirmed by the fact that, under Article 35(4), any Member State, whether or not it has made a declaration pursuant to Article 35(2), is entitled to submit statements of case or written observations to the Court in cases which arise under Article 35(1). That jurisdiction would be deprived of most of its useful effect if individuals were not entitled to invoke framework decisions in order to obtain a conforming interpretation of national law before the courts of the Member States. (...)

The second and third paragraphs of Article 1 of the Treaty on European Union provide that that treaty marks a new stage in the process of creating an ever closer union among the peoples of Europe and that the task of the Union, which is founded on the European Communities, supplemented by the policies and forms of cooperation established by that treaty, shall be to organise, in a manner demonstrating consistency and solidarity, relations between the Member States and between their peoples.[84]

In this revolutionary case, the ECJ uses the principle of loyal cooperation 'to take the next step'. It would be hard for the Union to obtain its objectives if the principle of loyal cooperation would not apply to the third pillar. Therefore, i.e., for reasons of 'effectiveness' amounting to the very stakes of European integration, the Court concluded that the principle of conforming interpretation was binding for third pillar framework decisions, as well. However, this obligation could be limited by general principles of law, especially the principles of legal certainty and non-retroactivity. Furthermore, it could form no basis for *contra legem* interpretation of national law. Finally, the ECJ held that it was for the national court to decide whether conforming interpretation is possible in a particular case. In this decision, it should also respect the constitutional traditions of the Member States and the ECHR, Article 6, in particular.

In this much discussed case, we see that the ECJ explicitly looks at the EU Treaty (what was then the third pillar) from a very specific perspective. It stresses that this Treaty is, first and foremost, a new step in the integration process that started with the Treaty of Rome. So, setting the 'ever closer union' as the goal, it then goes on to ask what would constitute the most effective means to reach it. So, the perspective of the *unity* of the integration process brings the ECJ into the situation that it is confronted once again with the very objectives underlying integration. Now, an attentive reading of the Court's reasoning reveals that these are not two distinct arguments, but actually, one and the same. One could reformulate its argumentation as follows. The EU Treaty, being a new step towards 'an ever closer Union', *implies* the application of the principle of loyal cooperation which, in turn, *implies* the obligation of conforming interpretation for national authorities. The Court thus uses teleological reasoning (posing the goal of the integration process) and, given this goal, concludes in favor of the *necessary implication* of the obligation of interpretation in conformity therewith. The Court of Justice links the objectives of the Treaty to the principle of loyalty, and then goes on to use this principle to derive the duty of conforming interpretation as its necessary corollary. The chiastic struc-

---

[84] Ibid., par. 36–38 and 41.

ture of constitution rises to the surface: The ECJ, defending the very objectives of European integration, and thus remaining faithful to the Treaty, metamorphoses its established meaning, and takes the next step. Once again, the ECJ's judgment is a 'coherent deformation'.

The same elements that were so important in the case law on 'federal common law' and European administrative law, reappear in the Pupino judgment. Crucial, however, is the principle of loyalty, or sincere cooperation. Broadly formulated and vague as it may be, this principle seems to go much further than the EU variant of principles such as *pacta sunt servanda,* or good faith. Nor is the principle of sincere cooperation the Union version of a blown-up *Verfassungspatriotismus.* Not unlike the concept of the common or internal market that forms the very core of European integration, the principle of loyalty reminds Member States of the promises they made for a common cause. What these promises entail, exactly, cannot be decided *a priori,* but only in the specific circumstances of the situation. Take the example of marriage. What it means to stay together 'for better or worse', and what specific duties and responsibilities this entails for the spouses, can only be judged by taking into account the specific circumstances. Loyalty in an institution is thus used to articulate the concrete value of a promise today. In the European Union, this principle allows the judge in different contexts to play the constituting role it is playing.

5.4   The Commonality of Traditions: A Court in Search of Human Rights

The third case study of this chapter will look into the protection of human rights in the European legal order. For a long time, the EU did not possess a legally binding catalogue of fundamental rights.[85] Yet, as early as the 1970s, the ECJ held that the institutions of the EC were all bound by fundamental rights.[86] The first of these judgments is the case of *Internationale Handelsgesellschaft.* The German judge was asked to leave out of consideration a measure of EC law, since it was in conflict with fundamental rights enshrined in the German constitution. In its preliminary ruling, the ECJ concluded the following:

> Recourse to the legal rules or concepts of national law in order to judge the validity of measures adopted by the institutions of the Community would have an adverse effect on the uniformity and efficacy of Community law. The validity of such measures can only be judged in the light of Community law. In fact, the law stemming from the Treaty, an independent source of law, cannot because of its very nature be overridden by rules of

---

[85] This changed with the entry into force of the Treaty of Lisbon on 1 December 2009, see Article 6 TEU. Yet, there is still the possibility to opt-out, as the Czech Republic, Poland and the United Kingdom show.

[86] A brief overview of the cases discussed in this section can be found in A. Arnull, o.c., pp. 337–340. As they were decided before the existence of the EU, in this section I will speak of EC (law).

national law, however framed, without being deprived of its character as Community law and without the legal basis of the Community itself being called in question. Therefore the validity of a Community measure or its effect within a Member State cannot be affected by allegations that it runs counter to either fundamental rights as formulated by the constitution of that State or the principles of a national constitutional structure.

However, an examination should be made as to whether or not any analogous guarantee inherent in Community law has been disregarded. In fact, respect for fundamental rights forms an integral part of the general principles of law protected by the Court of Justice. The protection of such rights, whilst inspired by the constitutional traditions common to the Member States, must be ensured within the framework of the structure and objectives of the Community. It must therefore be ascertained, in the light of the doubts expressed by the Verwaltungsgericht, whether the system of deposits has infringed rights of a fundamental nature, respect for which must be ensured in the Community legal system.[87]

In this famous judgment, the ECJ recognised fundamental rights as part of the principles of EC law.[88] Furthermore, it held that it could find inspiration for these rights in 'the constitutional traditions common to the Member States.' The ECJ, in the situation when the uniformity and efficacy of EC law were at stake, held that such a case could only be decided by taking the perspective of EC law. Then, it goes back to the *nature* of European law, as stemming from an independent source, to argue that national law cannot set aside EC rules without putting at risk the legal basis of the whole Community. This even holds for the highest national rules, those found in the constitution. So, taking up the situation of the Community as an independent, and thus autonomous, legal order, the ECJ was able to take the next step by following 'the constitutional traditions common to the Member States,' yet preserving for itself the ultimate decision what these traditions amounted to in the case at hand. The danger of such an approach is clear, as Craig and De Bùrca comment on this case: 'If the ECJ's interpretation of the requirements of these principles differs significantly from the interpretation of the Member States which also guarantee their protection, the legitimacy of the Court's adjudication is likely to be called into question.'[89]

Perhaps also for this reason, the ECJ kept searching for other sources to tap. A couple of years later, it found another spring that could help feed the general principles of EC law. In the case of *Nold,* the ECJ argued as follows:

As the Court has already stated, fundamental rights form an integral part of the general principles of law, the observance of which it ensures.

In safeguarding these rights, the Court is bound to draw inspiration from constitutional traditions common to the Member States, and it cannot therefore uphold measures which are incompatible with fundamental rights recognized and protected by the Constitutions of those States.

Similarly, international treaties for the protection of human rights on which the Member States have collaborated or of which they are signatories, can supply guidelines which should be followed within the framework of Community law. (…)[90]

---

[87] Case 11/70, *Internationale Handelsgesellschaft mbH v Einfuhr- und Vorratsstelle für Getreide und Futtermittel* [1970] ECR 1125, par. 3–4.

[88] See also Case 26/69 *Stauder v City of Ulm* [1969] ECR 419.

[89] P. Craig & G. de Bùrca, o.c., p. 383.

[90] Case 4/73, *Nold v Commission* [1974] ECR 491, par. 13.

Notice that the ECJ says that it should respect the constitutional traditions common to the Member States. The new element in this case is obviously the reference to international treaties signed by the Member States. Also, these may form guidelines for the Court asked to decide a case concerning fundamental rights. In 1979, the ECJ further elaborated on this approach when it had to take a decision in the case of *Hauer*. In a conflict concerning the right to property, the ECJ clarified its earlier case law, while calling to mind the fundamental issue underlying its case law on human rights:

> As the Court declared in its judgment of 17 December 1970, *Internationale Handelsgesell-schaft* [1970] ECR 1125, the question of a possible infringement of fundamental rights by a measure of the Community institutions can only be judged in the light of Community law itself. The introduction of special criteria for assessment stemming from the legislation or constitutional law of a particular Member State would, by damaging the substantive unity and efficacy of Community law, lead inevitably to the destruction of the unity of the Common Market and the jeopardizing of the cohesion of the Community.
>
> The Court also emphasized in the judgment cited, and later in the judgment of 14 May 1974, *Nold* [1974] ECR 491, that fundamental rights form an integral part of the general principles of the law, the observance of which it ensures; that in safeguarding those rights, the Court is bound to draw inspiration from constitutional traditions common to the Member States, so that measures which are incompatible with the fundamental rights recognized by the constitutions of those States are unacceptable in the Community; and that, similarly, international treaties for the protection of human rights on which the Member States have collaborated or of which they are signatories, can supply guidelines which should be followed within the framework of Community law. That conception was later recognized by the joint declaration of the European Parliament, the Council and the Commission of 5 April 1977, which, after recalling the case-law of the Court, refers on the one hand to the rights guaranteed by the constitutions of the Member States and on the other hand to the European Convention for the Protection of Human Rights and Fundamental Freedoms of 4 November 1950 (Official Journal C 103, 1977, p. 1).[91]

Thus, the ECJ starts by reiterating its judgment in *Handelsgesellschaft*. Yet, it chooses sharper wording to emphasize the risk posed by national courts reviewing EC measures by their own fundamental rights standard. This would mean to damage the 'substantive unity and efficacy of EC law' and 'destruct the unity' of the market, while putting at risk the 'cohesion' of the Community. These dangers cause the Court to take the next step. This step consists of an explicit reference to the European Convention of Human Rights.[92] The principles of EC law will thus include those fundamental rights that are to be found in the ECHR, and the constitutional traditions common to the Member States.[93]

However, something strange is happening here. For, from which perspective are those traditions to be seen as constituting a 'common' heritage, a source shared by

---

[91] Case 44/79, *Hauer v Land Rheinland-Pfalz* [1979] ECR 3727, par. 14–15.

[92] See also Case 260/89, *ERT* [1991] ECR 2925, par. 41. See also: Joined Cases C-402/05 P and C-415/05 P, *Yassin Abdullah Kadi and Al Barakaat International Foundation v. Council of the European Union*, judgment of 3 September 2008, par. 283–285 where the ECJ calls respect for fundamental rights one of the 'constitutional principles of the EC Treaty'.

[93] See now Article 6 TEU. In paragraph 2 of this article it says that the EU shall accede to the ECHR. This is one of the amendments made by the Treaty of Lisbon.

the Member States that can subsequently be used by the ECJ as an inspiration for the EC general principles? Surely, only in a particular *situation* do the traditions of the Member States appear as 'common'. The ECJ, confronted with the threat to the unity and efficacy of EC law, the unity of the market and the cohesion of the Community, is put in the specific situation of recognizing human rights as a part of the general principles of EC law. It does this in a very specific way. While emphasizing the autonomy and independence of these EC principles, at the very same time, the Court takes its cue from the rights found in international agreements, and the constitutional traditions common to the Member States. So, while constituting fundamental rights as an integral part of EC legal principles, the ECJ lets itself be guided by what the Member States already have in common.

Yet, there is more. The answer to the question at the beginning of the previous paragraph brings to light a circularity in the reasoning of the Court. Only from the perspective of the ECJ, situated in a field where general principles of EC law are called upon in order to avert the dangers to the integration process, do the constitutional traditions of the Member States appear as 'common'. However, why then should the ECJ be the sole judge authorised to set aside EC law that contradicts fundamental rights? What threats do national courts pose to the unity and cohesion of EC law, if they assess the compatibility of EC measures from '*common* traditions'? In what sense do national courts menace the unity of the market with '*special* criteria for assessment stemming from the legislation or constitutional law of a *particular* Member State,' if fundamental rights are exactly a part that constitutes traditions the Member States have *in common*? Here is the circularity in the reasoning of the Court: The commonness of constitutional traditions is only to be found by the ECJ, if it presupposes a commonness of traditions. The ECJ acts like a magician pulling from its hat a rabbit that it has first put there itself.

Before we move on to consider the way the ECJ regards its own task, it might be fruitful to quickly recapitulate what we have seen in the case studies discussed in the last three sections. In this respect, I would like to point to important similarities between the discussed cases, their further differences notwithstanding. First of all, there was an important similarity in the way in which the Court reasoned in the cases discussed. Again and again, we have seen that there was a certain circularity in the Court's reasoning, precisely at the crucial point when it introduced a new element in its case law, or a new reading of the Treaty. I argued that this is the way in which the ECJ takes the next step. Indeed, going from case to case, the ECJ invents the grounds for its rulings, while claiming to build on firm ground. This reveals, I held, that the constitutional activity of the ECJ should be understood in a chiastic way, to wit, as an interplay between constituent and constitutional power. Now, the passivity of this activity has not yet been fully elaborated. Passivity was mentioned in the context of the preliminary reference procedure, where it had the twofold meaning of the ECJ being placed 'before the decision', and open to the changing conditions in which European law should function, while proceeding from the line of decisions already taken. The way this passive dimension has emerged in the cases discussed, becomes clear when we direct our attention to a second similarity, to wit, a similarity in the grounds invoked by the ECJ in support of its decision. We have seen it referring to the objectives of the Community, the general system or whole scheme of the Treaty, the fundamental principles of the EC, the autonomous nature of the Treaty, the full effectiveness of Community law, the importance of the uniform application of Community law, the unity of the market, the effectiveness of EC law, the unity of the integration project, the cohesion of the Community, and the principle of loyal cooperation. A quick look at these rationales reveals that we are at the very heart of European integration. Jeopardising these grounds is an 'existential' danger to the European integration project. Secondly, I submit that these grounds are neither just normative, nor simply factual. Instead, one might say that they move between facts and norms. In other words, each of these grounds requires both a factual and a normative reading in order to make sense. For instance, as we have seen above, the effectiveness of Community law does not simply imply that Community law *ought* to be effectively implemented and enforced in the national legal orders. This demand should somehow be reconciled with the national legal order as it *is*. In the same vein, 'the unity of the integration project' is not something that can be determined *a priori*. To make sense of such a phrase, one needs to reconcile the normative demands of a uniting Europe with the factual, popular and political support for a united Europe. And that is exactly what these grounds do—they *make sense*. More precisely, they suggest a certain sense in which to proceed for whoever is situated, 'placed before the decision'. In the situation where the core of integration is at stake, the ECJ, confronted with the specific facts of the case, is being guided by these grounds, and perceives through them the direction to follow. The principle of loyalty, or sincere cooperation plays a special role in this respect. The power of loyalty resides in its ability to tie the goals of integration to the willingness, and the resulting promises made by the actors with which it all started. At the end of the day, integration cannot do without States that loyally uphold the obligations agreed upon. The principle of loyalty holds the different States to a mirror in which they see themselves from a Community perspective: As Member States. Under that guise only, their responsibilities become visible.

5.5   Constitutionalising Integration: Constitutional Charter, Constitutional Court

One last issue remains to be tackled: How are we to understand the relation between the ECJ's role in the constitution of the European legal order, and the task assigned to it according to its mandate? The ECJ has often been described as an activist court, increasing the powers of the European institutions at the cost of those of the Member States.[94] As we have seen in the first chapter of this study, it often did this by extensively interpreting the European Treaties, regarding the common or internal

---

[94] See Sect. 5.1. For a recent defense of the legitimacy of the ECJ, see: Q. L. Hong, 'Constitutional Review in the Mega-Leviathan: A Democratic Foundation for the European Court of Justice', *European Law Journal*, vol. 16 (2010), pp. 695–716.

market as the primal objective, or *telos,* of the integration process. This has led to the so-called constitutionalisation of European (Community) law. In a number of cases, the ECJ has interpreted the Treaty founding the European Community in a very specific way. Albeit concluded as a normal international treaty, the EC is now 'constitutionalised', and it is the Court who is responsible for this.[95] Before turning to some of these classic cases, the aspect that I would like to concentrate on first is the way in which the ECJ perceives the integration process as a whole, and how this goes hand in hand with a specific interpretation of its own role. One may say that recently the ECJ has extended its 'constitutional' case law. This has happened in the context of the EU, in cases where the Court was asked to decide over the relationship between the different pillars. Now, it is not my aim to give a full overview of this complicated and still evolving case law.[96] Yet, what I would like to do is to take a look at the way in which the ECJ has reasoned in a couple of recent cases. One of these is the case of Maria Pupino, discussed earlier in this chapter. In that case, the ECJ concluded that since the Treaty of Amsterdam was a new step in the integration process, the principle of loyal cooperation also applied in the third pillar. Interestingly, the Court could only come to this conclusion by taking a very specific perspective on the integration process. The ECJ regarded integration *sub specie unitatis*: Only in the light of the *unity* of the integration process does the EU Treaty (as amended by the Treaty of Amsterdam) constitute the next step. The ECJ seems more and more to emphasize the interrelatedness of the different pillars of the Union. As I have mentioned before, the Treaty of Lisbon has abolished the pillar structure. In a sense, the ECJ anticipated this abolition in the case law discussed here by its interpretation of the relationship between the pillars.

Another interesting case in this regard, is the Court's judgment in the case of *Segi.* This case concerned a Basque youth organisation that was put on a list of terrorist organisations, and suffered financial damage as a result. Segi held that its fundamental rights had been breached. Furthermore, it held that common position 2001/931/CFSP on the application of specific measures to combat terrorism was unlawful, and did not give them appropriate rights of defence. In this particular case, the question was whether a national judge could ask for a preliminary question concerning a common position, based on both Articles 15 EU (now Article 29 TEU) and 34 EU (now repealed). The problem was that following Article 35 EU (now repealed), the ECJ could not give preliminary rulings concerning common positions. The Court, however, concluded as follows:

> (...) A common position requires the compliance of the Member States by virtue of the principle of the duty to cooperate in good faith, which means in particular that Member States are to take all appropriate measures, whether general or particular, to ensure fulfilment of their obligations under European Union law (see Pupino, paragraph 42). (...) However, a common position is not supposed to produce of itself legal effects in relation

---

[95] For more on this process, see Chap. 1, Sect. 1.3 of this study.

[96] For more information, see: D.M. Curtin en R.A. Wessel, 'Rechtseenheid van de Europese Unie? De rol van het Hof van Justitie als constitutionele rechter', *SEW Tijdschrift voor Europees en economisch recht,* 2008, nr. 10, pp. 369–376.

to third parties. That is why, in the system established by Title VI of the EU Treaty, only framework decisions and decisions may be the subject of an action for annulment before the Court of Justice. The Court's jurisdiction, as defined by Article 35(1) EU, to give preliminary rulings also does not extend to common positions but is limited to rulings on the validity and interpretation of framework decisions and decisions, on the interpretation of conventions established under Title VI and on the validity and interpretation of the measures implementing them.

Article 35(1) EU, in that it does not enable national courts to refer a question to the Court for a preliminary ruling on a common position but only a question concerning the acts listed in that provision, treats as acts capable of being the subject of such a reference for a preliminary ruling all measures adopted by the Council and intended to produce legal effects in relation to third parties. Given that the procedure enabling the Court to give preliminary rulings is designed to guarantee observance of the law in the interpretation and application of the Treaty, it would run counter to that objective to interpret Article 35(1) EU narrowly. The right to make a reference to the Court of Justice for a preliminary ruling must therefore exist in respect of all measures adopted by the Council, whatever their nature or form, which are intended to have legal effects in relation to third parties (…).

As a result, it has to be possible to make subject to review by the Court a common position which, because of its content, has a scope going beyond that assigned by the EU Treaty to that kind of act. Therefore, a national court hearing a dispute which indirectly raises the issue of the validity or interpretation of a common position adopted on the basis of Article 34 EU, (…) would be able, subject to the conditions fixed by Article 35 EU, to ask the Court to give a preliminary ruling. It would then fall to the Court to find, where appropriate, that the common position is intended to produce legal effects in relation to third parties, to accord it its true classification and to give a preliminary ruling.

The Court would also have jurisdiction to review the lawfulness of such acts when an action has been brought by a Member State or the Commission under the conditions fixed by Article 35(6) EU.[97]

Even though, under the EU Treaty, the Court has no power to give a preliminary ruling on common positions, the ECJ still concludes that it is mandated to do so. Important in this respect is, again, the reference to the principle of loyalty or sincere cooperation that allows the Court to remind the Member States of their duties with regard to common positions, even to the extent that this would mean that the effects of this instrument will go further than the Treaty stipulates. The important criterion seems to be whether the instrument in question 'intended to have legal effects in relation to third parties.' However, again the ECJ seems to make use of a circular argument: The criterion it has formulated does not find its origin in the text of the Treaty. Article 35 (1) EU only enumerated several instruments, the interpretation of which could be the subject of a preliminary reference. A common position was not one of them. So, the criterion of 'intended to have legal effects in relation to third parties' only holds if one first presupposes that this criterion was indeed intended by the authors of the EU Treaty. That means that the ECJ could only uphold this conclusion in the specific situation where it was asked to give a decision concerning the right to effective judicial protection, being one of the fundamental rights, the protection of which is enshrined in Article 6 (2) EU (now Article 6 TEU). In this field, the ECJ let itself be guided not only by the principle of loyalty or sincere cooperation, but also by the system of judicial protection as embodied by the preliminary ques-

---

[97] Case C-355/04 P, *Segi and Others v. The Council* [2007] ECR I-1657, par. 52–55.

tion procedure.[98] The Court, guided by the principles mentioned above, was able to take the next step, and bring the third pillar a little bit closer to the first one. Just as the ECJ has played an important role for the legal protection of individuals in the first pillar, it wanted to do so in the third pillar of the EU, as well.

In another case, the ECJ has clarified how it saw the relationship between the three pillars of the Union. In the case of *Kadi*, following the Court of First Instance, the ECJ spoke of 'the coexistence of the Union and the Community as integrated but separate legal orders, and the constitutional architecture of the pillars, as intended by the framers of the Treaties now in force (...).'[99] Indeed, speaking explicitly of the '*constitutional* architecture of the pillars', the ECJ seems to revisit its own line of reasoning of the constitutionalisation of the EC Treaty. Now, however, the ECJ has the aim of bringing the different pillars closer together by starting from the perspective of the *unity* of the integration process, and its own task of guarding this unity. In this respect, it is interesting to come back to that older case law and see what the ECJ has concluded there. Generally speaking, one may say that it is the task of the ECJ to watch over the legislation of the Member States, and the actions of the EC institutions. True, the Court misses the power to declare a national rule void. Nevertheless, the preliminary question procedure of Article 267 TFEU, and the appeal procedures of Articles 258 and 259 TFEU against violation of the Treaty, make it possible for the Court to manifest itself as the final authority on the interpretation of Community law. Following Article 263 TFEU, also the actions of the EU institutions fall under the jurisdiction of the Court. In 1986, in the case of *Les Verts,* the Court explicitly stated how it saw its own task:

> It must first be emphasized in this regard that the European Economic Community is a community based on the rule of law, inasmuch as neither its Member States nor its institutions can avoid a review of the question whether the measures adopted by them are in conformity with the basic constitutional charter, the Treaty. In particular, in articles 173 [now Article 263 TFEU] and 184 [now Article 277 TFEU], on the one hand, and in article 177 [now Article 267 TFEU], on the other, the Treaty established a complete system of legal remedies and procedures designed to permit the Court of Justice to review the legality of measures adopted by institutions.[100]

As a legal community, a legal order with its own constitutional charter, the European Community respects the principle of protection by an independent and impartial judiciary. The entry into force of the Charter of Fundamental Rights of the European Union as a legally binding document could surely be regarded as a new step on this road, even if, as we have seen in the previous section, the protection of fundamental rights was no longer absent from the agenda of the community and the ECJ.

---

[98] See for an explanation of this procedure Sect. 5.1 above.

[99] Joined Cases C-402/05 P and C-415/05 P, *Yassin Abdullah Kadi and Al Barakaat International Foundation v. Council of the European Union,* judgment of 3 September 2008, par. 202.

[100] Case 294/83, *Les Verts v. Parliament* [1986] ECR 1339, par. 23. See also: Joined Cases C-402/05 P and C-415/05 P, *Yassin Abdullah Kadi and Al Barakaat International Foundation v. Council of the European Union,* par. 281.

The Court reiterated this 'constitutional' line of reasoning in Opinion 1/91, concerning the agreement between the Community and the EFTA-countries on the creation of a European Economic Area. The ECJ first looked at the different objectives of the EEA-Treaty, on the one hand, and the EC Treaty, on the other. It held that, whereas the former had only economic objectives, the EC Treaty went much further:

> the treaty aims to achieve economic integration leading to the establishment of an internal market and economic and monetary union. Article 1 of the Single European Act makes it clear moreover that the objective of all the Community treaties is to contribute together to making concrete progress towards European unity (...)
> [T]he EEC Treaty, albeit concluded in the form of an international agreement, none the less constitutes the constitutional charter of a Community based on the rule of law. As the Court of Justice has consistently held, the Community treaties established a new legal order for the benefit of which the States have limited their sovereign rights, in ever wider fields, and the subjects of which comprise not only Member States but also their nationals (see, in particular, the judgment in Case 26/62 Van Gend en Loos [1963] ECR 1). The essential characteristics of the Community legal order which has thus been established are in particular its primacy over the law of the Member States and the direct effect of a whole series of provisions which are applicable to their nationals and to the Member States themselves.[101]

The economic aims of the Treaty are thus only means that contribute to achieve a wider objective of European unity. This all follows from the special *nature* of the EC Treaty. Yet, it is the Court itself that has come up with the special nature-thesis. Paradoxically, the statement that the Treaty constitutes a 'constitutional charter', only holds when the ECJ constitutes it *as* a constitutional charter....

As was said before, the line of case law in which the ECJ has held that the EC Treaty is more than simply an international treaty, is known under the name of 'constitutionalisation'. Since we have already described this subject earlier, I simply want to look into the crucial link between the reasoning of the ECJ in some important cases, and its own mandate. Now, to find the first step in this process of constitutionalisation, we need to go back as far as 1962. In the classic case of *Van Gend en Loos,* the ECJ states that 'the objective of the EEC Treaty, which is to establish a common market, the functioning of which is of direct concern to interested parties in the Community, implies that this Treaty is more than an agreement which creates mutual obligations between the contracting states.'[102] According to the Court, this means that the European Communities form a new legal order to which the Member States have partly ceded their sovereignty. For this reason, the Treaty does not just address the Member States. Unlike ordinary rules of international law, EC rules can directly give rights to, and impose obligations on, the citizens of the Member States.[103] In this way, the Court establishes that Community law has direct effect, which means

---

[101] Opinion 1/91 [1991] ECR I-06079, par. 17 and 21.

[102] Case 26/62, *Van Gend & Loos* [1963] ECR 1.

[103] Ibid.: 'The Community constitutes a new legal order of international law for the benefit of which the states have limited their sovereign rights, albeit within limited fields, and the subjects of which comprise not only Member States but also their nationals. Independently of the legislation of Member States, community law therefore not only imposes obligations on individuals but is also intended to confer upon them rights which become part of their legal heritage.'

that the rules of community law, on the condition that they are sufficiently clear and precise, can be called upon by citizens before their national courts.[104]

With this judgment, the ECJ has given the (E)EC Treaty a meaning beyond that of an ordinary international agreement. The EC Treaty directly influences the rights and duties of the citizens of the Member States. Normally, international treaties only bind the signing parties, the states. This is captured in the well-known principle of international law, *pacta sunt servanda*. Any consequences for the citizens of the contracting states are an issue of national constitutional law. Even compared to international treaties that confer rights upon individuals, for instance, the various treaties on human rights, the EC Treaty goes further. It can not only give rights, but also impose obligations on the citizens of the Member States. According to the ECJ, the direct effect of Community law is an immediate consequence of the Treaty establishing 'a new legal order', and does not depend on what the constitution of a Member State says about the application of international law in the national legal order.

The argumentation the Court uses in its constitutionalising case law is thus that of the teleological interpretation: Given that the final objective (*telos*) of the Treaty is the establishment of a common or internal market, the direct effect of community law follows as the necessary instrument to attain this aim. Yet, it is important to keep in mind that this is not a kind of means/end rationality that would amount to simple instrumentalism. If the case studies of the previous sections have taught us something, it is that the interrelatedness between national and European legal order precludes the possibility of a straightforward view of European law as a means to attain ends. Hence, teleological interpretation should be understood differently. One might characterise it as a kind of thinking that points the way, the path to reach the goal. A path is, unlike a vehicle for example, not a means to reach an end. Rather, one might describe it as the end itself, as it shows itself 'in the meantime'.

Let us now connect this teleological reasoning with the ECJ's mandate. This mandate is formulated in Article 19 TEU, the first paragraph of which says:

> The Court of Justice of the European Union shall include the Court of Justice, the General Court and specialised courts. It shall ensure that in the interpretation and application of the Treaties the law is observed.

Setting the common or internal market as the main *telos* of integration, the Court has been able to come to the 'necessary' conclusion of such key doctrines as direct effect, and supremacy of European law. Yet, the question is from what perspective does a *telos* appear? A third person's perspective cannot make sense of a *telos*. Of course, when the game is an old one, and the rules well-known, a spectator understands what the ultimate goal is, and is able to define it in clear terms. However, in the case of European integration, this does not hold. Speaking of a *telos* of integration implies being immersed in a field, being situated in a concrete reality where it depends on the next step to be taken whether or not a *telos* comes closer. In

---

[104] For an examination of the constitutional value of this doctrine, see: S. Prechal, 'Direct Effect, Indirect Effect, Supremacy and the Evolving Constitution of the European Union', in: C. Barnard (ed.), *The Fundamentals of EU Law Revisited. Assessing the Impact of the Constitutional Debate*, Oxford (etc.): Oxford University Press 2007, pp. 35–70.

other words, it implies taking the agential point of view, the perspective of someone walking the path, step by step. The agent understands that the next step can only be taken by following the clues, dealing with practical difficulties on the road, and then proceeding towards an 'ever closer Union'. The Court is situated in this field by its own mandate. Constitutionalisation is, therefore, closely linked with the role the ECJ itself plays in integration. While saying something about the European integration project as a legal order, the ECJ says something about itself. Saying something about what a European legal *order* is as an autonomous order, the ECJ is itself *ordering* Europe legally.

In the case of *Kadi*, mentioned above, the ECJ explicitly called to mind the link between the autonomy of the EC legal order, and its own task:

> It is also to be recalled that an international agreement cannot affect the allocation of powers fixed by the Treaties or, consequently, the autonomy of the Community legal system, observance of which is ensured by the Court by virtue of the exclusive jurisdiction conferred on it by Article 220 EC [now Article 19 TEU], jurisdiction that the Court has, moreover, already held to form part of the very foundations of the Community (…)[105]

Remember Article 19 TEU, where the ECJ, a judicial body called into being by the Treaty, is thus given the task of 'ensuring that the law is observed'. This task is formulated broadly, even when taking into account the reference to the jurisdiction of the Court. This broad formulation immediately provokes the question what the last enigmatic part of the mandate means. What does 'the law' refer to in this article? One thing that does seem to be beyond doubt is that 'law' comprises more than simply the Treaties.[106] Looking at the way in which the ECJ has taken up its role, it seems fair to say that in the *praxis* of its case law, it has itself been giving meaning to what it entails that the 'law is observed' in the European legal order.

Now, this practice, as we have analysed it in this chapter, points to something else. Paradoxically, 'ensuring that the law is observed' can only be done by going beyond a simple textual explanation of the Treaty. So, the ECJ can only ensure the observance of the EU legal order by truly creative acts, acts of chiastic constitution. That is what constitutionalisation ultimately boils down to. Yet, this remains only half of the story. A full understanding of the process of constitutionalisation is only possible by taking into account that constitution and passivity go hand in hand. The ECJ can only *bind* others to the law, while *being bound* by the law. It stands on trial while sitting at the trial. As said, the mandate plays a crucial role in this respect because it situates the ECJ. In this way, it is guided by the rule, and able to take the next step. Therefore, it might not come as a surprise that a close

---

[105] Joined Cases C-402/05 P and C-415/05 P, *Yassin Abdullah Kadi and Al Barakaat International Foundation v. Council of the European Union,* par. 282.

[106] Cf. R. Barents & L.J. Brinkhorst, *Grondlijnen van Europees Recht,* Deventer: Kluwer 2006, p. 55 and A. Arnull, o.c., p. 335: 'The reference in Article 220 EC to "the law", unless nothing more than "a pious aspiration or a harmless piece of padding", must have been intended to embrace something more than the law expressly laid down by or under the Treaty itself.' See also: H. Schepel and E. Blankenburg, 'Mobilizing the European Court of Justice', in: G. de Bùrca, and J.H.H. Weiler, *The European Court of Justice,* Oxford (etc.): Oxford University Press 2001, pp. 9–42, at p. 10.

reading of the ECJ's mandate reveals something peculiar. In ensuring that the law is observed (interpreting and applying the Treaty, and thus also, all secondary legislation stemming from it) ... the law is observed. There remains a sense of 'the law' that is not available for autonomous activity of the ECJ. There remains a sense of 'the law' that is not at the disposal of the judge, but that makes it possible for him to perform his task, in the first place. There remains a sense of 'the law' that comes *to* the European legal order, rather than simply from it. One can, of course, speculate as to what is exactly meant by 'the law'. It might be more fruitful, however, to first ask the question what it means 'to ensure that the law is *observed*'? What does it take '*to observe* the law'? 'Observare' in Latin has the meaning of 'to heed', 'to respect', 'to esteem'. In this way, the European judge is reminded of what Rousseau once called the first law, that the laws should be observed.[107] This calls into mind the very *prudentia* involved in juris-prudence. Now, in what way should the ECJ be prudent? What is the passivity that the ECJ should reckon with in its own activity? As the principle of loyalty or sincere cooperation is used, time and again, to point to the obligations of Member States towards the Union, one might almost forget that it also works the other way around. Indeed, if the principle makes clear that there is no European integration without Member States, it also hints at the passivity that European institutions furrow as a fertile soil for integration. Any European institution involved in constitutional activity will engage the constitutional traditions of the Member States. In this respect, Article 4, paragraph 2 TEU is important, where the Union (and thus all its institutions) is called upon to 'respect the equality of Member States before the Treaties as well as their national identities, inherent in their fundamental structures, political and constitutional, inclusive of regional and local self-government.' The ECJ is no exception to this. Time and again, it will have to operate with a certain vigilance in order to avoid the pitfalls that are inherent to legal power, as it constantly moves between power *in* and power *over* the law. Perhaps, it is this vigilance that is needed to fulfil those words of Husserl, that a tradition entails '*the power to forget origins* and to give to the past not a survival, which is the hypocritical form of forgetfulness, but a new life, which is the noble form of memory.'[108] Then, this memorising would be an oblique way to reckon with a passivity *of* constitution. It is of this 'constitutional passivity' that the ECJ has to give evidence in all of its judgments.[109]

---

[107] J.-J. Rousseau, 'Discourse on Political Economy', in: *The Social Contract and Other Later Political Writings,* ed. and trans. V. Gourevitch, Cambridge: Cambridge University Press 1997 [1755], pp. 3–38, at p. 11. In the same vein, see also: B. Waldenfels, *Phänomenologie der Aufmerksamkeit,* Frankfurt am Mein 2005, pp. 270–271 and B. van Roermund, *Het verdwijnpunt van de wet. Een opstel over symboolwerking van wetgeving,* Deventer: Tjeenk Willink 1997.

[108] M. Merleau-Ponty, *Signs,* trans. R. McCleary, Evanston, Ill.: Northwestern University Press 1964, p. 59./M. Merleau-Ponty, *Signes,* Paris: Gallimard 2003 [1960], p. 95. [Italics in the original]

[109] For the notion of 'constitutional passivity', see: M. Merleau-Ponty, *L'institution. La passivité. Notes de cours au Collège de France (1954–1955),* Paris: Belin 2003, p. 182.

5.6   Conclusion

In this chapter, I have returned to the legal problems underlying this study. My hypothesis was that only a chiastic relationship between constitution and passivity can make sense of the relationship between constituent and constituted power in the context of competence issues in EU law. In the first section, I have looked into the preliminary ruling procedure as the specific institutional constellation to accomplish legal certainty in the European legal order. I showed how this procedure is characterised by the chiastic interplay between national courts and ECJ. Then, I turned to some exemplary episodes in the ECJ's case law concerning competences. First, I analysed the cases on European "federal common law" and implied powers, and showed how the structure of implication was a direct result of the specific situation of the court, and the need to protect the unity and autonomy of the European legal order. In the same vein, in the following sections, I analysed European administrative law, the case of Maria Pupino, and the Court's case law on human rights. I have shown that one can only make sense of this case law by taking into account a theory of chiastic constitution in passivity. In the final section, I looked into recent and classic cases concerning the constitutionalisation of the integration process. Stressing the importance of the principle of loyal cooperation, and the mandate of the ECJ, I argued that the Court may obliquely reckon with the passivity in activity by prudently dealing with the constitutional traditions of the Member States in its own constitutionalising activity.

Conclusive Summary

We have scrutinised the 'creeping competences' of the European Union. These competences are the legal powers to enact binding legislation. In the first chapter, we started from the present division of powers between the Union and its Member States. This division is ruled by the principle of conferred powers that holds that the Union has only those competences that are given to it. Accordingly, the competences of the Union can be divided into exclusive, concurrent (sub-divided into exhaustible and non-exhaustible powers) and supporting powers. While this distinction seems rather clear-cut, the so-called doctrine of implied or implicit powers questions the rule of conferred powers. This doctrine, an emblematic case of creeping competences, was first developed by the U.S. Supreme Court, and now forms a classic in the law of international organisations. The European Court of Justice (ECJ) developed its doctrine of implied powers of the European Community in several cases in the 1970s. In a basic formulation, the doctrine holds that the EC does not only have the competences explicitly given to it by the Treaties, but also possesses those powers that are necessary to make use of the explicit powers. While these cases were mostly about external powers of the Community, the existence of several broadly formulated Treaty articles makes clear that implied powers are not a marginal phenomenon in the European legal order. The existence of this doctrine has made us turn our attention to the role of the ECJ in the European legal order. According to its rather vaguely formulated mandate, Article 19 TEU, the ECJ should 'ensure that the law is observed.' For this purpose, the Court has jurisdiction in several procedures, of which the preliminary reference procedure is the most important. In this procedure, the ECJ answers questions on European law posed to it by national courts. With this procedure, the ECJ has become the final legal authority on EU law, and developed this law into something that goes beyond normal international law. This latter ongoing development, by which the Treaties gained in importance, has been called the 'constitutionalisation' of the Treaties. It is exactly this 'constitutionalisation' that has given EU law a much bigger than expected role in every-day life, and that has been one of the phenomena causing the problems falling under the term 'competence creep'. On a deeper level, this 'competence creep' brings with it serious questions concerning authority. Two interrelated questions can be discerned. First, who has ultimate authority to attribute competences? Secondly, who has the judicial power to decide over the previous question? On a deeper level, however, both defenders and critics of implied powers have something in common. Both take their cue from a strict separation of law and politics: The legal powers of international organisations are regarded as purely functional, as legal means to meet (pre-given) political ends. One influential institution addressing these issues was the German Federal Constitutional Court (FCC) in its judgment on the Treaty of Maastricht. Starting from a strict interpretation of the principle of conferred powers, the doctrine of implied powers was severely criticised. Notwithstanding that the FCC has a point, its own solution to the problem of creeping competences is highly problematic from the viewpoint of European integration, since it would completely hand over the future of the integration process to the whims of national courts. I advanced the thesis that there was more at stake in the doctrine of implied powers than meets the eye, and that this 'more' would take us right to the heart of constitutional theory.

This voyage into constitutional theory was undertaken in Chap. 2. Starting from the core of the Maastricht Decision, linking the theme of legal powers with that of constitution-making, a distinction between two traditions of constitutional thinking was made. First of all, there is a revolutionary tradition, originating in France and the Unites States of America. On the other hand, there is an evolutionary tradition, born in Germany and the United Kingdom. The former, the tradition that puts emphasis on the concept of constituent power and upholds the primacy of politics over law, was scrutinised by analysing the work of Sieyès and Negri. While both regard revolution as the paradigm of constituent power, their first interest is in who is the subject of the revolution, and thus of constituent power. While Sieyès assigns this role to the nation, and ultimately rests his theory on a social contract, Negri points to the multitude as the supreme political actor. Their differences notwithstanding, both ultimately fall prey to circular reasoning: Sieyès, because he presupposes who the parties to the contract are; Negri, because he alludes to a necessary moment of representation, a concept he had explicitly rejected. The second tradition is the one of constitutionalism. This theory of constitution-making stresses the need to limit the power of government, to tame political power. St. John Bolingbroke and Böckenförde are amongst the many defenders of this viewpoint. Though constitutionalism certainly has its strengths, I found that there remains a fallacy in this approach, too, because it can only defend the case of limiting powers by presupposing that power is necessarily limited. Finally, I reread (parts of) the discussion between Carl Schmitt and Hans Kelsen, as an example of a real debate between a defender of the revolutionary tradition (Schmitt) and the evolutionary one (Kelsen). Or, in their own terminology, Schmitt is defending a dualism of law and state, while Kelsen advocates a monism of law and state. Yet, here again, Kelsen's monism ultimately rests on the very same dualistic presupposition as Schmitt holds: a strict separation of law and politics. It is exactly this dualism that has appeared under different guises in all the positions discussed in this chapter. Taking their differences into account, one could consider the two traditions of constitution-making as completely mirroring one another. On a deeper level, however, it is the commonly held dualism between politics and law, absolute power and limited power, presence and absence, formless forming and form, *Geist* and expression, original and representation, that makes their divergences possible. It is also this dualism that underlies the discussions on implied powers. Conceptualising legal power as essentially limited, both traditions of constitution-making reject the implied powers doctrine of the ECJ. Since, however, neither tradition can offer a tenable alternative, I suggested to re-think constitution-making in order to conceptualise legal power in such a way that we are able to make sense of creeping competences in general, and implied powers in particular. I proposed to re-describe, rather than to judge the phenomenon.

Chapter 3 was the first step in this process. I started by showing how theories of constitution-making take up the question of creation of law. The dualism that both traditions take for granted entails that they also think of creation in a dualistic way. The revolutionary tradition regards creation as an act *ex nihilo*. The tradition of constitutionalism basically regards creation as a process of copying a pre-given reality. Philosophically speaking, we encounter here two version of representational thinking. The problem of this way of conceptualising creation is that the act of creation itself is not taken seriously. Taking my cue from the work of Maurice Merleau-Ponty, I proposed rethinking constitution-making by making use of the model of creation as expression, or metamorphosis, as 'coherent deformation'. Expression should then be taken as the constitution of sense, with legal-political constitution-making as a species of a more encompassing genus. This model of creation was explained by the relationship between speaking speech and spoken speech. This is an analytical distinction between two ways in which the expressive force of language appears. The two poles do not exist in a pure form; they are mutually dependent, internally related in a paradoxical way, but they cannot ever completely coincide. In short, this relationship is chiastic. This has consequences for an understanding of historicity, to wit, of expression *in time*. Following Merleau-Ponty, a distinction was made between two forms of historicity. The first form was the historicity of the Museum. This is the historicity of death, because it only regards the unity of painting retrospectively. A second form of historicity starts from the act of painting itself, that binds all painters to one and the same task. This is the historicity of life, where tradition refers to 'the power to forget the origin.' This understanding of the unity of painting brings with it a view of history as the advent of meaning. In a more full-blown philosophy of history that plays a role in politics, this opens up the dimension of the symbolic. Indeed, political action, understood as action in history, always unfolds in a symbolic field. The specific concept of the symbolic referred to in this regard, always points to the symbolic dimension of a concrete constellation of things or actions. This dimension (the 'depth' of the world) is opened to us by our body. For Merleau-Ponty, perception is the privileged *locus* of access to the world. This means that in perception, we understand that our relationship towards the world is not, first of all, that of a subject towards an object. No, we are, first of all, in a practical relationship with the world, i.e., the subject is a *Je peux* rather than a *Je pense*. This *Je peux* hovers between 'being able' and 'being enabled'. Our relationship is, therefore, one of bodily sense-constitution, according to the chiastic model described earlier. Rereading some examples of political theorists, I showed how, in law and politics, this has consequences for our understanding of revolution, the role of representation in democracy, and the relationship between rule of man and rule of law. The relationship between law and politics needs to be understood chiastically.

In Chap. 4, I continued this line of thought by a critical reading of Descombes's book on the subject in modern philosophy, especially in the field of law. Descombes argues that he can find an autonomous subject of rule-following by taking his cue from Wittgenstein's thoughts on this phenomenon. Crucial in this theory is the example of teaching someone to play chess and Wittgenstein remarks that what is involved here are 'customs'. An analysis of this situation has Descombes pointing to the need for conventions: Teaching someone to play chess boils down to teaching someone a set of conventions. With Anscombe, Descombes then holds that such a set of conventions should finally rest on a 'practical necessity'. My problem with this position is that a reference to conventions begs the question, since conventions are exactly part of what needs to be explained, and not the solution. I proposed an alternative reading of Wittgenstein's thoughts on rule-following, especially of the crucial notion of 'customs'. Rereading Wittgenstein, I argued that he regards rule-following as a pre-reflective activity. Indeed, rules guide me in a bodily way, like signposts do. That is how I understand Wittgenstein saying that rule-following is a 'practice'. In order to make sense of the latter notion, I propose to regard Merleau-Ponty's work as the better interpretative grid of what Wittgenstein had in mind. There, I argued, we can find an understanding of practice that regards it as a bodily activity. This reading of practice is needed in order to make sense of rule-following as a pre-reflective activity. This notion of practice is also where the account of perception has led us. I started out with perception in art. Both the experience of the artist, and that of the art viewer (the latter is derived from the former) should be understood as one in which the constituting activity is rooted in passivity; or rather, that there is an intertwinement of activity and passivity. Five points were important, in this respect. First of all, perceiving always means being bodily situated in a field. Secondly, there is a specific bodily way of dealing with the situation at hand, and the tasks that need to be performed. Thirdly, it is my perceiving body that constitutes sense by taking its cue from (in both the active and the passive sense of the word) the sense of the world. Fourthly, the intimate bond between subject and world is caught in the new notion of the subject as '*j'en suis*'; I am in the world and of the world. Lastly, this notion involves a chiasm of passivity and activity in sense-constitution. In other words, I argued that Wittgenstein's thoughts on rule-following are to be understood starting from a bodily subject as is explicated in the work of Merleau-Ponty. Confronting this interpretation of Wittgenstein with Descombes's, I proposed an alternative interpretation of the crucial concept of customs. Going back to the original Wittgensteinian word '*Gepflogenheiten*', I argued that the customs of rule-following are not to be understood as conventions, but rather as 'habits' in the deeper sense (rendered by the Oxford English Dictionary as 'archaic') of 'bodily apparel or attire', a clothing or garment as the interface that is as much part of me as it is of the world. Wittgenstein teaches us that rule-following is, first and foremost, a bodily activity that forces me in a certain situation that I can take up and take further by going along with the movement of the world. In short, I can only follow rules as I follow sign-posts, i.e., by attaching myself to them in a bodily way.

In the fifth and last chapter, I returned to the problem of creeping competences that was central to the first chapter of this inquiry. What has the detour via philosophy contributed to an understanding of the competence creep? To answer this question, I first looked at the specific situation of the ECJ; subsequently, I analysed some specific areas of case law in which competences could be said to be 'creeping'. To situate the ECJ, I analysed the specific place this court holds in the EU legal order by looking at its role in the preliminary question procedure, and its own case law on the so-called *acte clair*. Rejecting the claim that the ECJ had simply installed a doctrine of precedent, I pointed to how answers in the preliminary reference procedure are basically concerned with the future application of EU law, and not with the past (as the term precedent stipulates). What is rather at stake is the nature of legal certainty in the European legal order. What the preliminary reference procedure and the *acte clair*-doctrine show is the responsive structure of legal certainty on a European level. The intertwinement of question and response, as emphasized by Waldenfels, has helped us to understand better how legal unity is constituted in Europe. This has consequences for the notion of judicial *Kompetenz-Kompetenz*: It points to a moment of passivity in legal constitution, a moment that cannot be captured legally. I argued that there is a passivity of adjudication in Europe in the two-fold sense of the ECJ being placed 'before the decision' and open to the changing conditions in which European law should function, while proceeding from the line of decisions already taken. This way of following the rule was examined in three case studies of constitution in case law, where the chiasm appeared again and again, in a circular moment in the reasoning of the ECJ. First of all, I returned to the doctrine of implied powers by showing that the structure of implication is also to be found in the case law wherein "federal common law" was created. This shed new light on how the structure of implication should be understood: The market as the ultimate goal of the integration process, and the emphasis on effectiveness, are connected in such a way that the argument necessarily appears in the form of an implication. The argument of a *telos* (the common or internal market) as an ultimate goal in the *future*, only works by pointing to commitments taken up in the *past* (the system of the Treaty, the principle of loyal cooperation). These, then, from the perspective of the *present*, appear as implied. The implication shows what is finally philosophically at stake in creeping competences, to wit, how legal power moves between power *in* and power *over* the law. The second case study concerned the principles of sincere cooperation and effectiveness, as appearing in several cases of the ECJ with regard to "European Public Law". Also in these cases, the structure of implication returns. The special emphasis on the principle of loyal cooperation was explained by arguing that this principle shows the Member States their respective responsibilities in an emblematic way. The third case study looked into the ECJ's case law on human rights. In this respect, I pointed out that the ECJ's reference to 'common constitutional traditions' is only tenable by presupposing that the Member States indeed hold these traditions in common. After these three case studies, I turned to the recent case law of the ECJ concerning the constitutionalisation of the EU Treaty. Pointing back once more to the broadly formulated mandate of the ECJ, I argued that observing the law can only be done by acts that metamorphose the existing meaning of the Treaty. So, the ECJ can only observe the EU as a legal order by truly creative acts, acts of chiastic constitution. Yet, at the same time, it should not forget that its constituting activity always roots in an insurmountable passivity. The problem of 'creeping competences' can never be completely avoided because it is inherent in the concept of legal power itself, as moving between power *in* and power *over* the law. Yet, this may be obliquely recognised by the ECJ by exercising a certain vigilance, while engaging with the constitutional traditions of the Member States. It is of this 'constitutional passivity' that the ECJ should give evidence, this is the *prudentia* involved in jurisprudence.

So what does this mean for the problem of creeping competences in the European Union? As a study in philosophy of law, this book does not aim to come up with solutions. Instead, a new framework of addressing the problems was presented. The analysis of legal power in this book has shown that, contrary to what is upheld by the main traditions of constitutional thinking, legal power is not simply power *in* law. Rather, taking my cue from a chiastic understanding of the relationship between constituent and constitutional power, I have argued that legal power always moves between power *in* and power *over* law. This means, first of all, that creeping competences are not so much an exception to the rule, but rather, what is at stake in creeping competences is the very structure of competence as legal power. It is inherent to competence to creep, i.e., to move between the two poles of constituent and constitutional power. Furthermore, my analysis also shows that this is the way legal power *ought* to behave. The relationship between constituent and constitutional power should work in a chiastic way in order to make change and innovation possible. Only a chiastic account of the relationship between constituent and constitutional power captures their specific interrelatedness (which is an advantage, in comparison with the traditional theories of constitution-making). The normative value of this last point emerges more fully when we ask ourselves what the theory expounded in this study can say of a possible limit to creeping competences. Even given that creeping competences tell us something about the nature of legal power itself, this does not preclude the possibility that there remain aspects of this phenomenon that are dangerous to the constitutional state, or *Rechtsstaat* itself. I have alluded to these dangers when the spread (*écart*) of the chiasm between constituent and constitutional power was discussed. In the vocabulary of this study, a legal order that denies the spread between the two poles cannot credibly make the claim of being a constitutional state. Of course, these claims cannot be made by the legal order itself, but rather by the institutions of the legal order, by the bodies of constitutional power. If such a body denies the constitutive significance of the others for its own legitimacy, this claim can be regarded as one denying the spread between constituent and constitutional power. In other words, this would be a constitutional power that assumes to be constituent power; there would be a coincidence of the two poles. My theory has shown that coincidence is ever imminent: The spread is a critical distance that precludes a fusion of constitutional power and constituent power.

Throughout this study on the phenomenon of creeping competences in the EU, I have paid special attention to the role of the ECJ because it is often considered to be part of the problem, instead of part of the solution. One of my conclusions is that the critique of the ECJ is in so far unjustified that it is inherent to legal power to be creeping. In other words, it is too simple to blame the ECJ for overstretching the boundaries of EU competences. Yet, this does not mean that the ECJ, too, cannot overstep its mandate and forget its role as constitutional power. A situation like this might arise when the ECJ does not take care to motivate its decisions as accurately as possible (e.g., by referring only to general principles, and not also to provisions of primary or secondary EU law), when it tries to harmonise areas that are explicitly precluded from harmonisation, when it makes decisions without taking into consideration the principles of subsidiarity and proportionality, if it does not strictly monitor the use of the so-called functional provisions in the Treaties and when it considers issues or gives its opinion on points not raised by the litigants of a dispute. In this regard, it is important to keep in mind that in the particular institutional structure of the EU, issues of competence or legal power touch both on the *horizontal* division of powers (between the different EU institutions) and on the *vertical* division of powers (between the EU and its Member States). The ECJ is the spider in this net, and it has to take the responsibility of passively constituting the next step in the case at hand in order to keep the promise of 'an ever closer union'.

What my analysis of the relationship between constituent and constitutional power has shown is that there is no balance in legal power. Moreover, there *should* be no balance in legal power, since this would be a petrified form of competence. Legal power is constantly out of joint. Indeed, it is precisely because it is out of joint that it can function. The constitutional powers in the European legal order ought to preserve the tensions between them, and render this order a *Rechtsstaat* in their constant reminder that there is no definitive balance possible, that there is no final claim to justice that stands beyond contestation.

Bibliography

Arendt, H. *On Revolution*, London: Penguin 1973 [1963].

Aristotle, *Politics*, trans. E. Barker, Oxford (etc.): Oxford University Press 1995.

Arnull, A. *The European Union and its Court of Justice* (2nd edition), Oxford (etc.): Oxford University Press 2006.

Audi, R. *Epistemology. A Contemporary Introduction to the Theory of Knowledge*, London (etc.): Routledge 1998.

Barak, A. *The Judge in a Democracy*, Princeton, NJ: Princeton University Press 2008 [2006].

Barbaras, R. *De l'être du phénomène. Sur l'ontologie de Merleau-Ponty*, Grenoble: Éditions Jérôme Millon 2001.

Baquero Cruz, J. 'The Changing Constitutional Role of the European Court of Justice', *International Journal of Legal Information*, vol. 34 (2006), pp. 223-245.

Baquero Cruz, J. 'The Legacy of the Maastricht-Urteil and the Pluralist Movement', *European Law Journal*, vol. 14 (2008), pp. 389-422.

Barents, R. & L.J. Brinkhorst, *Grondlijnen van Europees Recht*, Deventer: Kluwer 2006.

Bloor, D. *Wittgenstein, Rules and Institutions*, London and New York: Routledge 1997.

Böckenförde, E-W. 'Die verfassunggebende Gewalt des Volkes – Ein Grenzbegriff des Verfassungsrechts', in E-W. Böckenförde, *Staat, Verfassung, Demokratie. Studien zur Verfassungstheorie und zum Verfassungsrecht*, Frankfurt am Main: Suhrkamp 1991, pp. 90-112.

Bogdandy, A. von and J. Bast, The European Union's Order of Competences: The Current Law and Proposals for its Reform, *Common Market Law Review*, vol. 39 (2002), pp. 227-268.

Bogdandy, A. von and J. Bast, 'The Vertical Order of Competences', in A. von Bogdandy and J. Bast (eds.), *Principles of European Constitutional Law*, Oxford (etc.): Hart 2006, pp. 335-372.

Brown, L.N. & T. Kennedy, *The Court of Justice of the European Communities* (5th edition), London: Sweet & Maxwell 2000.

Bulygin, E. 'On Norms of Competence', *Law & Philosophy*, vol. 11 (1992), pp. 201-216.

Búrca, G. de 'The European Court of Justice and the Evolution of EU Law', in T.A. Börzel and R.A. Cichowski (eds.), *The State of the European Union: Law, Politics and Society* (vol. 6), Oxford (etc.): Oxford University Press 2003, pp. 48-75.

Búrca G. de & B. de Witte, 'The Delimitation of Powers Between the EU and its Member States', in A. Arnull & D. Wincott (eds.), *Accountability and Legitimacy in the European Union*, Oxford: Oxford University Press 2002, pp. 201-222.

Carbone, K. 'Viva Le Louvre! At 20, I.M. Pei's Controversial Pyramid Defies Critics', available at: http://www.fastcompany.com/blog/ken-carbone/yes-less/viva-le-louvre-20-im-peis-controversial-pyramid-defies-critics [visited on 29 October 2009].

Carbone, M. *La visibilité de l'invisible. Merleau-Ponty entre Cézanne et Proust*, Hildesheim (etc.): Georg Olms Verlag 2001.

Carman, T. 'The Body in Husserl and Merleau-Ponty', *Philosophical Topics,* vol. 27 (1999), pp. 205-226.

Castiglione, D. 'The Political Theory of the Constitution' in R. Bellamy and D. Castiglione (eds.), *Constitutionalism in Transformation: European and Theoretical Perspectives*, Oxford (etc.): Blackwell 1996, pp. 5-23.

Chase, W.G. and H. Simon, 'Perception in Chess', *Cognitive Psychology*, vol. 4 (1973), pp. 55-81.

Claes, M.L.H.K. *The National Courts' Mandate in the European Constitution*, Oxford (etc.): Hart Publishing 2006.

Conway, G. 'Conflicts of Competence Norms in EU Law and the Legal Reasoning of the ECJ', *German Law Journal*, vol. 11 (2010), pp. 966-1005.

Cotté, S. 'I.M. Pei, l'architecte des musées', in M. Laclotte (ed.), *Le nouveau visage du Louvre. Numéro spécial de la Revue du Louvre et des Musées de France*, Paris: Conseil des Musées Nationaux 1989, pp. 13-15.

Craig, P. 'The Jurisdiction of the Community Courts Reconsidered', in: G. de Bùrca and J.H.H. Weiler (eds.), *The European Court of Justice*, Oxford (etc.): Oxford University Press 2001, pp. 177-214.

Craig, P. & G. De Bùrca, *EU Law. Text, Cases, and Materials* (4th edition), Oxford (etc.): Oxford University Press 2008.

Curtin, D.M. en R.A. Wessel, 'Rechtseenheid van de Europese Unie? De rol van het Hof van Justitie als constitutionele rechter', *SEW Tijdschrift voor Europees en economisch recht*, 2008, nr. 10, pp. 369-376.

Cummings, E.E. *50 Poems*, New York: Duell, Sloan and Pearce 1940.

Dashwood, A. and J. Heliskoski, 'The classic authorities revisited', in A. Dashwood and Ch. Hillion (eds.), *The General Law of E.C. External Relations*, London: Sweets & Maxwell 2000, pp. 3-19.

Davies, G. 'Subsidiarity: The Wrong Idea, In the Wrong Place, At the Wrong Time', *Common Market Law Review*, vol. 43 (2006), pp. 63-85.

Delcò, A. *Merleau-Ponty et l'expérience de la création. Du paradigme au schème*, Paris: Presses Universitaires de France 2005.

Denys, C. *Impliciete bevoegdheden in de Europese Economische Gemeenschap. Een onderzoek naar de betekenis van 'implied powers'*, Antwerpen: Maklu 1990.

Descombes, V. *Le complément de sujet. Enquête sur le fait d'agir de soi-même*, Paris: Gallimard 2004.

Everling, U. 'The Court of Justice As a Decisionmaking Authority', *Michigan Law Review*, vol. 82 (1983-1984), pp. 1294-1310.

Giardina, A. 'The Rule of Law and Implied Powers in the European Communities', in *The Italian Yearbook of International Law. Volume I*, Napoli: Editoriale Scientifica 1975, pp. 99-111.

Gollin, R. 'De viool als verlengstuk van haar wezen. Dinsdagprofiel Janine Jansen', *de Volkskrant*, 16 October, 2007.

Goucho Soares, A. 'The Principle of Conferred Powers and the Division of Powers between the European Community and the Member States', *Liverpool Law Review*, vol. 23 (2001), pp. 57-78.

Hamrick, W. S. *An Existential Phenomenology of Law: Maurice Merleau-Ponty*, Dordrecht (etc.): Nijhoff 1987.

Harris, J.W. *Legal Philosophies* (2nd edition), London (etc.): Butterworths 1997.

Hart, H.L.A. *The Concept of Law* (2nd edition), Oxford (etc.): Oxford University Press 1994.

Hartley, T.C. *The Foundations of European Community Law* (3rd edition), Oxford: Clarendon 1994.

Herlin-Karnell, E. 'Subsidiarity in the Area of EU Justice and Home Affairs Law – A Lost Cause?', *European Law Journal*, vol 15 (2009), pp. 351-361.

Hohfeld, W. N. *Fundamental Legal Conceptions as Applied in Judicial Reasoning and Other Legal Essays* (ed. W. W. Cook), New Haven: Yale University Press 1923.

Hong, Q. L. *The Legal Inclusion of Extremist Speech*, Nijmegen: Wolf Legal Publishers 2005.

Hong, Q. L. 'Constitutional Review in the Mega-Leviathan: A Democratic Foundation for the European Court of Justice', *European Law Journal*, vol. 16 (2010), pp. 695-716.

Honig, B. *Emergency Politics: Paradox, Law, Democracy*, Princeton and Oxford: Princeton University Press 2009.

Itzcovich, G. 'The Interpretation of Community Law by the European Court of Justice', *German Law Journal*, vol. 10 (2009), pp. 537-560.

Jacqué, J-P. 'The Principle of Institutional Balance', *Common Market Law Review*, vol. 41 (2004), pp. 383-391.

Jans, J.H., R. de Lange, S. Prechal and R.J.G.M. Widdershoven, *Europeanisation of Public Law*, Groningen: Europa Law Publishing 2007.

Kelsen, H. *General Theory of Law and State*, New York: Russel & Russel 1961.

Kelsen, H. 'Das Wesen des Staates', in H. Klacatsky, R. Marcić and H. Schambeck (eds.), *Die Wiener Rechtstheoretische Schule*, Wien (etc.): Europa Verlag 1968, pp. 1713-1728.

Kelsen, H. 'Law, State, and Justice in the Pure Theory of Law', in H. Kelsen, *What is Justice? Justice, Law, and Politics in the Mirror of Science. Collected Essays by Hans Kelsen*, Berkeley (etc.): University of California Press 1971, pp. 288-302.

Kelsen, H. *Introduction to the Problems of Legal Theory*, Oxford: Clarendon Press 1992.

Kelsen, H. 'On the Essence and Value of Democracy', trans. B. Cooper and S. Hemetsberger, in A.J. Jacobson and B. Schlink (eds.), *Weimar: A Jurisprudence of Crisis*, Berkeley (etc.): University of California Press 2002 [1929], pp. 84-109.

Klabbers, J. 'Over het leerstuk van de impliciete bevoegdheden in het recht der internationale organisaties', in J.D.M. Steenbergen (ed.), *Ongebogen recht*, Den Haag: Sdu Uitgevers 1998, pp. 1-12.

Klabbers, J. *An Introduction to International Institutional Law*, Cambridge: Cambridge University Press 2002.

Knook, A. *Europe's Constitutional Court: The Role of the European Court of Justice in the Intertwined Separation of Powers and Division of Powers in the European Union*, Doctoral Thesis, Utrecht University, Utrecht 2009.

Labelle, G. 'L'oeuvre deWeber et ses prolongements selon Merleau-Ponty: de l'historicité à la recherche de l'absolu dans le relatif', in Christian Nadeau (ed.), *La philosophie de l'histoire. Mélanges oferts à Maurice Lagueux*, Québec: PUL 2007, pp. 395-434.

Labelle, G. 'Maurice Merleau-Ponty et la genèse de la philosophie politique de Claude Lefort', *Politique et Sociétés*, vol. 22 (2003), pp. 9-44, available at: http://id.erudit.org/iderudit/008849ar [visited on 29 October 2009].

Laclotte, M. 'Le nouveau visage du Louvre', in M. Laclotte (ed.), *Le nouveau visage du Louvre. Numéro spécial de la Revue du Louvre et des Musées de France*, Paris: Conseil des Musées Nationaux 1989, pp. 5-12.

Lawlor, L. *Thinking through French Philosphy: The Being of the Question*, Bloomington: Indiana University Press 2003.

Lefort, C. *Democracy and Political Theory*, trans. D. Macey, Cambridge: Polity Press 1988 [1986].

Lefort, C. 'Le sens de l'orientation', in M. Merleau-Ponty, *Notes de cours sur L'origine de la géométrie de Husserl*, Suivi de Recherches sur la phénoménologie de Merleau-Ponty, R. Barbaras (ed.), Paris: Presses Universitaires de France 1998, pp. 221-238.

Lenaerts, K. and K. Gutman, '"Federal Common Law" in the European Union: A Comparative Perspective from the United States', *The American Journal of Comparative Law*, vol. 54 (2006), pp. 1-121.

Lindahl, H. 'European Integration: Popular Sovereignty and a Politics of Boundaries', *European Law Journal*, vol. 6 (2000), pp. 239-256.

Lindahl, H. 'Acquiring a Community: the *Acquis* and the Institution of European Legal Order', *European Law Journal*, vol. 9 (2003), pp. 433-450.

Lindahl, H. 'Constituent Power and Reflexive Identity: Towards an Ontology of Collective Selfhood', in M. Loughlin and N. Walker (eds.), *The Paradox of Constitutionalism: Constituent Power and Constitutional Form*, Oxford (etc.): Oxford University Press 2007, pp. 9-24.

Lindahl, H. 'The paradox of constituent power. The ambiguous self-constitution of the European Union', *Ratio Juris: An International Journal of Jurisprudence and Philosophy of Law*, vol. 20 (2007), pp. 485-505.

Lo Giudice, A. *Il soggetto plurale. Regolazione sociale e mediazione simbolica*, Milano: Giuffrè 2006.

Loose, D. *Democratie zonder blauwdruk. De politieke filosofie van Claude Lefort*, Best: Damon 1997.

Loughlin, M. and N. Walker (eds.), *The Paradox of Constitutionalism: Constituent Power and Constitutional Form*, Oxford (etc.): Oxford University Press 2007.

Malanczuk, P. *Akehurst's Modern Introduction to International Law*, London (etc.): Routledge 1997.

Mancini, G.F. 'The Making of a Constitution for Europe', *Common Market Law Review*, vol. 26 (1989), pp. 595-614.

Mayer, Z.C. 'Competences – Reloaded? The Vertical Division of Powers in the EU and the new European Constitution', *International Journal of Constitutional Law*, vol. 3 (2005), pp. 493-515.

McIlwain, C.H. *Constitutionalism: Ancient and Modern*, Indianapolis: Liberty Fund 2008.

Ménasé, S. *Passivité et création. Merleau-Ponty et l'art moderne*, Paris: Presses Universitaires de France, 2003.

Merleau-Ponty, M. *The Structure of Behavior*, trans. A.L. Fisher, Boston: Beacon Press 1963 / M. Merleau-Ponty, *La structure du comportement*, Presses Universitaires de France: Paris 1942.

Merleau-Ponty, M. *Phenomenology of Perception*, trans. C. Smith, London and New York: Routledge 2003 / M. Merleau-Ponty, *Phénoménologie de la perception*, Paris: Gallimard 1945.

Merleau-Ponty, M. *Sense and Non-sense*, trans. P.A. Dreyfus, Evanston, Ill.: Northwestern University Press / M. Merleau-Ponty, *Sens et non-sens*, Gallimard: Paris 1996 [1948].

Merleau-Ponty, M. *Un inédit de Maurice Merleau-Ponty*, in M. Merleau-Ponty, *Parcours deux 1951-1961*, Verdier: Lagrasse 2000, pp. 36-48 [1951].

Merleau-Ponty, M. *In Praise of Philosophy and Other Essays*, trans. by J. O'Neill, Evanston, Ill.: Northwestern University Press 1988 / M. Merleau-Ponty, *Éloge de la philosophie et autres essays*, Paris: Gallimard 2002 [1953].

Merleau-Ponty, M. *Adventures of the Dialectic*, trans. J. Bien, London: Heinemann 1974 / M. Merleau-Ponty, *Les aventures de la dialectique*, Paris: Gallimard 2000 [1955].

Merleau-Ponty, M. *Signs*, trans. R.C. McCleary, Evanston, Ill.: Northwestern University Press 1964 / M. Merleau-Ponty, *Signes*, Paris: Gallimard 2001 [1960].

Merleau-Ponty, M. 'Eye and Mind', in T. Baldwin (ed.), *Merleau-Ponty. Basic Writings*, London and New York: Routledge 2004, pp. 290-324 / M. Merleau-Ponty, *L'Oeil et l'Esprit*, Paris: Gallimard 2003 [1964].

Merleau-Ponty, M. *The Visible and the Invisible*, trans. A. Lingis, Evanston, Ill.: Northwestern University Press 1968 / M. Merleau-Ponty, *Le visible et l'invisible*, Paris: Gallimard 2003 [1964].

Merleau-Ponty, M. *The Prose of the World*, trans. J. O'Neill, Evanston, Ill.: Northwestern University Press 1964 / M. Merleau-Ponty, *La prose du monde*, Paris: Gallimard 1969.

Merleau-Ponty, M. *Husserl at the Limits of Phenomenology*, Including texts by Edmund Husserl, trans. and eds. L. Lawlor with B. Bergo, Evanston: Northwestern University Press 2002 / M. Merleau-Ponty, *Notes de cours sur L'origine de la géométrie de Husserl*, Suivi de Recherches sur la phénoménologie de Merleau-Ponty, R. Barbaras (ed.), Paris: Presses Universitaires de France 1998.

Merleau-Ponty, M. *L'institution. La passivité. Notes de cours au Collège de France (1954-1955)*, Paris: Belin 2003.

Möllers, Ch. 'Pouvoir Constituant-Constitution-Constitutionalisation', in A. von Bogdandy and J. Bast (eds.), *Principles of European Constitutional Law*, Oxford (etc.): Hart 2006, pp. 183-226.

Mullen, D.C. *Beyond Subjectivity and Representation: Perception, Expression, and Creation in Nietzsche, Heidegger and Merleau-Ponty*, Lanham (etc.): University Press of America 1999.

Murakami, H. *What I Talk About When I Talk About Running*, New York: Knopf 2008.

Negri, A. *Insurgencies. Constituent Power and the Modern State*, Minneapolis (etc.): University of Minnesota Press 1999.

Nijhuis, M. 'Echoes of Brushstrokes', Paper presented at '100 Years of Merleau-Ponty, A Centenary Conference',14-16 March 2008, Sofia University, Bulgaria.

Ovid, *Metmorphoses*, trans. M. Innes, London (etc.): Penguin 1955.

Perelman, Ch. *Logique juridique: Nouvelle rhétorique*, Toulouse: Dalloz 1976.

Pernice, I. *Rethinking the Methods of Dividing and Controlling the Competences of the Union*, Walter Hallstein-Institut für Europäisches Verfassungsrecht Humboldt-Universität zu Berlin, October 2001, available at: www.whi-berlin.de/pernice-competencies.htm [visited on 29 October 2009].

Phelan, D. R. *Revolt or Revolution: The Constitutional Boundaries of the European Community*, Dublin: Round Hall Sweet & Maxwell 1997.

Pollack, M.A. 'Creeping Competence: The Expanding Agenda of the European Community', *Journal of Public Policy*, vol. 14 (1994), pp. 95-145.

Prechal, S. 'Direct Effect, Indirect Effect, Supremacy and the Evolving Constitution of the European Union', in C. Barnard (ed.), *The Fundamentals of EU Law Revisited. Assessing the Impact of the Constitutional Debate*, Oxford (etc.): Oxford University Press 2007, pp. 35-70.

Prechal, S. and B. van Roermund (eds.), *The Coherence of EU Law: The Search for Unity in Divergent Concepts*, Oxford (etc.): Oxford University Press 2008.

Prechal, S., S. de Vries and H. van Eijken, 'The Principle of Attributed Powers and the "Scope of EU Law"', in L. Besselink, F. Pennings and S. Prechal (eds.), *The Eclipse of Legality in Europe*, Kluwer Law International, forthcoming 2011.

Poiares Maduro, M. 'Europe and the constitution: what if this is as good as it gets?', in J.H.H. Weiler and M. Wind, *European Constitutionalism Beyond the State*, Cambridge (etc.): Cambridge University Press 2003, pp. 74-102.

Radbruch, G. 'Legal Philosophy', in *The Legal Philosophies of Lask, Radbruch, and Dabin*, trans. K. Wilk, Cambridge, Mass.: Harvard University Press 1950, pp. 47-226.

Rainville, M. *L'expérience et l'expression: essai sur la pensée de Maurice Merleau-Ponty*, Montréal: Éditions Bellarmin 1988.

Rasmussen, H. 'The European's Court *Acte Clair* Strategy in *CILFIT*', *European Law Journal*, vol. 9 (1984), pp. 242-259.

Ricoeur, P. 'Husserl et le sens de l'histoire', *Revue de métaphysique et de morale*, vol. 3-4 (1949), pp. 280-316.

Ricoeur, P. *Oneself as Another*, trans. K. Blamey, Chicago and London: The University of Chicago 1994 [1990].

Rousseau, J.-J. 'The Social Contract', in *The Social Contract and Other Later Political Writings*, ed. and trans. V. Gourevitch, Cambridge: Cambridge University Press 1997 [1762], pp. 39-152.

Rousseau, J.-J. 'Discourse on Political Economy', in *The Social Contract and Other Later Political Writings*, ed. and trans. V. Gourevitch, Cambridge: Cambridge University Press 1997 [1755], pp. 3-38.

Schepel, H. and E. Blankenburg, 'Mobilizing the European Court of Justice', in G. de Bùrca and J.H.H. Weiler, *The European Court of Justice*, Oxford (etc.): Oxford University Press 2001, pp. 9-42.

Schmidt, J. *Maurice Merleau-Ponty: between phenomenology and structuralism*, London: Macmillan 1985.

Schmitt, C. *Political Theology. Four Chapters on the Concept of Sovereignty*, trans. G. Schwab, Chicago: The University of Chicago Press 1985 [1922].

Schmitt, C. *The Crisis of Parliamentary Democracy*, trans. E. Kennedy, Cambridge, Mass.: MIT Press 1985 [1923].

Schmitt, C. *Verfassungslehre*, Berlin: Duncker & Humblot 1970 [1928].

Schmitt, C. *The Concept of the Political*, trans. G. Schwab, Chicago: The University of Chicago Press 1996 [1932].

Schütze R. 'Supremacy without Pre-emption? The very slowly emergent Doctrine of Community Pre-emption', *Common Market Law Review*, vol. 43 (2006), pp. 1023-1048.

Senden, L. *Soft law in European Community law. Its Relationship to Legislation*, Nijmegen: Wolf Legal Publishers 2003.

Senden, L. 'Twintig jaar Europese rechtsontwikkeling: Versterking van het effet utile van het Europese recht', in A.M.J. van den Biggelaar et al. (eds.), *Twintig jaar rechtsontwikkeling*. Bundel ter gelegenheid van het vierde lustrum van JUVAT, Nijmegen: Wolf Legal Publishers 2008, pp. 107-132.

Sieyès, E. J. *What is the Third Estate?*, trans. M. Blondel, London: Pall Mall Press 1963 [1789].

Skubiszewski, K. 'Implied Powers of International Organizations', in Y. Dinstein (ed.), *International Law at a Time of Perplexity*, Dordrecht: Kluwer Academic 1989, pp. 855-868

Slater, D. 'The scope of EC harmonizing powers revisited?', *German Law Journal*, vol. 4 (2003), pp. 137-147.

Slatman, J. *L'expression au-delà de la représentation. Sur l'aisthêsis et l'esthétique chez Merleau-Ponty*, s.n. 2001.

Slatman, J. 'The Sense of Life: Husserl and Merleau-Ponty on Touching and Being Touched', *Chiasmi International*, no. 7 (2005), pp. 305-325.

Snyder, F. 'The unfinished constitution of the European Union: principles, processes and culture', in J.H.H. Weiler and M. Wind, *European Constitutionalism Beyond the State*, Cambridge (etc.): Cambridge University Press 2003, pp. 55-73.

Spaak, T. 'Norms that Confer Competence', *Ratio Juris: An International Journal of Jurisprudence and Philosophy of Law*, vol. 16 (2003), pp. 89-104.

Stadlmeier, S. 'Die "Implied Powers" der Europäischen Gemeinschaften', *Zeitschrift für öffentliches Recht*, vol. 52 (1997), pp. 353-388.

Stein, E. 'Lawyers, Judges, and the Making of a Transnational Constitution', *American Journal of International Law*, vol. 75 (1981), pp. 1-27.

Taylor, C. *Sources of the Self. The Making of the Modern Identity*, Cambridge (etc.): Cambridge University Press 1989.

Tietz, J. *Geschiedenis van de architectuur in de 20e eeuw*, vertaling J. B. Kanon en D. Antoons, Keulen: Könneman 1999.

Timmermans, Ch. 'Foreword', in J.H. Jans, R. de Lange, S. Prechal and R.J.G.M. Widdershoven, *Europeanisation of Public Law*, Groningen: Europa Law Publishing 2007, pp. v-vi.

Tsagourias, N. (ed.), *Transnational Constitutionalism. International and European Perspectives*, Cambridge (etc.): Cambridge University Press 2007.

Vallier, R. 'Institution. The Significance of Merleau-Ponty's 1954 Course at the Collège de France', *Chiasmi International*, no. 7 (2005), pp. 281-303.

Van der Tang, G.F.M. *Grondwetsbegrip en grondwetsidee*, Gouda: Quint 1998.

Van Ooik, R.H. *De keuze der rechtsgrondslag voor besluiten van de Europese Unie*, Deventer: Kluwer 1999.

Van Ooik, R. 'The European Court of Justice and the Division of Competence in the European Union', in D. Obradovic and N. Lavranos (eds.), *Interface between EU Law and National Law*, Groningen: Europa Law Publishing 2007, pp. 11-40.

Van Roermund, B. *Het verdwijnpunt van de wet. Een opstel over symboolwerking van wetgeving*, Deventer: Tjeenk Willink 1997.

Van Roermund, B. 'Constituerende macht, soevereiniteit en representatie', *Tijdschrift voor Filosofie*, vol. 64 (2002), pp. 509-532.

Van Roermund, B. 'First-Person Plural Legislature: Political Reflexivity and Representation', *Philosophical Explorations*, vol. 6 (2003), pp. 235-250.

Van Roermund, B. 'Introduction: Law - the Order and the Alien,' *Ethical Perspectives: Journal of the European ethics network*, vol. 13 (2006), pp. 331-357.

Van Roermund, B. 'The Origin of Legal Rules', Paper presented on the Conference 'The Species of Origin', Glasgow, 13-14 December 2007. Available at: www.speciesoforigin.org/FCKeditor/File/BVR_Origin.pdf [visited on 25 October 2009].

Visker, R. *Truth and Singularity. Taking Foucault into Phenomenology*, Deventer (etc.): Kluwer 1999.

Visker, R. *The Inhuman Condition: Looking for Difference After Levinas and Heidegger*, Dordrecht (etc.): Kluwer Academic 2004.

Waele, H. de *Rechterlijk activisme en het Europees Hof van Justitie*, Den Haag: Boom Juridische Uitgevers 2009.

Waldenfels, B. *Antwortregister*, Frankfurt am Main: Suhrkamp 1994.

Waldenfels, B. 'Das Paradox des Ausdrucks', in B. Waldenfels, *Deutsch-französische Gedankengänge*, Frankfurt am Main: Suhrkamp 1995, pp. 105-123.

Waldenfels, B. *Order in the Twilight*, trans. D. J. Parent, Athens, Ohio: Ohio University Press 1996.

Waldenfels, B. *Vielstimmigkeit der Rede: Studien zur Phänomenologie des Fremden 4*, Frankfurt am Mein: Suhrkamp 1999.

Waldenfels, B. *Das Leibliche Selbst. Vorlesungen zur Phänomenologie des Leibes*, Frankfurt am Mein: Suhrkamp 2000.

Waldenfels, B. *Verfremdung der Moderne. Phänomenologische Grenzgänge*, Göttingen: Wallstein Verlag 2001.

Waldenfels, B. *Phänomenologie der Aufmerksamkeit*, Frankfurt am Mein: Suhrkamp 2005.

Walker Bynum, C. *Metamorphosis and Identity*, New York: Zone Books 2001.

Weatherill, S. 'Competence' in B. de Witte (ed.), *Ten Reflections on the Constitutional Treaty for Europe*, European University Institute, Robert Schuman Centre for Advanced Studies and Academy of European Law, San Domenico di Fiesole 2003, pp. 45-66.

Weatherill, S. 'Activism and Restraint in the European Court of Justice', in P. Capps, M. Evans and S. Konstadinidis (eds), *Asserting Jurisdiction: International and European Legal Perspectives*, Portland (Oregon): Hart 2003, pp. 255-282.

Weatherill, S. 'Competence Creep and Competence Control', in P. Eeckhout and T. Tridimas (eds.), *Yearbook of European Law*, vol. 23 (2004), pp. 1-55.

Weiler, J.H.H. 'Does Europe Need a Constitution? Demos, Telos and the German Maastricht Decision', European Law Journal, vol. 1 (1995), pp. 219-258.

Weiler, J.H.H. 'A Constitution for Europe? Some Hard Choices', *Journal of Common Market Studies*, vol. 40 (2002), pp. 563-580.

Weiler, J.H.H., A.-M. Slaughter, A. Stone Sweet, 'Prologue – The European Courts of Justice', in A.-M. Slaughter, A. Stone Sweet and J.H.H. Weiler, *The European Court and National Courts – Doctrine and Jurisprudence. Legal Change in Its Social Context*, Oxford: Hart 1998, pp. v-xiv.

Wessel, R. 'Integration by Stealth: On the Exclusivity of Community Competence. A Comment on the Ronald van Ooik Contribution', in D. Obradovic and N. Lavranos (eds.), *Interface between EU Law and National Law*, Groningen: Europa Law Publishing 2007, pp. 41-49.

Wittgenstein, L. *Philosophical Investigations*, Oxford: Blackwell 1967.

Wittgenstein, L. *Remarks on the Foundations of Mathematics*, Oxford: Blackwell 1978.

Wittgenstein, L. *On Certainty*, Oxford: Blackwell 1979.

Table of Cases

A. European Court of Justice

L. Corrias, *The Passivity of Law*,
DOI 10.1007/978-94-007-1034-4, © Springer Science+Business Media B.V. 2011

B. Other courts

Documents

Declaration of 9 May 1950, available at http://europa.eu/abc/symbols/9-may/decl_en.htm [visited on 18 October 2009].

Declaration on nationality of a Member State, attached to the Maastricht Treaty.

Declaration no. 23 attached to the Treaty of Nice, Declaration on the Future of the Union, December 2000.

Delimitation of competence between the European Union and the Member States – Existing system, problems and avenues to be explored, CONV 47/02.

Presidency Conclusions of the Laeken European Council (14 and 15 December 2001): Annex I: Laeken Declaration on the future of the European Union, in Bulletin of the European Union. 2001, No. 12, pp. 19-23.

L. Corrias, *The Passivity of Law,*
DOI 10.1007/978-94-007-1034-4, © Springer Science+Business Media B.V. 2011

Lightning Source UK Ltd.
Milton Keynes UK
UKOW05n0714250517
301980UK00015B/385/P